The Definitive Guide to Magento

A Comprehensive Look at Magento

Adam McCombs

Robert Banh

Apress®

The Definitive Guide to Magento: A Comprehensive Look at Magento

Copyright © 2009 by Adam McCombs and Robert Banh

ISBN-13 (pbk): 978-1-4302-7229-8

ISBN-13 (electronic): 978-1-4302-7228-1

9 8 7 6 5 4 3 2 1

President and Publisher: Paul Manning
Lead Editor: Michelle Lowmann
Technical Reviewers: Robert Banh, Gordon Forsythe
Editorial Board: Clay Andres, Steve Anglin, Mark Beckner, Ewan Buckingham, Gary Cornell, Jonathan Gennick, Jonathan Hassell, Michelle Lowman, Matthew Moodie, Duncan Parkes, Jeffrey Pepper, Frank Pohlmann, Douglas Pundick, Ben Renow-Clarke, Dominic Shakeshaft, Matt Wade, Tom Welsh
Coordinating Editor: Jim Markham
Copy Editors: Katie Stence, Nancy Sixsmith
Production Support: Patrick Cunningham
Indexer: Julie Grady
Artist: April Milne
Cover Designer: Anna Ishchenko

Distributed to the book trade worldwide by Springer-Verlag New York, Inc., 233 Spring Street, 6th Floor, New York, NY 10013. Phone 1-800-SPRINGER, fax 201-348-4505, e-mail orders-ny@springer-sbm.com, or visit http://www.springeronline.com.

For information on translations, please contact Apress directly at 2855 Telegraph Avenue, Suite 600, Berkeley, CA 94705. Phone 510-549-5930, fax 510-549-5939, e-mail info@apress.com, or visit http://www.apress.com.

Apress and friends of ED books may be purchased in bulk for academic, corporate, or promotional use. eBook versions and licenses are also available for most titles. For more information, reference our Special Bulk Sales–eBook Licensing web page at http://www.apress.com/info/bulksales.

The source code for this book is available to readers at http://www.apress.com.

To my wife and brother, Esther and Mark
—Adam McCombs

To my mother and sister, Jenny and Annie
—Robert Banh

Contents at a Glance

Contents

About the Authors

Adam McCombs is a trained musician who accidentally stumbled into the fun-filled world of web design and development. His journey began several years ago while attending Texas State University as a music education major. Adam decided to build a simple site to display his photography work, so he taught himself the basic fundamentals of good graphic and web site design. One site led to another, then to a couple of clients; the next thing he knew, he was more interested in typography than Bach (although he still enjoys a good fugue every now and then).

Adam is currently a full-time designer and developer who specializes in adapting open source frameworks such as Magento, Wordpress, Joomla!, and Drupal into functional custom web site solutions for clients of small and medium-sized businesses. He loves helping clients fulfill their visions and bring their ideas to life. Adam has also donated his work and time to nonprofit organizations, charities, and many broke musicians.

When he can bring himself to part with his computer, Adam enjoys photography and running after his two rambunctious Labradors with his wife.

Robert Banh is an accomplished developer, working in code since the existence of Pluto. He often hacks core systems and deploys web sites during his down time. Robert specializes in building custom PHP/MySQL web applications, using technologies such as Zend framework and CodeIgniter. Depending on the project, he's known to jump from the content management system of Wordpress, Drupal, and Expression Engine to the eCommerce solutions of Magento and Shopify. When Robert is not coding, he plays with Adobe Photoshop and aligns hand-drawn boxes into a 960 grid. He also dreams in hex colors.

Robert's passion lives on the Web, designing and building custom solutions for clients stemming from IBM, HP, Unisys, and KLRU to small mom-and-pop shops and nonprofit organizations. He is currently employed at the University of Texas at Austin, where they let him run free to code in multiple frameworks and experiment taking over the world with unofodox designs for the Web.

Robert has a computer science degree from the University of Texas at Austin. If he's not mentoring or tweeting, you can find him attending Refresh Austin each month.

About the Technical Reviewers

 **Gordon Forsythe** has been developing web applications with PHP since 2000. He has worked on many open source applications and has developed programs for various fields including education, health care, real estate, and telecommunications. Gordon currently resides in Phoenix with his wife, three cats, two dogs, and five fish.

Acknowledgments

First of all, I'd like to thank my wife Esther. Without her support, I would not have the opportunity to pursue my dreams and career (or finish this book).

To my brother Mark, who always reminds me that there is more to life than work.

To Robert Banh for always keeping me grounded and supporting me in all my Magento endeavors. Thanks for stepping in to help with this book. I think we did a great job of documenting Magento, for our own sakes, if nothing else.

To Michelle Lowman and James Markham for not only giving me the opportunity to write this book but for all their patience and guidance along the way.

To Katie Stence for her editing advice and transforming my ideas into coherent thoughts.

To Roy Rubin and everyone at Varien for developing the Magento platform.

Finally, a big thank you to Cecy Correa, Rob MacKay, Jason Lengstorf, Nadine Gilden, Mike Conaty, Chad Engle, and all the #DCTH gang.

Adam McCombs

I want to first thank my mother, Jenny Banh, and my sister Annie. Without their encouragement, I wouldn't be where I am today. They believed in me countless times and always encouraged me to pursue my dreams.

To Adam McCombs for bringing me along for all these crazy Magento projects that somehow turned us into pseudo experts. I owe my future gray hairs to him and Magento.

To Esther for putting up with me and cooking those delicious meals as Adam and I debugged Magento for the 900th time. The solution wouldn't be complete until we went through our chaotic routine.

To Krist for being my positive beacon after long hours of writing this book. Her positive advice and suggestions were invaluable. Thank you for teaching me that the cup is never half empty.

To Michelle Lowman and James Markham for being outstanding mentors. Thank you for giving me guidance throughout the whole process. I couldn't ask for a better team.

To Gordon Forsythe: without your technical guidance I would be lost! Thank you for poring through my code, I know it's not an easy feat.

To Nancy Sixsmith: you are truly a masterpiece. I'm certain any paragraph you edit can be turned into a great piece of writing. Thank you turning my bad grammar into legible words.

And finally, to all my geeky friends who were there from the beginning of this book process: Cecy Correa, Alex Jones, Rob MacKay, Jason Lengstorf, Andrea La Valleur, Sarah Whinnem, Nadine Gilden, Tomo Kawai, James Bowman, Mike Conaty, Chad Engle, and the whole #DCTH crew. Thanks for all the great discussions and laughter.

Robert Banh

Introduction

The Definitive Guide to Magento takes a comprehensive look at Magento, a robust and flexible e-commerce platform built on the Zend framework. With more than 750,000 downloads, Magento is the fastest-growing open source e-commerce solution. This book walks you through all the steps of building a fully functional Magento-based web site. It also includes information on managing products, customers, and orders.

This book is meant to be a desktop reference when working with Magento. Not only does it take a look into some of the finer points of Magento (including walkthroughs of the public and administrative interfaces, and modifying the default Magento theme) but we also included a comprehensive API reference for developers looking to extend Magento beyond its basic functionality.

Who This Book Is For

This book has two primary audiences. The first includes website designers and developers looking for an eCommerce solution for clients. Magento can not only be manipulated in terms of design but it can meet some of the most complex development requirements.

The second audience includes small to medium-sized business owners who are looking to establish an online eCommerce presence. For most business, Magento is ready to perform right after installation. You can easily configure Magento with very little knowledge of PHP or HTML. Magento also allows you to install themes to modify your store's appearance.

Magento is the ideal eCommerce solution for anyone looking to easily install, customize, and run an online store.

How This Book Is Structured

This book is dived into two major sections. Part One: Getting Started with Magento provides a brief history of Magento; walkthroughs of the public and administrative interfaces; and in-depth looks at customers, products, and orders. Part Two: Advanced Magento Development dives deeper into Magento and how to manipulate Magento's appearance, install and build Magento extensions, and how to utilize Magento's built-in API as well as some Magento tips and tricks.

Prerequisites

There are no prerequisites to using Magento. Magento can be installed and configured with a basic understanding of how to upload and download files and the use of a file transfer protocol (FTP) application.

For designers and developers looking to extend Magento beyond its basic functionality and design, Magento can be customized with a basic understanding of HTML, CSS, and XML. Although we recommend having a beginning understanding of PHP and MySQL, it is not required for basic store operations and use.

Contacting the Authors

We always welcome your questions and feedback regarding the contents of this book. You can reach Adam McCombs at adamjmccombs@gmail.com and visit his web site at http://www.mccombs.me/. You can reach Robert Banh at robertbanh@gmail.com and visit his site at http://www.htmltree.com.

PART 1

Getting Started with Magento

In chapters 1-6, we will walk you through how to install Magento and the public and administrative interfaces, how to work with products, customers, and orders as well as configuring Magento for use.

CHAPTER 1

■ ■ ■

Introduction to Magento

What Is Magento?

Magento is a full-fledged, open source eCommerce platform aimed at web site designers, developers, and business owners who are looking for a complete eCommerce web site solution. Magento's open source architecture enables the user to maintain complete control over the structure and functionality of a web site.

Varien, the company responsible for building Magento, has set a new standard for open source applications. One of the most impressive aspects of Magento is the use of the Zend Framework. This allows for separation of the Model-View-Controller (MVC) which separates its core operations from functionality and appearance. Magento offers a stable eCommerce environment and gives you the flexibility to completely customize the web site to suit your business needs.

What Is Open Source Software?

Open Source Software (OSS) is a unique approach to the development and distribution of software. Open Source Software must not only offer access to the source code, but also be distributed as open source software. This allows users the rights to use, modify, and redistribute the software in either a modified or unmodified format.

In 1983, Richard Matthew Stallman launched the GNU Project to create a free UNIX-type operating system. The GNU Project led to the creation of free software such as gcc, the GNU C Compiler, and other free software instrumental in the birth of Linux. The GNU Project is also responsible for the GPL, or GNU General Public License, setting the stage for the creation of other free software licenses.

As more people started to realize that there was money to be made with free software, the free software approach took a more commercial turn in 1998 with the founding of the Open Source Initiative (OSI) by Eric S. Raymond and Bruce Perens. OSI is responsible for creating the Open Source Definition (OSD), and it reviews licenses to determine if they fit the OSD. The OSD-compliant list currently includes over 60 licenses, including GPLv2 and GPLv3.

Linux is probably the most famous software developed under the free software/open source ideology. Originally written in 1991 by Linus Torvalds, Linux is now one of widely distributed software, powering five out of ten of the world's webhosting and server type enviroments. Much of Linux success can be attributed to its open source approach.

For more information about open source visit: http://www.opensource.org.

Magento Versions and License

There are currently two versions of Magento: the Magento Community Edition and the Magento Enterprise Edition.

The Magento Community Edition is licensed under the Open Software License (OSL) v3.0. The Magento Enterprise Edition is available under a commercial license and requires an annual fee. Both editions share the same underlying framework. The Enterprise Edition includes several additional features that are not included with the Community Edition, including gift certificates, customer store credits, and strong data encryption.

Full details about Magento licensing can be found at: http://www.magentocommerce.com/license.

The History Behind Magento

Varien began developing Magento in January of 2007. It was their vision to establish an eCommerce platform unlike anything else on the market. Varien originally planned on building an eCommerce platform based on a fork of osCommerce, but decided to write their own system using the Zend Framework instead. During Varien's six month beta period, they had over 225,000 downloads of Magento. The first public release of Magento, version 1.0, was released on March 31, 2008.

Shortly after, Magento 1.1 was released. Magento 1.1 fixed many bugs found in version 1.0, but also included a faster and more informative administrative user interface. Magento 1.2 was released on December 29, 2008. This version included several upgraded Zend Framework libraries and a new feature: downloadable products.

The current version of Magento 1.3 was released on March 30, 2009. This version increased Magento's speed in both public and administrative views. The Magento Enterprise Edition version 1.3 Enterprise was released on April 15, 2009. This version requires a service agreement with Varien and costs $8,900 USD per year and it includes technical support which is not available with the Community Edition.

Zend: Magento's Workhorse

The Zend Framework, the platform Magento is built upon, is an open source, object-oriented application framework that uses PHP 5. Zend was released in 2005 under the Open Source Initiative (OSI)-approved New BSD License. The Zend Framework, often referred to as ZF, is built to be a lightweight yet flexible platform. ZF tries to follow the best programming practices and has been adopted for use by several major corporations including IBM, Adobe, and Oracle.

The Zend Framework provides Magento with an open source architecture and framework. ZF is really the engine that makes an application like Magento possible. Using the Zend Framework made it possible for Varien to develop Magento in a relatively short amount of time.

Who Should Use Magento?

Magento has two primary audiences: web site developers and businesses looking to expand in the online eCommerce marketplace. Regardless of your level of expertise, Magento has been designed in a way that is easily approachable. Magento is built to work straight out of the box with very little customization. It is easy to update your web site by adding new products and managing orders. While Magento has the flexibility to be applied to advanced eCommerce situations, basic operations of the site can be handled with little training.

Magento can be customized with a basic understanding of HTML, CSS, and XML. While it's recommended to have a beginning understanding of PHP and MySQL, it is not required for basic store operations and use. PHP for Absolute Beginners is a great starting point for anyone just getting started with learning php. Developers who are looking to apply Magento to more custom eCommerce web sites should have an advanced knowledge of PHP and a working knowledge of the Zend Framework.

Why Magento?

In addition to a solid architecture and framework, there are several unique reasons why Magento makes a great choice for an eCommerce solution.

- One of the most amazing features about Magento is that you can design and develop multiple web sites and they store and share one administrative interface. This extremely flexible feature allows you to modify and control multiple web sites. All of your products inventory and pricing can be controlled from one central location. There is no longer a need to login to multiple locations to handle multiple web sites. Magento has the ability to control them all.

- Magento supports over sixty languages, multiple currencies, and tax rates. This gives you the ability to easily expand in the global market.

- Layered navigation gives users customized browsing options when viewing products by categories. You can now sort products by price, size, color, and other customizable attributes.

- Magento also has built-in web services. This flexibility allows external applications to access magento's data without changing the underlying core code. Currently, SOAP and XML-RPC protocols are available out of the box.

- Magento has Search Engine Optimization (SEO) built in from the start. It has the ability to handle friendly URL rewrites which make it easy for search engines to index your store and products.

- Not only does Magento offer real-time carrier rates and quotes, users can ship products from one order to multiple shipping address. This makes gift shopping especially easy.

- Magento also has several reporting features built in. These allows for easy view of sales reports, best-selling products, and customer reporting. They can even be exported in a CSV format to integrate with excel and other database programs.

- Magento has designed its file structure to three major sections: core, functionality, and design. This allows for easy updating of images and CSS styling without affecting the functionality of the site. Store functionality can also be easily customized without affecting the Magento's core. As a result, you can modify Magento without having to worry about upgrading to newer versions in the future.

- Magento has a huge community backing. In addition to a public forum and bug tracking, Magento also has its own public repository of extensions called Magento Connect. These extensions can be found at `http://www.magentocommerce.com/magento-connect`. Magento Connect features both free and commercial extensions to enhance the functionality of your web site.

- Since Magento is released under the Open Software License (OSL), the Magento Community Edition is available at no cost. In turn, this allows web site developers and eCommerce web site owners to cut down on software costs.

Beyond This Guide

This guide is only a starting point for using a platform like Magento. We highly recommend building a test environment to get comfortable and play around with Magento. It can be very overwhelming at first, but getting your hands dirty in a test environment is a great way to learn about Magento's features and flexibility.

Another great resource is Magento's main web site: `http://www.magentocommerce.com`. Aside from a huge community forum which is supported by the staff at Varien, there is an ever expanding Wiki Knowledge Base, screencasts, and other technical documentation.

CHAPTER 2

■ ■ ■

Installing Magento

The community version of Magento is designed to run under the power of your own web server. In this chapter, you will be reviewing the standard installation process for version 1.3.2.3. Magento can also be installed on local host environments for testing and development. A local host installation follows a similar process that we've outlined in this chapter as well. For additional information about installation on a local host system, you can visit http://www.magentocommerce.com.

System Requirements

Before you begin the installation process, it is important that your server meets the requirements to install and run Magento:

- Linux x86, x86-64.

- Apache Web Server (1.x or 2.x).

- PHP 5.2.0 or newer, (PHP4 with limited support).

- Certain PHP extensions are required. Check Magento's web site for a full list of required PHP extensions.

- Magento requires safe mode to be turned off to run Magento.

- MySQL 4.1.20 or newer.

Additional details regarding system requirements can be found at: http://www.magentocommerce.com/system-requirements.

If you are not sure whether your hosting server meets these requirements, a simple script is available for download to determine your server's abilities. Visit http://www.magentocommerce.com/knowledge-base/entry/how-do-i-know-if-my-server-is-compatible-with-magento for more information.

■ **Note** While not a requirement, Magento is SSL ready and is recommended for sites performing transactions involving credit card purchases.

Automatic Install

Many webhosts provide automatic installations. This allows you to install Magento with a few simple clicks. While it is important to understand the installation process, an automatic installation can save time. Contact your web site host to find out if they support automatic installations. If they do not, Magento must be installed manually.

■ **Tip** Be aware that automatic installations can sometimes erase entire directories during the installation process. It is recommended that you back up all files before you begin a new installation process, regardless of whether it is automatic or manual.

Getting Started

If your web server has met the system requirements, you are ready to install Magento by following these six steps:

1. What and where to download

2. Uploading Magento for installation

3. Setting correct file permissions

4. Setting up a Magento database

5. Installing Magento

6. Configuring Magento

The following steps outline standard installation. If you have SSH access and are more comfortable using SSH instead of a web-based installation than you can visit the following link for more information: http://www.magentocommerce.com/wiki/groups/227/installing_magento_via_shell_ssh.

Installation Step 1: What and Where to Download?

To get started visit: http://www.magentocommerce.com/download. As shown in Figure 2-1, Magento offers three different files you can download. Each file is offered in either zip, tar.gz, or tar.bz2 formats.

- *Downloader*: The downloader is a small file that installs the full release.

- *Full release*: This file is a full release of Magento. It contains all necessary files needed to install and run Magento. The full release is considered an alternative to the downloader file. No additional files are needed if you choose to use this option.

- *Sample Data*: This file is optional and is only required if you want to install sample data to your initial installation of Magento. Sample data is not included with either the downloader or full release. If you have never worked with Magento before, it is highly recommended that you install sample data.

Figure 2-1. A quick look at the download page. Magento offers three files to download: Downloader, Full Release, and Sample Data.

This guide will follow the steps using the downloader file, but if you choose to download the full release file, the process will be relatively similar.

Installation Step 2: Uploading Magento for Installation

Once you have downloaded the downloader file and/or the sample data file, you will need to transfer the files to your server.

You should have downloaded a file name similar to: magento-downloader-**1.3.2.3**.zip. Unzip these files and upload them to your server under the directory path of your choice. If you are using FTP to upload, you will need to place the files inside of your web directory (examples). Alternatively, you can upload these files to a nonroot directory path such as www.domainname.com/magento or www.domainname.com/store.

If you have chosen to install the sample data, the file you downloaded should look similar to: magento-sample-data-x.x.x.zip. Unzip this file and you will notice that it contains two files, magento_sample_data_for_1.2.0.sql, which will be used later, and a folder called media. Upload the media folder to the same directory that the downloaded files were uploaded to. Again, this step is optional, but is recommended if you have previously never installed or worked with Magento.

Installation Step 3: Setting Correct File Permissions

For the installation process to work properly, Magento requires certain permissions be given to the top-level directory (where you uploaded the Magento files) and all Magento directories underneath it.

Note Each server is different and may not require changes to be made. You can quickly test your folders permissions by visiting your Magento directory. If the page loads without errors, you can skip this step and move on to section "Installation Step 4: Setting Up a Magento database."

Using an FTP client, navigate to your Magento directory. Use the Change Permissions or Change Mode function built into your FTP client. Note that with previous command line installation often times you can click on the folder and change the permissions this way.

Permissions are usually set in one of two ways, either by a number or organized by groups. If your FTP uses numbers, set the number to 777 or 0777. If your FTP client organizes permissions by groups, make sure that every group has access under Reading Writing and Execute, often times abbreviated as RWX.

Note If your server has suPHP or suEXEC enabled, you will need to use permission 755 instead of 777.

Figure 2-2 is an example of permissions set to 777 or 0777.

Figure 2-2. An informational view of a folder. This allows you to easily adjust permission.

If you are not using an FTP program, file permissions can also be set using a file browser from within your webhost cpanel or another administrative interface. Simply navigate to your Magento folder and adjust the permissions using the previous process detailed.

Note While Magento's documentation suggests that the directories be set to 777, this may not be the case in your specific situation. If setting your folder permissions to 777 does not work, try 755. This error is due to your hosting server having suPHP or suEXEC-enabled.

Installation Step 4: Setting up a Magento Database

Before you begin installing Magento, you will need to set up a database for Magento to use.

Login to your webhost access panel or cpanel and navigate to the MySQL Databases section. Create a new database and a user that has all the privileges to access the database (see Figure 2-3).

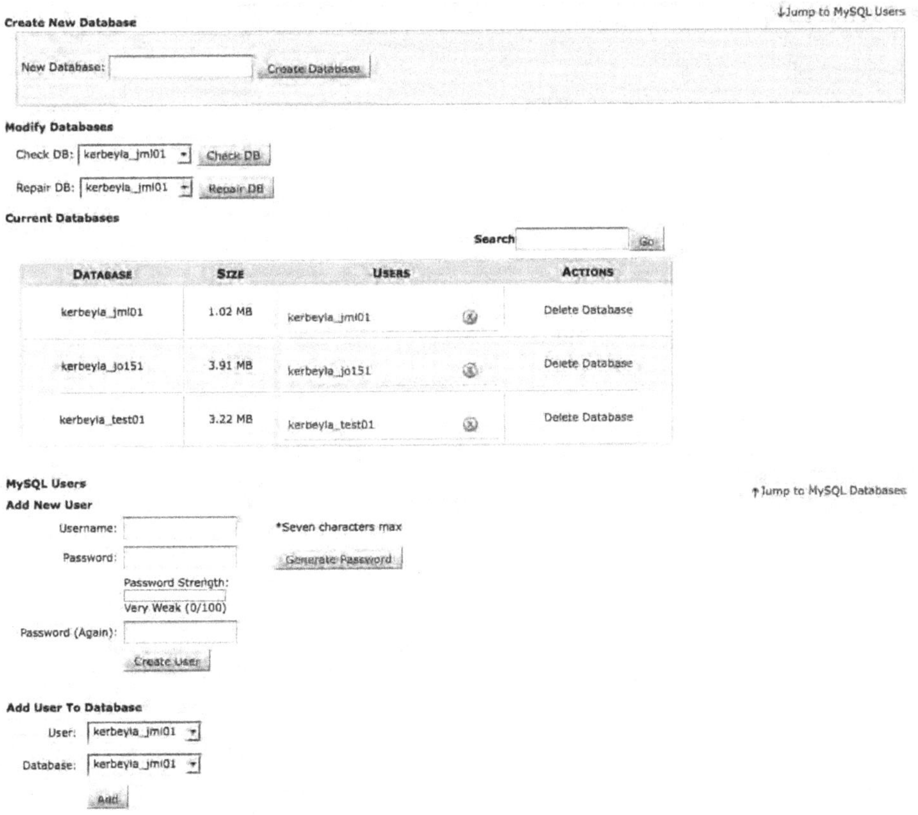

Figure 2-3. *A detailed view of MySQL Database page. This page is used to set up new databases and users. You can assign users to specific databases after they have both been created.*

If you have chosen to use the sample data, login to your phpMyAdmin and open the database you just created. Click the import tab and locate the file you downloaded inside magento-sample-data-x.x.x.zip, called magento_sample_data_for_1.2.0.sql. This should import all of the sample data contained in this file.

Installation Step 5: Installing Magento

1. Using your web browser, navigate to where you have uploaded the Magento files. If everything has been uploaded and extracted correctly, you should see the Magento Installation Wizard, as shown in Figure 2-4.

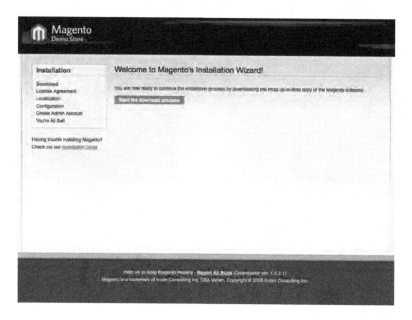

Figure 2-4. *This is the default view for the Magento Installation Wizard.*

If Magento is displaying any errors, they must be resolved before you continue the installation process.

■ **Note** If an error occurs refer to the previous section on setting correct file permissions.

---

2. To start the installation process, simply click Start the download process. A black downloader box will appear and begin downloading all the remaining files necessary to run Magento.

3. After all of the remaining files have been downloaded, a button will appear that says Continue Magento Installation. Click this button to continue the installation.

4. A user license will be loaded, you must read and agree to the license before continuing.

5. Next is the Localization step. Here you choose the stores default location, time zone, and currency. While Magento does allow the set up of multiple eCommerce stores this installation process will only cover the one Magento store. This information is for the set up of the default store.

6. Database configuration. This page is broken up into several different sections.

7. Create Admin Account that includes your first name, last name, email address, username, and password (see Figure 2-5).

Figure 2-5. Configuration of the Magento installation

- *Database connection*: Enter in your host name, database name, user password, and tables prefix. This can be found through your web hosting cpanel or another administrative interface.

- Web access options: Simply enter in the URL of your Magento store, for example *http://www.domainname.com*. For Admin Path it should prefill with admin is customizable. If you have an SSL, it is recommended that you check the Use Secure URLs (SSL) box.

- Session storage options: You can choose either File System or Database. Storing sessions in the database is better for security, but might cause additional load on your database. Session storage that uses File System allows easy access to session information via FTP.

Once you have finished the last step, you will be given an encryption key, as shown in Figure 2-6. It is very important that you save this key for future reference. This encryption key is used to encrypt passwords, credit card numbers, and other important information.

Understand that every Magneto store that is installed, regardless of whether you install sample data, is initially set up as a demo store. There are several areas that need to be customized before you begin selling products.

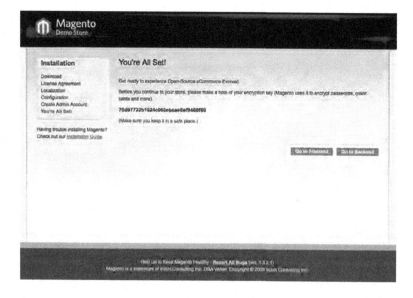

Figure 2-6. *A successful installation of Magento*

What's Next?

Chapter 3 will be an overview of both the frontend and backend sections of Magento. If you are already familiar enough with these sections move ahead to Chapter 4, which will give an in-depth list of items necessary to turn your Magento store from Demo mode to a production store.

CHAPTER 3

■■■

The Public Interface Walk-through

Through the Looking Glass

Magento is made up of two different interfaces. There is the public interface that is open to anyone who visits the web site and an administration interface, which can only be seen to those who have access. Figure 3-1 shows a quick glance at both interfaces.

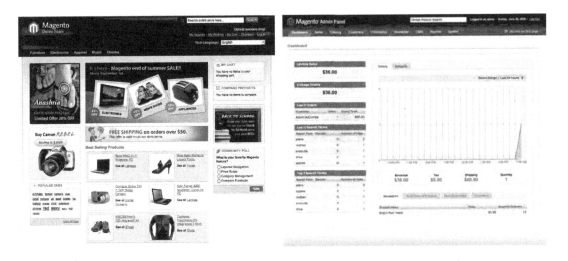

Figure 3-1. *On the left is the public interface of Magento. On the right is administration interface. The administration interface is not viewable by the public.*

The public interface of Magento allows a user to manipulate how the store is designed and the ability to change how you promote your products. With Magento, you are able to edit layout, color schemes, photos, and content to fit your unique situation. Even if you choose not to install the sample data provided by Magento, your store will initially be set up as a demo store. For more information about configuring your store and removing all of the demo information and functionality, take a look at Chapter 8.

In this chapter, you will be exploring the following sections of the public interface: page header, categories and category views, product page, compare products, and CMS pages and static blocks (see Figure 3-2).

Figure 3-2. *A close-up look at the Magento Demo store home page and numbered list of sections you'll be touring.*

Page Header

As shown in Figure 3-3, the top of Magento's store is the page header. The page header provides some important functionality to your customers. It also includes a welcome message that you can customize to give customers an unique greeting.

Figure 3-3. *Your Magento store's page header includes a search bar, language select, and several acount links.*

You can replace the Magento Demo Store logo with your company logo on the left-hand side of the page header. For more information on how to replace this logo you can refer to Chapter 8.

On the right-hand side, there is a search bar. Customers can search for products by using keywords or searching for text used in product descriptions. As an administrator, you have the ability to configure search terms that can be used on your site. This means that if someone searches for MP3 player you can direct them to either a specific MP3 player you want to promote or the MP3 player category.

Below the welcome message are several links aimed at providing customers with additional information. They include the following:

- *My Account*: This link allows customers to view their order history, place product reorders, and view account information. The tab includes addresses associated with their account, lists of product reviews, and newsletter subscription management.

- *My Wishlist*: If customers are not ready to purchase a product they can add it to their wishlist. After products are added to the list customers can view their wishlist by clicking on the "my wishlist" link or the "my account" link in the header.

- *My Cart*: Customers can review, update, and delete products they have added to their shopping cart. Customers are also able to proceed to checkout from the My Cart page.

- *Checkout*: This link will take customers directly to the checkout process with any products they currently have in their cart.

- *Login*: Once they have registered, returning customers have the ability to login to the web site. Registered customers can save items to their cart and wishlist. Registering also allows for customers to sign up to receive newsletters. Once logged in, this link will change to a logout button.

Underneath the list of links, there is also a drop down menu that displays the current language of the Magento Demo Site. Magento offers flexibility by offering your eCommerce store in multiple languages without having to install multiple copies of Magento in other languages. By default, Magento includes three languages, English, French and German. If one of these languages does not suffice, you can download one of 63 additional languages from `http://www.magentocommerce.com/magento-connect`.

Categories and Category Views

By default, top-level categories, known as anchor categories, are listed horizontally just below the header and above the content area of the web site. Rolling over each one of these categories will show a drop down listing of any subcategories.

These use Javascript and if the user has javascript turned off these menus will not expand. Magento will also display a user-friendly message telling the user that Javascript is required to utilize the full functionality of the site (see Figure 3-4).

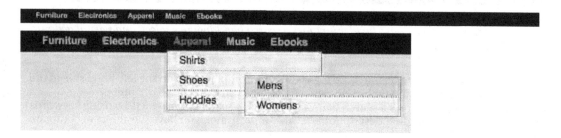

Figure 3-4. *An expanded view of root level categories and subcategories. Magento has menu drop downs already built in.*

Each category and subcategory has a landing page similar to the one shown in Figures 3-4 and 3-5. There are a number of different sections on category landing pages. Landing pages display an up loadable category image, category sorting options, and product listings in each category.

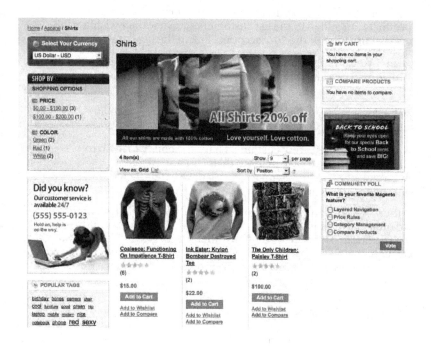

Figure 3-5. *A category landing page that displays a category image, sorting features, and products listed under this category.*

On the category landing pages, you can display your products in both grid and list type layouts. Customers have the ability to change their view, as well as sorting options for the number of products shown and how they are sorted. Products can be sorted by position, name, price, and quantity ratio (see Figure 3-6).

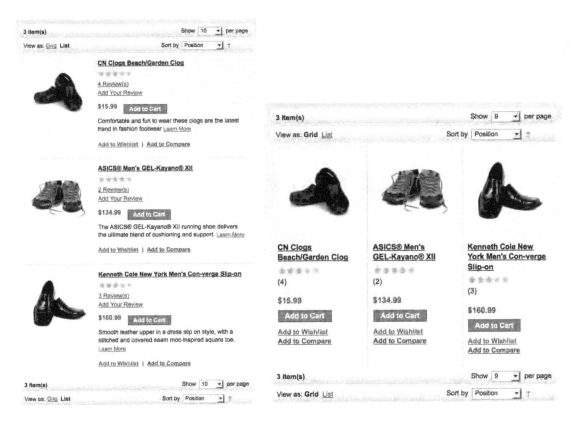

Figure 3-6. *Shows the two different layouts in which products can be displayed, grid and list style layouts. This allows for complete flexibilty as customers are browsing your site.*

Customers can also control how products are displayed by selecting the filter options on the left-hand side of the screen. Display options are listed under the SHOP BY title. Filter options can include price, color, and manufacturer. To apply these filters, simply click on one of the links. Customers can apply multiple filters to category listings. To remove these filters, simply press the clear all items option (see Figure 3-7).

Figure 3-7. *This shows some examples of filtering options displayed under the shop by section. The information shown in this figure was derived from information contained within the sample data installation.*

You may also notice there is a Popular tag box on the left-hand column. Products can be given tags so customers can easily find similar related products. This provides customers with an alternative method for browsing your web site and finding products they need. We will be discussing product tags and other products they contain in Chapter 5.

Product Page

Without a doubt the product page is the most important page inside of your eCommerce. Product pages allow you to communicate important information about your products to customers. As shown in Figure 3-8, Product pages contain product descriptions, pricing, and additional photos. Magento offers the following options when building your product pages:

- *Product images*: Magento allows you to upload multiple images of your products. Customers can also zoom in and view images larger than the provided area, assuming javascript is enabled on the customer's computer.

- *Product descriptions*: There are two types of product descriptions: quick overview and product description. These sections are used to describe a product in detail and provide customers with all the information they might need to make an informed purchase.

- *Product price*: Magento has the ability to include standard pricing for products and specify pricing for certain customer groups. Pricing can also be set based upon product quantities to offer volume discounts. We'll discuss customer groups and group pricing more in Chapter 6.

- *Additional information*: This section is used for providing additional technical information that might normally be included in a quick overview or product description.

- *Product tags*: Product pages display tags that have been assigned to each product. Customers can navigate to other products which share the same tag.

- *Product options*: Magento provides you with the flexibility to give products additional options. These options are customized to product specifics and include such examples as sizes, colors, and dimensions.

- *Product reviews*: Customers can rate and review products on an individual basis. Administrators have the ability to edit and remove each review.

- *Upsell products*: Upsell products are listed under the section "you may also be interested in the following product(s)." This allows you to promote related products on each product page.

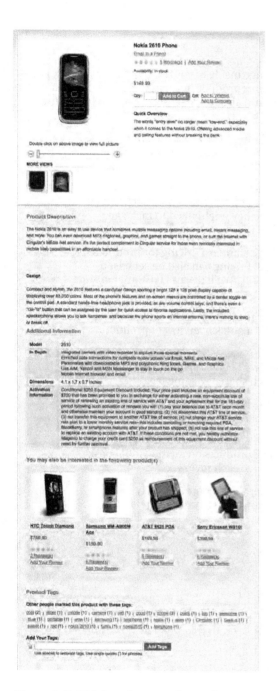

Figure 3-8. *This is a close-up of a product page. Each of the sections, including quick descriptions, product descriptions, and additional information are updatedable and customizable.*

Compare Products

Another great feature that Magento includes is giving a customer the ability to compare products side by side. Not only can customers compare pricing between two items, but they can also compare other information such as product descriptions, product skus, and other customizable options.

To compare items, customers must first add a product using the compare button which is found either on the category page or the product page. It's also noteworthy again that if a customer has javascript turned off they will not be able to compare products. Once the customer has more than one item in their compare products area, they may compare products. Customers also have the ability to "print this page," if they choose to compare products (see Figures 3-9 and 3-10).

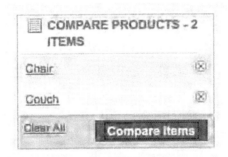

Figure 3-9. Products must first be added to the compare list by clicking the link underneath the add to cart button. Customers must add a minimum of two products to their compare items list before they can compare products.

Compare Products

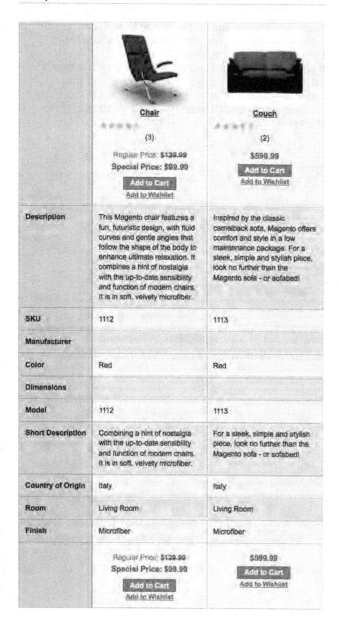

	Chair	Couch
	★★★★☆	★★★★☆
	(3)	(2)
	Regular Price: $139.99	$599.99
	Special Price: $99.90	Add to Cart
	Add to Cart	Add to Wishlist
	Add to Wishlist	
Description	This Magento chair features a fun, futuristic design, with fluid curves and gentle angles that follow the shape of the body to enhance ultimate relaxation. It combines a hint of nostalgia with the up-to-date sensibility and function of modern chairs. It is in soft, velvety microfiber.	Inspired by the classic camelback sofa, Magento offers comfort and style in a low maintenance package. For a sleek, simple and stylish piece, look no further than the Magento sofa - or sofabed!
SKU	1112	1113
Manufacturer		
Color	Red	Red
Dimensions		
Model	1112	1113
Short Description	Combining a hint of nostalgia with the up-to-date sensibility and function of modern chairs. It is in soft, velvety microfiber.	For a sleek, simple and stylish piece, look no further than the Magento sofa - or sofabed!
Country of Origin	Italy	Italy
Room	Living Room	Living Room
Finish	Microfiber	Microfiber
	Regular Price: $139.99	$599.99
	Special Price: $99.99	Add to Cart
	Add to Cart	Add to Wishlist
	Add to Wishlist	

Figure 3-10. *The Compare Products window. Here customers can compare different products and product details.*

CMS Pages and Static Blocks

In addition to being a top-notch eCommerce platform, Magento has the ability to display pages called CMS pages or content management system pages. CMS pages refer to any non-product page. These pages can include additional information about your eCommerce store, such as company information, about us, payment terms, and customer service. CMS pages are given their own URL address and can be customized in both appearance and layout. These pages allow you to include images and content in addition to your products. Figure 3-11 is an example of how CMS pages look on the public interface.

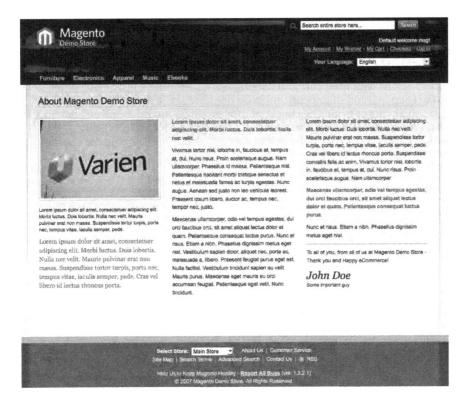

Figure 3-11. *This is a CMS page. It allows you to provide customers with important information about your store.*

Magento also provides another form of content management called static blocks. Static blocks are a great way of implementing editable content into your eCcommerce web site. The footer shown in Figure 3-12 is a perfect example of how to use static blocks. The footer, like other static blocks, is fully editable inside of Magento's administrative section. Static blocks can be used for news, upcoming events, and web site updates. If you understand the basics of HTML and PHP, you can place static blocks anywhere within your web site.

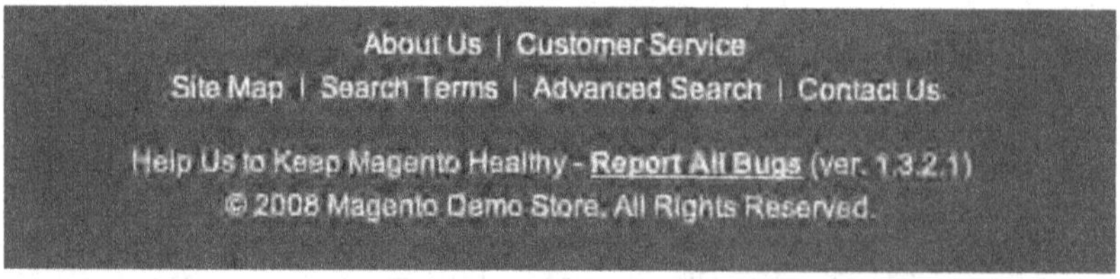

About Us | Customer Service
Site Map | Search Terms | Advanced Search | Contact Us

Help Us to Keep Magento Healthy - Report All Bugs (ver. 1.3.2.1)
© 2008 Magento Demo Store. All Rights Reserved.

Figure 3-12. The web site footer is a static block and can be edited through Magento's administrative interface.

The Checkout Process

A customer's checkout process begins with their cart and making any last minute adjustments before checking out. It's important to keep in mind that if customers do not have javascript enabled they will not be able to add products to their cart or begin the checkout process. Magento has done an amazing job at condensing and streamlining the checkout process into a single page. From a technical standpoint, Magento uses Ajax to reduce page transitions and save bandwidth by keeping the checkout process to one page. Customers can review their checkout information during the checkout process without having to visit another page (see Figure 3-13).

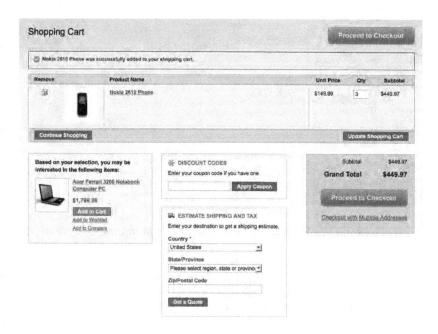

Figure 3-13. The shopping cart. This is the last stop before the checkout process begins. Customers can update products, enter discount codes, and get estimates on shipping.

Step 1: Checkout Method

Once customers review their shopping cart and click Proceed to Checkout, they will be presented with Magento's one-page checkout process. In the first of this process, customers must either checkout as a guest, register, or enter in login information if they are returning customers. Magento allows you to disable the ability for customers to check out as guests. This feature can be disabled from the Magento's administrative section (see Figure 3-14).

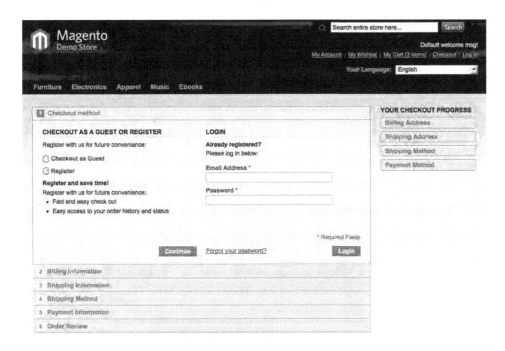

Figure 3-14. *Step 1 of the one-page checkout process. Customers have the ability to login, register, or checkout as a guest.*

Step 2: Billing Information

In this step, customers must enter in their Billing Information which includes name, company, email, mailing address, city, state, zip, country, and phone number. Customers can choose to ship to the same address and skip to step 4. If at any point the customers want to change this information they can go back to one of the previous steps by clicking one of the previous bars. After an Address is used for the first time, it will be associated with the customer's account and they will be able to select a previously used address from a drop down menu (see Figure 3-15).

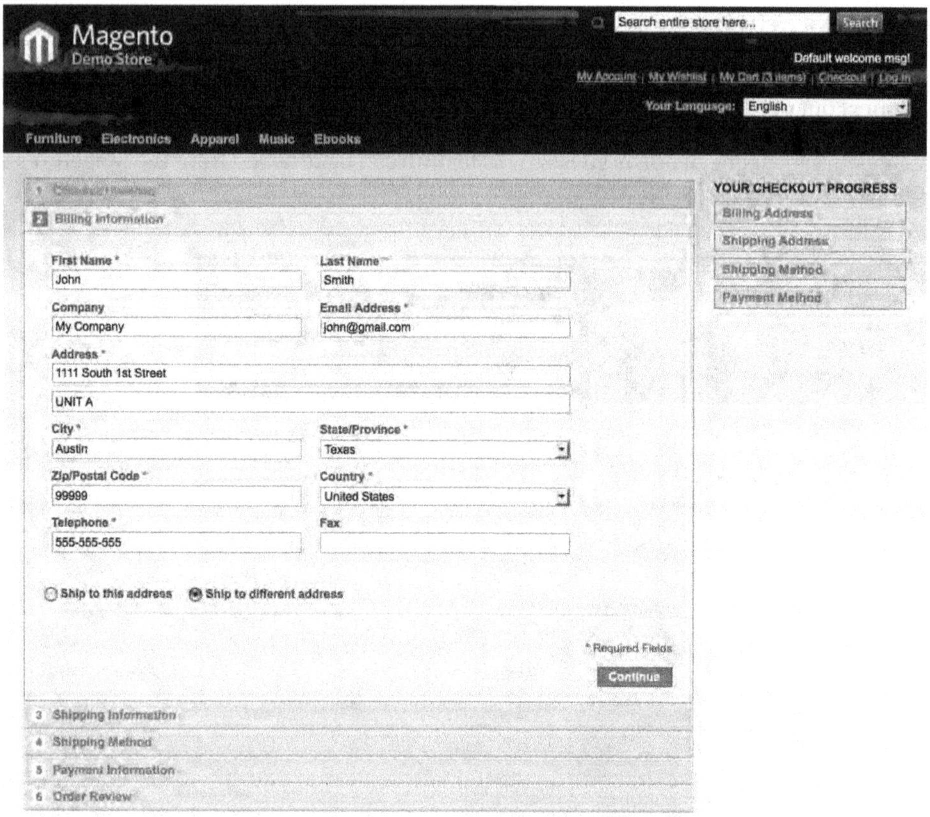

Figure 3-15. Step 2 of the onepage checkout process. Customers must enter in their billing information.

Step 3: Shipping Information

In step 3, customers must enter their shipping information. Similar to the billing information, this information will be accessible to the customer next time they start the checkout process (see Figure 3-16).

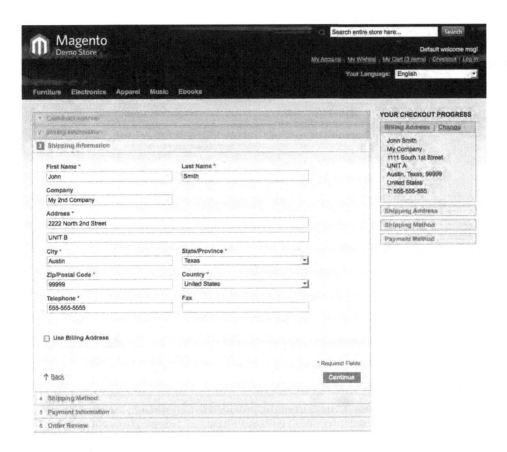

Figure 3-16. *Step 3 of the onepage checkout process. Customers must enter in their shipping information.*

Step 4: Shipping Method

In this step, customers must choose their shipping method to continue the checkout process. Magento provides complete control over the shipping options. Administrators can not only control which shipping auctions are available, but exactly how much shipping should cost. Magento also has UPS and FedEx shipping calculators built in. This allows for real-time shipping quotes by both the UPS and FedEx online shipping calculators. Customers can also enter in a gift message if their purchase is a gift (see Figure 3-17).

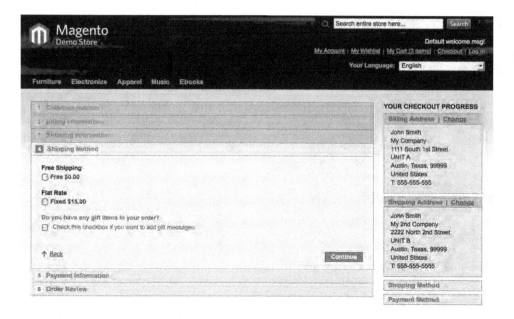

Figure 3-17. *Step 4 of the onepage checkout process. Customers must enter in their shipping information.*

Step 5: Payment Method

In step 5, customers must select a payment method from the provided list. By default, Magento offers several different payment options including integration with authorize.net, Google checkout, purchase orders, checks and money orders, and credit card storing for offline manual processing. There are also over 200 hundred different payment modules available on `http://www.magentocommerce.com/magento-connect`. For more information about installing and configuring extensions please refer to Chapter 10 (see Figure 3-18).

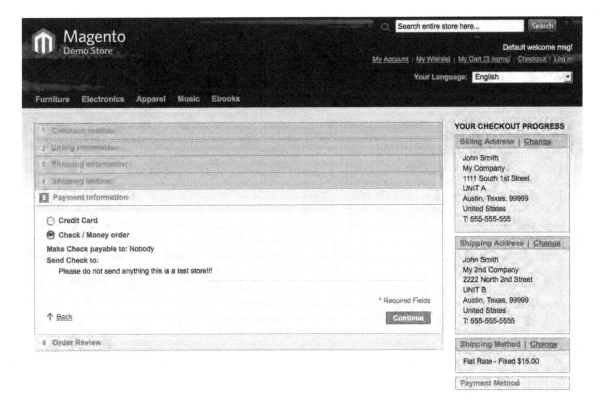

Figure 3-18. *Step 5 of the onepage checkout process. Selecting a payment method for the purchase.*

Step 6: Order Review

The sixth and the final step of the checkout process is called Order Review. Not only are customers given an itemized listing and order totals, but they can easily review their shipping address, billing address, shipping method, and payment method in the boxes on the right-hand side of the screen (see Figure 3-19).

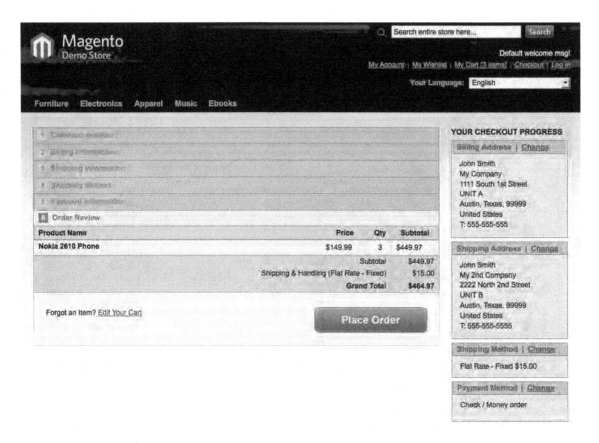

Figure 3-19. *Step 6 of the onepage checkout process. Customers must review an order and confirm it.*

At this point, customers can edit any other information before they submit their order. Once customers have placed their orders, they will be redirected to an order confirmation page. An e-mail will be sent to the customer and to the Magento store administrator. If customers choose to register during the checkout process and not check out as a guest they can view their order information using their My Account link.

Ship to Multiple Addresses

One of the interesting features about Magento is that customers have the ability to ship orders with multiple products to multiple addresses. While this may sound confusing, Magento does a great job of simplifying the process. After selecting destinations for each of the products in their orders, products are reorganized by destination. Customers can even select different shipping methods to different destinations. Orders are then processed and given unique order numbers based upon their destination.

Shipping to multiple addresses is not available to guests, so unlike the main checkout process, customers must register before they can begin the checkout process. If shipping to multiple addresses is not a feature you want to use in your store, administrators can also disable shipping to multiple addresses from inside the administration interface.

Step 1: Select Addresses

After reviewing their carts, customers can choose to ship their products to multiple addresses. Although not a one page checkout, the Shipping to Multiple Addresses option allows customers the ability to ship specific products and product quantities to different shipping addresses. Customers can add additional addresses by clicking the Enter a New Address button (see Figure 3-20).

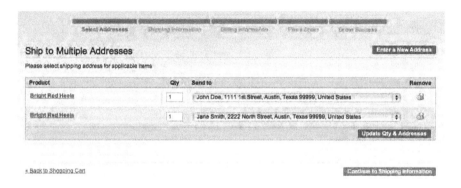

Figure 3-20. *Step 1 of the Ship to Multiple Address checkout process. Customers assign specific shipping address to each product and quantity.*

Step 2: Shipping Information

Once customers have selected addresses for each of their products and quantities, they will move to the shipping information page. Magento will separate and reorganize the order based upon the shipping addresses selected in step 1. Customers can select different shipping methods for each address. This is a great option for customers purchasing gifts or for wholesalers looking to ship similar products to multiple addresses (see Figure 3-21).

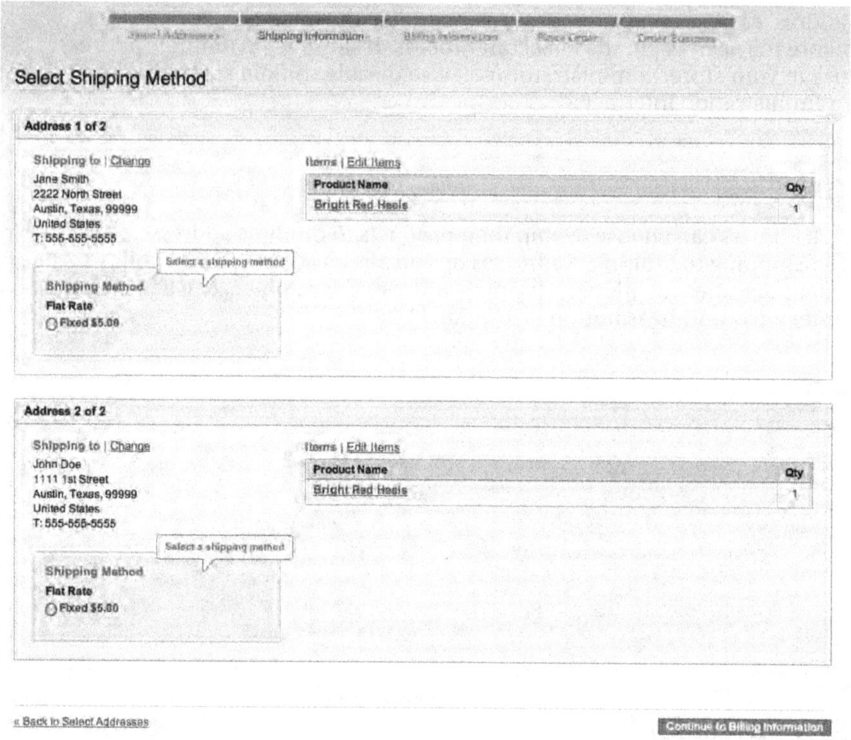

Figure 3-21. *Step 2 of the Ship to Multiple Address checkout process. Magento will reorganze orders based on the shipping address selected in step 1.*

Step 3: Billing Information

In step 3, customers must enter in their billing information and select a payment method for the orders. It is important to note that while customers can ship products to multiple addresses there can only be one billing address and payment method (see Figure 3-22).

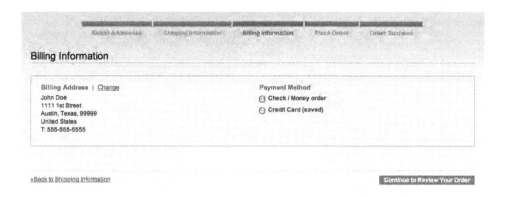

Figure 3-22. Step 3 of the Ship to Multiple Address checkout process. Selecting a billing address and a payment method.

Step 4: Place Order

Once customers have entered the information, they are presented with a Review Order page. This page displays the billing information, payment method, shipping information, and totals for each of the orders that are about to be placed. For easy management, Magento separates each unique shipping address into a new order. The customer will only be charged one time, but separating each order by shipping address allows for easy updating and product tracking (see Figure 3-23).

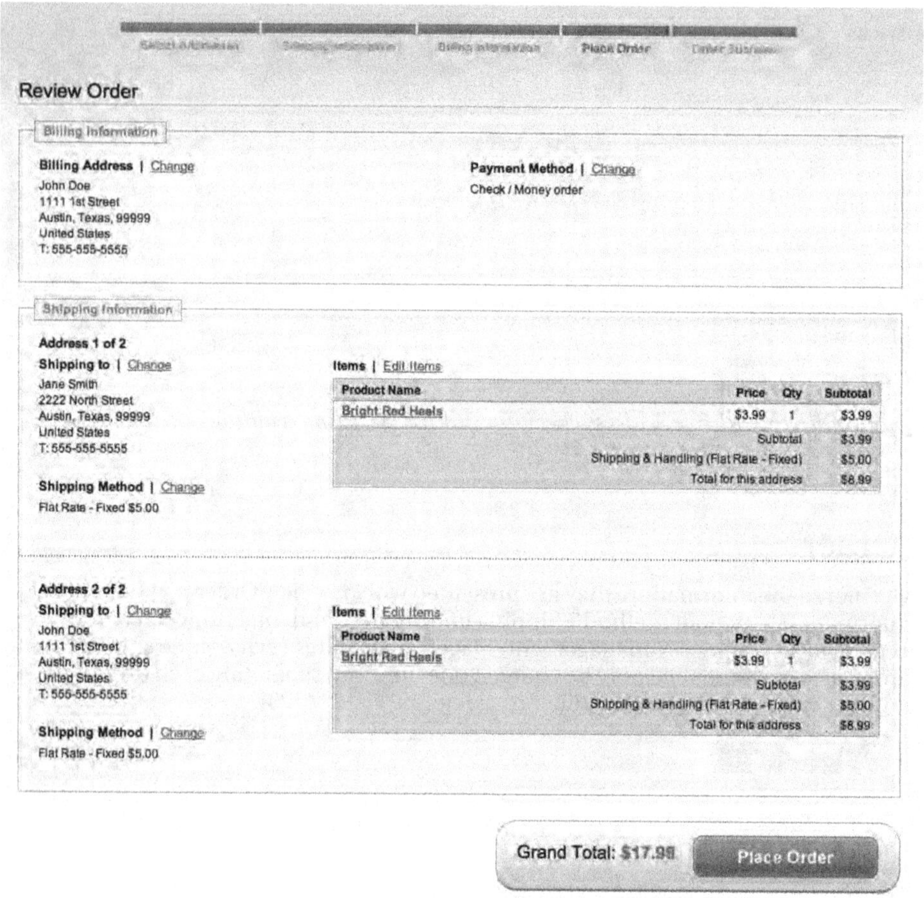

Figure 3-23. Step 4 of the Ship to Multiple Address checkout process. Customers must review thier orders before completing the process.

Step 5: Order Success

This case simply thanks a customer for placing their order and provides them with a list of order numbers that were placed. Both the customer and store administrators should receive an e-mail containing order confirmation (see Figure 3-24).

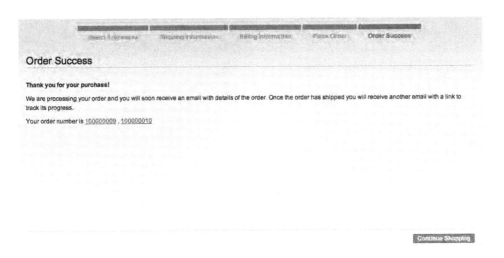

Figure 3-24. *Step 5 of the ship to multiple address checkout process. The order process is complete.*

Everything reviewed in this chapter in reference to the public interface is completely customizable and we will be going into details on how to customize the public interface in Chapter 9.

What's Next?

That's about all for the public interface, but that is only half of Magento. In Chapter 4, you'll be taking a similar look at the administrative interface. Once your store has been designed and built, the administrative interface is probably where you will spend the majority of your time monitoring your site and orders.

If you are already comfortable with the administrative interface and you are looking to jump in and configure your store by removing all of the demo information and functionality please take a look at Chapter 8.

CHAPTER 4

■ ■ ■

The Administration Interface Walk-through

The Administration Interface: The Dashboard

The administration interface is responsible for controlling everything you see on the public interface. You can view and manage orders, update customer information, and add new products to your store.

Before you login it's important to know that the administrative interface relies heavily on javascript, and if you do not have javascript running on your browser you will not be able to login or be able to use the administrative interface at its full capacity (see Figure 4-1).

You can login to your site's administrative interface by visiting: `http://www.yourdomain.com/index.php/admin/`.

Figure 4-1. The login panel to the administration interface

Once logged in, you will be redirected to the dashboard. The dashboard gives a quick overview of all the recent activity with your web site. You can view overviews of lifetime sales, average order totals, order transaction totals over a given period, and recent product searches by customers (see Figure 4-2).

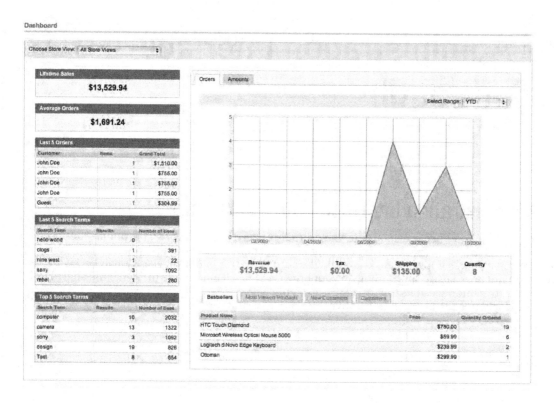

Figure 4-2. *The administration interface dashboard. Review recent sales, transaction amounts, and searches.*

The dashboard is the gateway to every other section in the administration interface. From the dashboard, you can navigate to each of these different sections:

- *Sales*: View orders, invoices, shipments, or create new orders

- *Catalog*: Create and manage products, categories, product attributes, and tags

- *Customers*: Create new customer accounts, edit existing customer accounts, and manage customer groups

- *Promotions:* Set up discount codes and shopping cart rules called promotions

- *Newsletter*: Manage newsletter subscribers, edit existing newsletters, or build new newsletters

- *CMS*: Manage non-product pages and static blocks

- *Reports*: View and export reports on a variety of different topics from sales, products, customers, and product reviews

- *System*: Contains all of the configuration details of your store, including individual store options, shipping settings, and cache management

The Administration Interface: Sales

The sales drop down contains six different areas: Orders, Invoices, Shipments, Credit Memos, Terms, and Conditions and Tax.

The Administration Interface: Sales—Orders Grid

Orders are a vital part of your store. Once an order has been placed in one of your stores, it will appear in the order grid page. The order grid serves three main purposes: reviewing orders by filtering options, bulk order actions, and creating new orders. As Figure 4-3 shows, orders are organized in pages in increments of 20, 30, 50, 100, and 200.

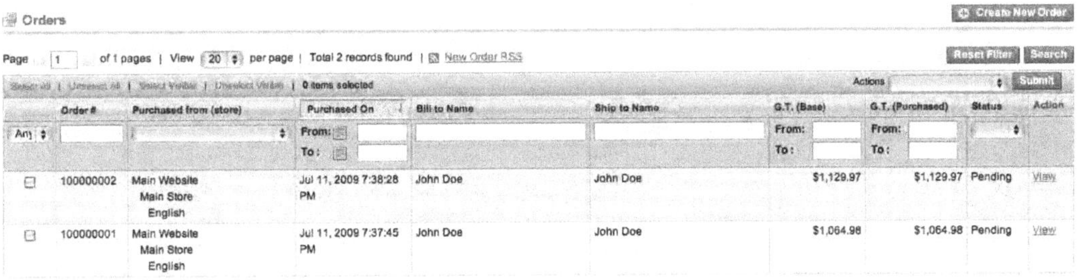

Figure 4-3. *A look at the Orders grid. Here you can filter which orders are displayed, change bulk order status, and create new orders.*

By default, orders are listed by the most Purchased On filter which displays orders from the most recent to the oldest. You can sort orders by clicking on any of the columns headers listed above the orders. These include: Order #, Purchased from (store), Purchased On, Bill to Name, Ship to Name, G.T. (Base), G.T. (Purchased), Status, and Action. Below the column headers are additional filtering options that include specific searching information, like a specific order number, purchase date, name, total amount, or status. To use the additional search features, enter in the specific information you are looking for and press search. Clicking the reset filter button to return the view to its default state.

From the sales order grid, you can also manage orders in bulk using the pulldown labeled Actions. Here you can modify multiple orders from the settings canceled, hold, and unhold. You can also print invoices, packing slips, and credit memos.

From the sales order grid, you can also create customer orders from inside the admin interface. To create a new order, simply click the Create New Order button on the Orders grid page (see Figures 4-4 and 4-5).

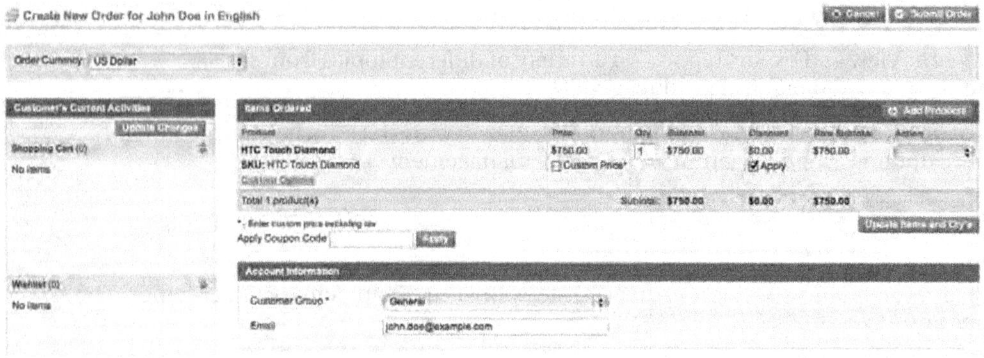

Figure 4-4. *Part 1 of creating an order from within the admin interface. View customer recent ativities and add products to the order.*

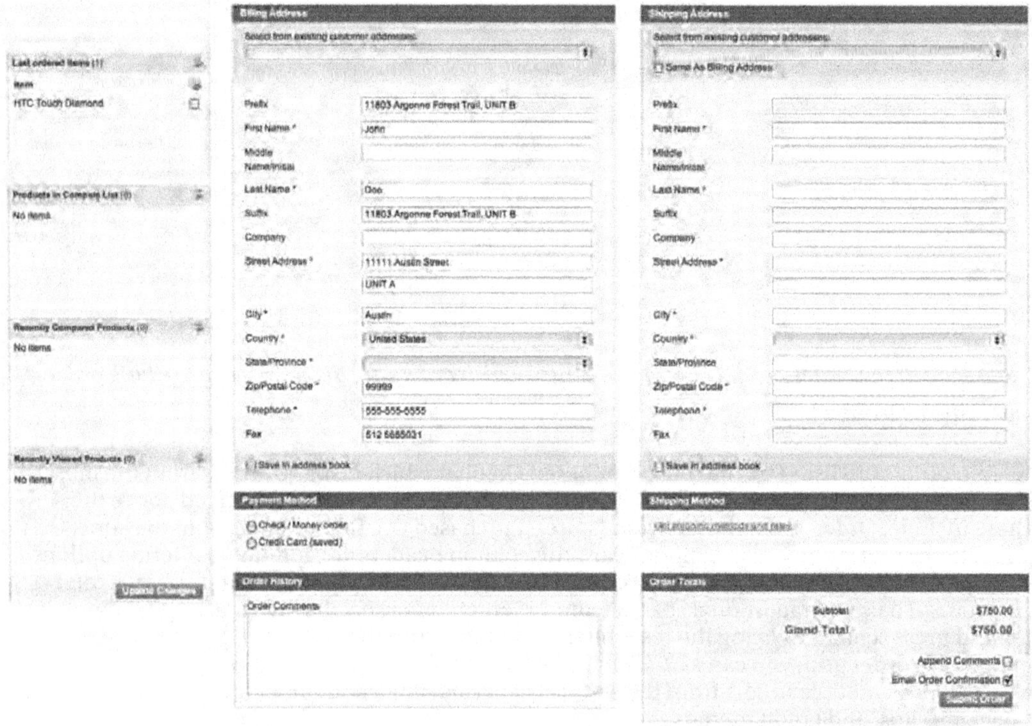

Figure 4-5. *Part 2 of creating an order from within the admin interface. Enter customer billing and shipping information, payment method, shipping method, comments, and submit the order.*

There are several steps involved with creating an order from inside the admin interface. They are the following:

- *Select a customer*. To begin the process, you must first either select an existing customer or click the create new customer button. If you choose the create new customer button, you can create a new customer and a new order at the same time.

- *Select a store*. If you have multiple stores set up, Magento will prompt you to select which store the order is for. While products and other content can be shared between different stores, customer accounts and orders are unique to individual stores. Customer registration is also unique to each store. As an example, if a customer is registered on store A and store B, but the order was placed under store A, it will not display under store B.

- *Add products to the order*. After selecting a customer and which store the order should be placed from, the next step is to add products to the order. If you selected an existing customer, a block called Customer's Current Activities will be displayed on the left-hand side. Customer's Current Activities provides an overview of products your customer has viewed, compared, and ordered. If the order is for a new customer, you will have to click the Add Products button. This will bring up a list of all available products. Click the checkbox next to the item and enter in the desired quantity for each product and click the Add Selected Product(s) to Order button. The page should refresh with all of the selected products. Now, you can update product quantities and set custom pricing for each item.

- *Enter customer information*. Next, enter in the customer's information including email address, billing address, and shipping address. If the order is using an existing customer, you can select previously used addresses from the Add New Address dropdown. If the address information is new and you'd like to save it for a future purchase, click the Save in address book checkbox on the bottom of both the billing and shipping address.

- *Payment method*. Select one of the payment options listed. If the payment method uses a credit card you will need to enter in that information as well.

- *Shipping method*. Select one of the shipping options listed. You must enter in a shipping address before shipping can be calculated.

- *Order comments*. If you need to add comments to the order, use the order comments field found within the Order History section. Order History stores comments and changes to order status and is viewable by customers. This is an optional area.

- *Order Totals:* Before you submit an order there are two additional checkboxes. If you added a comment to the order, make sure you select the Append Comments checkbox. You also have the ability to send the customer an email containing all order information by selecting the Email Order Confirmation checkbox.

Once you submit an order, you will be taken to the order details page. This page allows you to review and manipulate orders on an individual basis. Alternatively, you can reach this page by clicking on any order on the sales grid page (see Figure 4-6).

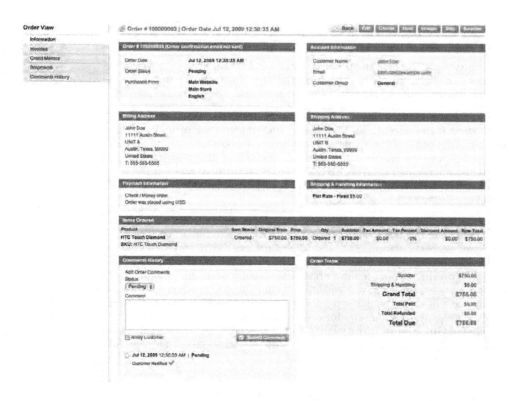

Figure 4-6. *The order details page. Here you can review and process orders through the various states including: Invoice, Ship,Cancel, Credit Memo, Reorder, and Ship.*

■ **Note** If you create a new order or a customer places an order its status will be set to PENDING.

The Administration Interface: Sales—Invoices Grid

The next step in processing a sales order is to create an invoice. Invoices can be created from the order details page (shown previously in Figure 4-5). Invoicing is a great way to notify customers that they still have an outstanding balance that needs to be paid. This is especially helpful if customers have the option to pay by check, money order, or purchase orders. You can also create multiple invoices per sales order. For example, if a customer orders two of product A and two of product B, you can invoice those two groups individually.

Once an order has been invoiced, it will appear on the Invoices Grid. The Invoices Grid uses a very similar layout to the sales order grid. Invoices can be filtered and searched for using the provided fields (see Figure 4-7).

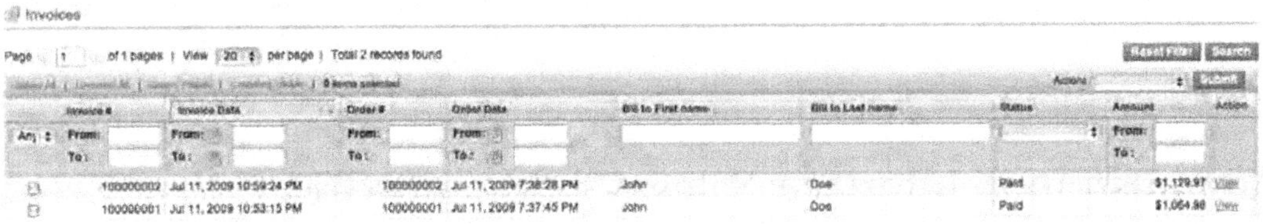

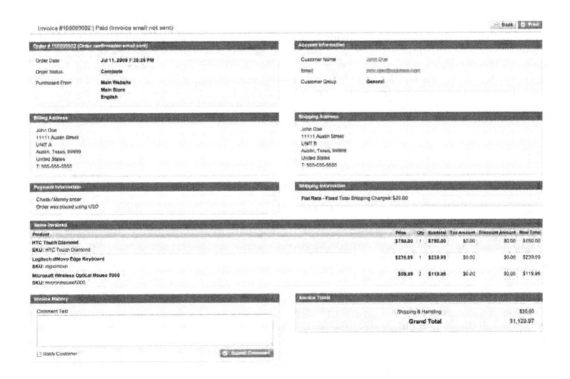

Figure 4-7. *This is a look at the invoice orders grid. Orders must be invoiced before they will appear on this list.*

If you click on any of the invoices you may be taken to the invoice detail page shown in Figure 4-8. At first glance, this might look identical to the sales order detail page, and while the information and layout is nearly identical it is important to understand that invoices cannot exists without a sales order being placed or created first.

Figure 4-8. *Similar to sales orders, invoices display all information necessary to invoice a customer.*

■ **Note** When you create an invoice for an order, this will change the order status from PENDING to PROCESSING.

The Administration Interface: Sales—Shipments Grid

Similar to invoices, shipment orders are created from the sales order detail page. During the shipment order process, Magento gives you the ability to create individual shipping orders, per specific product quantities depending on which products have shipped out. To do this, simply modify the Qty to Ship fields next to each product.

■ **Note** Chapter 7 will cover what to do if you need to cancel an order.

Alternatively, during the invoice creation process, there is a checkbox located under the shipping method box. If you select this checkbox, you will create a shipment order and can enter in one or more tracking numbers at the same time. If the notify customer checkbox is selected while the shipment order is being created, the customer will receive an email containing the tracking number information. Once added to shipment orders, customers can view tracking numbers by logging into the public interface and viewing their order history. Use this feature carefully because if you create a shipment order at the same time you are creating an invoice you will not be able to separate product quantities into different shipments (see Figure 4-9).

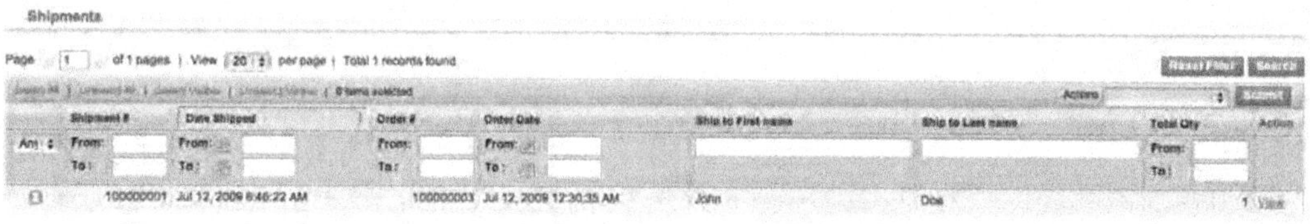

Figure 4-9. *Shipments order grid. Similar format to sales order grid and the invoice order grid.*

Individual shipment orders display all the necessary order information plus any tracking information that is associated with this shipment orders. While shipment orders share all of the same order information, if there are multiple shipping orders that have their own unique tracking information, each order with have to be updated individually (see Figure 4-10).

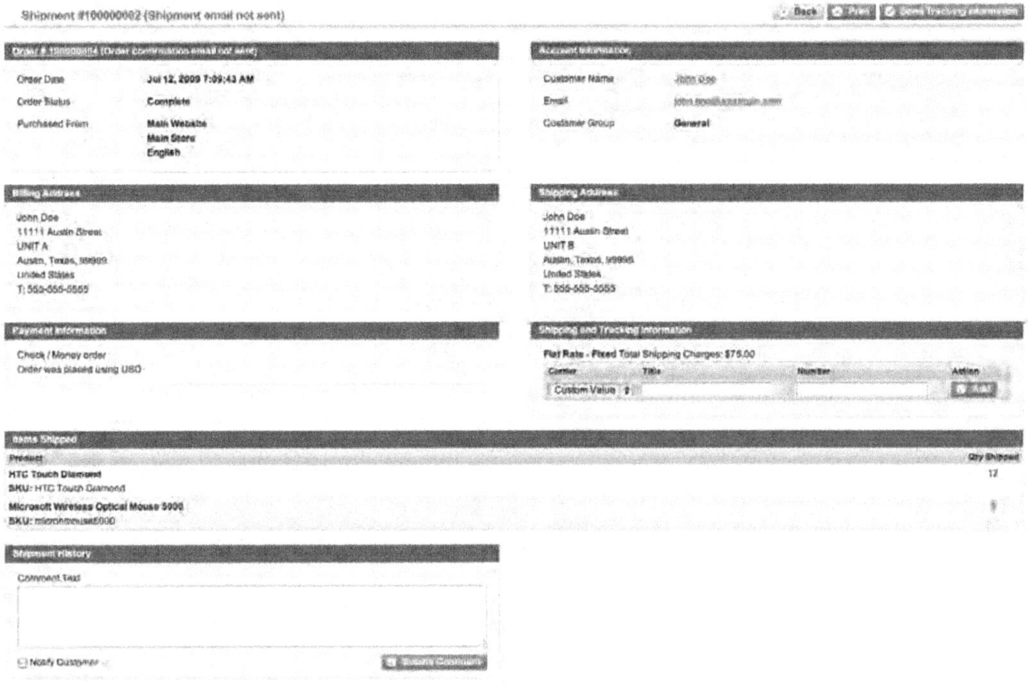

Figure 4-10. Similar to sales orders and invoices, shipment orders display order information and tracking information.

Note When you create a shipment for an order, this will change the order status from PROCESSING to COMPLETE. If an invoice for the order has not been created, a PENDING status will be changed to PROCESSING when you create a shipment order.

The Administration Interface: Sales—Credit Memos

Credit Memos are used to provide customers with refunds. Credit memos can be issued at any part in the process once an order has been placed. To create a credit memo, you must visit a sales order detail page. Credit memos allow you to either credit entire orders back to customers or select specific product quantities to refund to the customer. You can also fund a portion of the shipping price (see Figure 4-11).

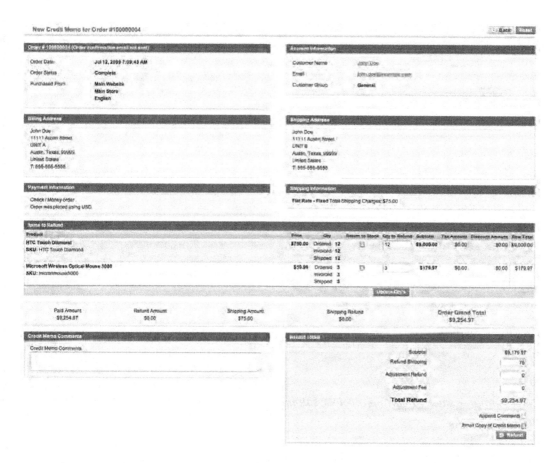

Figure 4-11. *Creating a credit memo from a sales order. Credit memos can refund portions or entire orders to customers.*

Once a credit memo has been created, it will be listed in the credit memo grid page. This grid page shares the same filtering options as orders, invoices, and shipments (see Figure 4-12).

Figure 4-12. *Creating a credit memo from a sales order. Credit memos can refund portions or entire orders to customers.*

> ■ **Note** Creating a credit memo will change the order status to COMPLETE regardless of what the previous status is set to.

The Administration Interface: Sales—Terms and Conditions

Terms and Conditions is the information the customers must agree to before purchasing products from your store. By default, Terms and Conditions are not active and will not display when customers checkout form your store. To activate them, Configuration ➤ System ➤ Checkout ➤ Checkout Options and set enable Terms and Conditions to yes and click the save config button. Once Terms and Conditions have been enabled, you can set up the additional information with this menu item.

Since you can set up Terms and Conditions for multiple stores, the first page of the Terms and Conditions menu page displays all Terms and Conditions in a grid format (see Figure 4-13).

Figure 4-13. *A grid view of all Terms and Conditions for each individual store*

With the detail view you can specify not only the terms and conditions that customers must agree to, but which store these terms and conditions should be displayed within. Terms and Conditions can be displayed as either Text or HTML. Terms and Conditions can also be enabled and disabled as needed (see Figures 4-14 and 4-15).

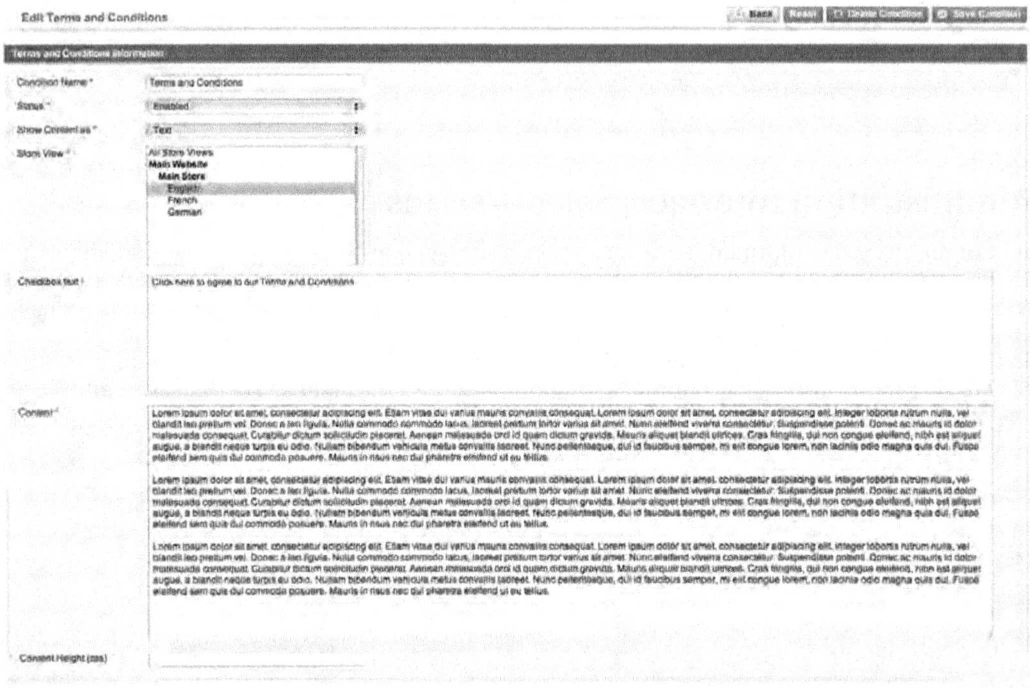

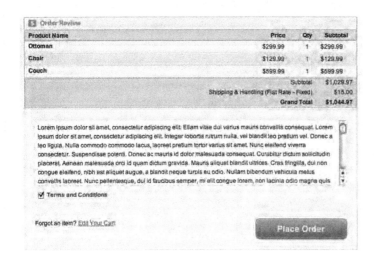

Figure 4-14. Edit Terms and Conditions Page

Figure 4-15. Terms and Conditions Displayed on the public interface during checkout

The Administration Interface: Sales—Tax

The Tax menu is only a placeholder for five submenus: manage tax Rules, manage tax zones and rates, import / export tax rates, customer tax classes, and product tax classes. Each one of these pages is responsible for configuring and modifying how your store uses taxes.

Tax can be configured based upon specific customers, products, and locations. For more information about taxes and how to configure and modify tax rates and classes, please refer to Chapter 5.

The Administration Interface: Catalog

The Catalog drop down of the administration interface gives you complete control over products, categories, tags, product attributes, and product reviews.

The Administration Interface: Catalog—Manage Products

The Manage Products links take you to another grid interface that display products by id, name, type, attributes, sku, price, quantity, and which web site the product is listed under (see Figure 4-16).

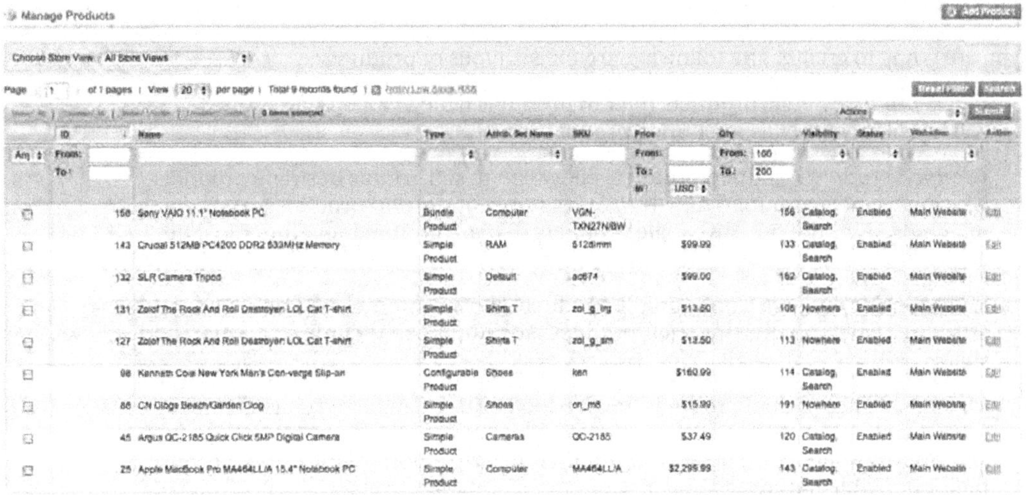

Figure 4-16. *A grid overview of all products currently in your Magento store. You can sort and search products.*

Clicking on any of these products will take you to the product details page. While somewhat overwhelming at first, the product detail page allows you to edit any of the following information related to your product: Name, sku, price, images, categories, attributes, and which web sites the product should be listed on (see Figure 4-17).

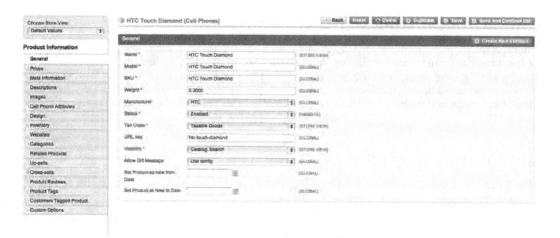

Figure 4-17. A product detail page. You can modify product names, pricing, images, and other product specific information.

Jumping back to the product grid overview, you can also create new products by clicking the Add Product button in the upper right-hand corner. To get started, you will need to select what type of product you are going to create. The following are the six types of products:

- *Single product:* Single products refer to products which can be sold individually or will be sold together as a grouped product.

- *Grouped product:* Grouped products allow you to sell groups of single products which have been grouped together. An example of a group product could be a matching shirt and tie. Any single products that are grouped together must be created first.

- *Configurable product:* Configurable products allow customers the ability to choose attributes when purchasing their product. Attributes can include size, color, and shape.

- *Virtual product:* Virtual products are products which can be purchased but are typically not physical products. Virtual Products can include additional product warranties or services. These products do not carry a normal inventory because of their intangible nature.

- *Bundle product:* Bundled products are products that are sold as a single product, but have several possible configurations. Computers are a perfect example of bundled products. Configuration options might include: Cases, CPU's, Hard Drives, ram and monitors.

- *Downloadable product:* Downloadable products are products that can be downloaded once purchased. After customers have purchased the product, they will be emailed a link to download the files they just purchased.

Once you have selected which product you want to create, you will be presented with a blank version of the product details page, as shown in Figure 4-18. You will need to fill out any information that is required before you can create the product. Required information is notated with an orange star. Don't worry if you miss any information, if you attempt to save the product with missing information, Magento will provide you with an alert and notification or what information is missing.

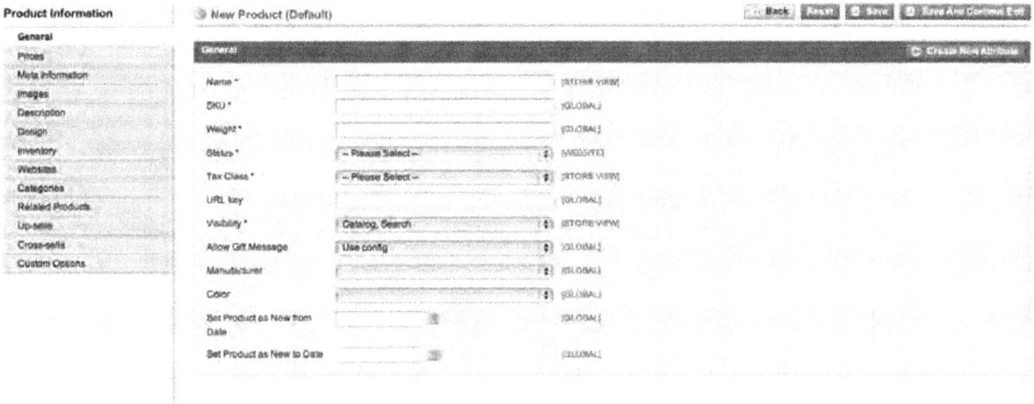

Figure 4-18. Creating a new product.Provide all information relevant to the product you are creating.

For more information on how to work with products, refer to Chapter 5.

The Administration Interface: Catalog—Manage Categories

Categories allow you to give your store structure and form.

Magento's category structure works differently than most. Each Magento store you create is assigned a unique Root category. Any other category that you want to use in your store must be created as a sub-category, even though all categories are considered sub-categories because you are placing them under the Root category. If you want a specific category to appear in your top-level navigation you will need to make sure you make that category an anchor category. Anchor categories will display in the top navigation and display any subcategories which are assigned below the specified anchor category.

The only problem with anchored categories is that you have a limited amount of horizontal space, so you are limited to the number of categories you can choose to anchor, as shown in Figure 4-19.

The break down looks something like the following:

Root Category

- Toys (anchored category)
  - Toy Category 1
  - Toy Category 2

- Games (anchored category)
  - Game Category 1
  - Game Category 2
- Stuffed Animals (anchored category)
  - Stuffed Animals Category 1
  - Stuffed Animals Category 2

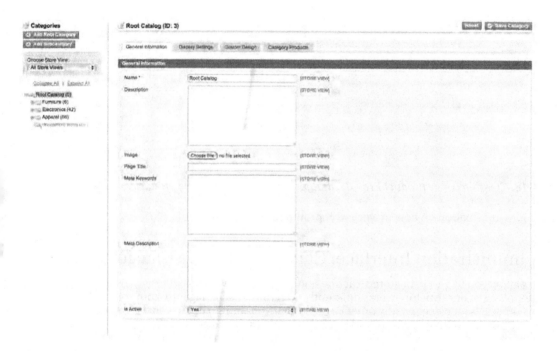

Figure 4-19. Managing Categories overview page. Edit Category name, photos, and descriptions.

■ **Tip** Creating a root category will not place it in the main navigation. You must select the Is Anchor drop down under the Display Settings tab.

The Administration Interface: Catalog—Attributes

Attributes are additional information provided to the clients that enable them to make informed decisions about the products they are looking at. Some examples of attributes are color, size, design, and

The Administration Interface: Catalog—Reviews and Ratings

One great feature about Magento is that it gives customers the ability to rate and review products. Both of these sections are represented underneath the Reviews and Ratings menu. Magento uses a 1–5 star rating system for product ratings. When customers fill out a review they are required to also include their 1–5 star rating on each of the rating topics. Price, quality, and value are all sample ratings shown in Figure 4-24.

Figure 4-24. *The Manage Ratings allows you to create new required rating options.*

Once you have set up your required ratings information and customers begin to complete reviews on your products, they will appear under Catalog ➤ Reviews and Ratings ➤ Customer Reviews ➤ Pending Reviews. Ratings must be approved before they will appear on the public web site. This helps to cut down on spam and unwarranted information.

Once ratings have been approved, they will be listed under Catalog ➤ Reviews and Ratings ➤ Customer Reviews ➤ Pending Reviews and appear in a list similar to Figure 4-25. This allows you to edit or delete reviews as necessary.

Figure 4-25. *The All Reviews page provides a list of product reviews written by customers. Reviews must be approved before appearing on the public interface.*

The Administration Interface: Catalog—Tags

Tags are an easy way to associate products with specific keywords. For example, if you are selling a cell phone, some example tags that might be associated with this product would be phone, camera, LC, sleek, and touchscreen. Tags can be added when the product is first created, but can also be added by customers from the public.

Underneath the Tags menu there are two menu choices: Pending Tags and All Tags. Pending Tags are Tags that have been suggested by customers, but must be approved before they will appear on the public interface. They will be listed under the Pending Tags menu item until they are approved.

Once you have created a tag for your products or customers tags have been approved, they will be listed under the Tags ➤ All Tags menu. You can see how many products have been tagged with specific keywords, edit tags, or delete tags (see Figure 4-26).

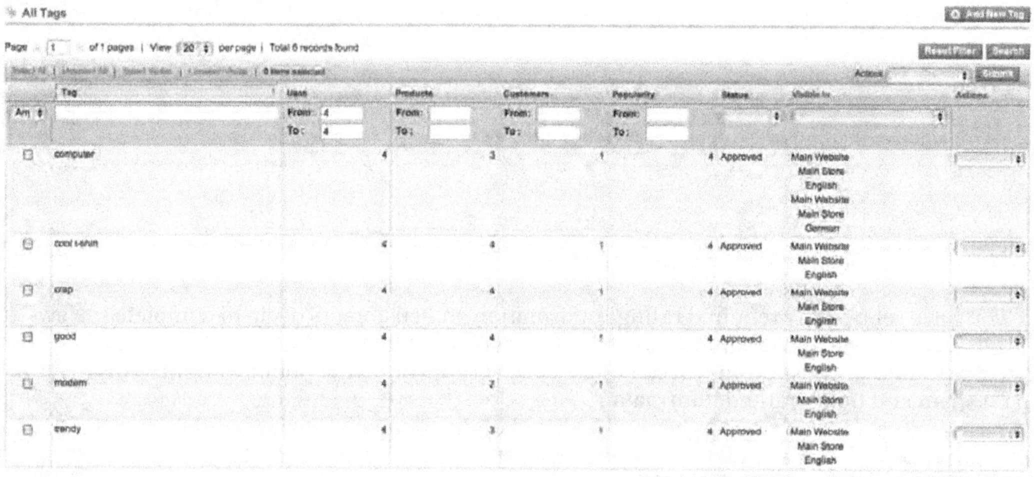

Figure 4-26. *The All tags overview page. Here you can edit or delete tags.*

The Administration Interface: Catalog—Google Base

Google Base, currently still in public Beta status, is an application that lets users submit all types of data to Google. If the information is relevant to a particular search, Google will display the information in Google search results, Google maps, and other search specific areas. It's an open effort aimed at helping Google's search results be more accurate and drive more traffic to your web site. It is in your store's benefit to take advantage of this service.

To take advantage of these services, you must visit `http://www.google.com/base/` and sign up for an account. Then, enter in your login information by going to System ➤ Configuration ➤ Sales ➤ Google API ➤ Google Base.

After you've signed up for an account and entered your information, you can begin adding products to your Google base account by using the inventory of your Magento store (see Figure 4-27).

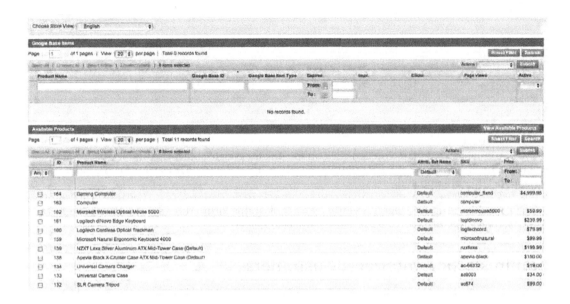

Figure 4-27. Adding products from your Magento store to Google Base.

■ **Note** If are using multiple stores, you can only submit products from the same store that you registered your Google base account with. Otherwise, Google base will not accept your products.

For more information on Google Base, you can visit Google's help section which is located at: `http://base.google.com/support/?hl=en&gl=us`

The Administration Interface: Catalog—Google Sitemap

Google sitemaps allow Google to quickly index your store. Sitemaps include additional information about your store. It is important to update your sitemap whenever you make changes to your store, so the next time your site is indexed, Google or any other search engine will pick up the changes.

To add a new sitemap to one of your stores, click the add sitemap button. You will need to enter a file name, path, and storeview to save your sitemap. If you choose to use a new folder, which is highly recommended, you must first create a folder using your FTP client that will share the same name you are going to use to store your sitemap (see Figure 4-28).

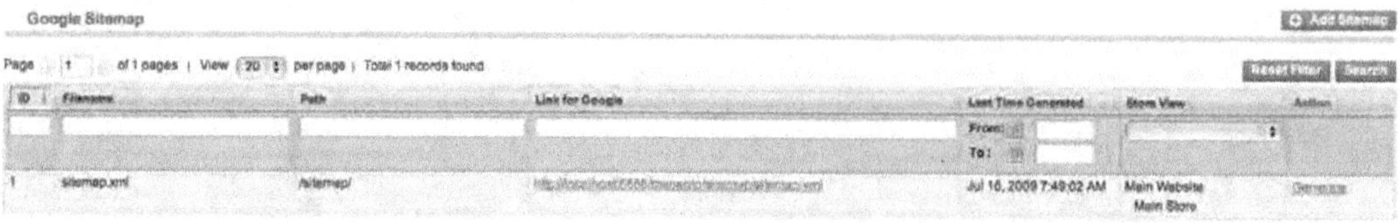

Figure 4-28. Google Sitemap provides a list of available sitemaps.

Once you've created a sitemap, you can click on the link for google categories and it will give you a preview of what the file looks like. It will contain page URLs, dates that the URLs were last modified, and how frequent the URLs are updated.

If you're trying to set up a google site map and are unable to do so, it might be because cron is not enabled. To find out more about Magento's cron take a look at this forum thread and link to Magento's wiki: `http://www.magentocommerce.com/boards/viewthread/13982/`.

The Administration Interface: Customers

The customers tab allows you to add new customers, manage existing customers, create or modify customer groups, and view online customers.

The Administration Interface: Customers—Manage Customers

The manage customers link provides an overview of every customer currently registered with your store. The overview page displays customer names, email address, customer group, telephone numbers, and additional information. You can filter how the overview page displays the list of customers or search for specific information in any of the provided fields: id number, name, email, group, telephone number, zip code, state/province, sign up date, and which web site they are assigned to.

The overview page also allows you to apply bulk actions to customers. You can delete customers, subscribe customers to newsletters, unsubscribe customers to newsletters, and assign customers to specific customer groups (see Figure 4-29).

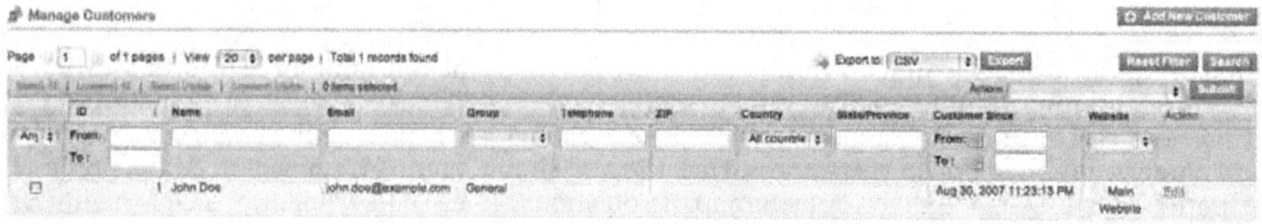

Figure 4-29. Manage Customer grid view provides an overview of all the customers who have registered or placed orders from your store.

Clicking on any of the customers listed in the manage custmers grid view will bring up the customer details page. The customer details page includes customer account information, a list of address they've used, their order history, and items they currently have in their shopping cart. The customer details page also keeps organized totals on how much customers have bought total and how much their average purchases were for (see Figure 4-30).

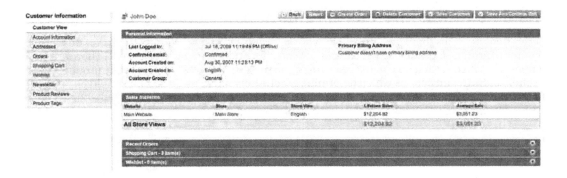

Figure 4-30. *The customer details page provides an in-depth look at a customer's details, including orders, wish lists, and product reviews.*

The Administration Interface: Customers—Customer Groups

Setting up customer groups allow you to establish multiple options for different customer groups. You can also assign different quantity pricing to products, depending on which group a customer is assigned to. This allows you to offer both retail pricing, wholesale pricing, and volume discounts through one web site. Customer groups also allow you to set up specific tax classes for customers. This provides control over tax. For example, typically wholesalers do not have to pay tax on wholesale purchases, but most retail customers are required to pay tax depending on their billing location. By assigning customers to specific groups depending on their requirements, this allows you complete control over product pricing and tax.

The Administration Interface: Customers—Online Customers

The online customers section displays a listing of all the customers currently browsing your store. This list includes customers who are not logged in. This page also displays the customers IP address, time their session started, and the most recent URL. If the customer is logged in the website, Magento will display their first and last name. If you click on a customer, you will be taken to their Manage Customer detail page that provides detailed information about the customer, items in their shopping cart, and their recent purchases.

The Administration Interface: Promotions

There are two different areas under promotions: Catalog Price Rules and Shopping Cart Price Rules. Catalog Price Rules are rules that affect the catalog only while Shopping Cart Price Rules are applied to items that are placed within a customer's cart.

The Administration Interface: Promotions—Catalog Price Rules

Catalog Price rules are rules that affect pricing for your entire store catalog. With this feature, you can bulk discounts to groups of products or single out one specific product to offer a discount. There are two main components when setting up catalog price rules: the rules themselves, which specify products by name, quantity or SKU, and actions which determine exactly how much of a discount should be applied to each product. For example, you can give discounts to products that are purchased together or discounts if a specific product quantity is purchased (see Figure 4-31).

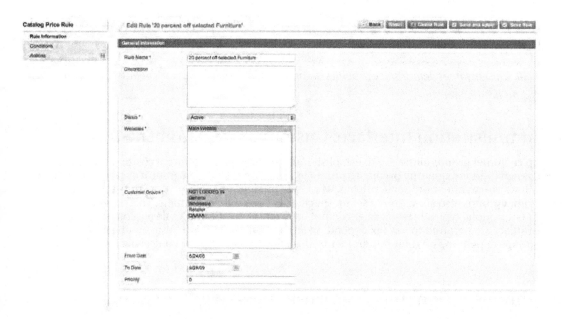

Figure 4-31. *Catalog Price rules are designed to modify products and offer discounts to customers.*

Rules are not retroactive, meaning if customer A purchases a product before the catalog price rule is applied, the rule will not update the previous order.

When establishing a catalog price rule it is important to know that if the today's date falls within the from date and the to date, the rules are instantaneous so once you've applied a catalog price rule it will immediately affect any products the rules apply to.

■ **Note** Customers have the ability to save products to their carts. If these products are modified by using the Catalog price rules, any saved items that have been modified will be removed from the customer's carts. Customers will have to add the same products to their carts again before they can checkout.

The Administration Interface: Promotions—Shopping Cart Price Rules

Unlike catalog price rules, shopping cart rules only affect customers during the checkout process. There are two types of shopping cart price rules, those that require a coupon code and those that do not require a coupon code. If the Shopping Cart Price Rules requires a coupon code; the customer is required to enter the coupon during checkout. Otherwise, it will not take effect. The shopping Cart Price rules that do not require a coupon code will automatically take effect once a customer has added the specific required products to their carts (see Figure 4-32).

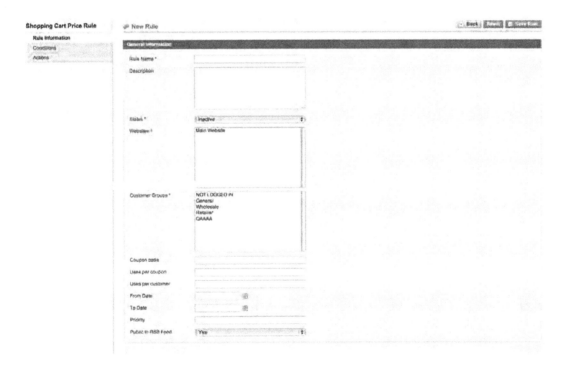

Figure 4-32. *Shopping Cart Price rules are designed to modify products and offer discounts to customers.*

The Administration Interface: Newsletter

Newsletters are a great way to keep customers informed of sales, new products and other store news. Customers can choose to receive your newsletter when they register for an account on your site or you can manually subscriber customers by visiting the Customer ➤ Manage Customers.

To send out newsletters from within your Magento interface, you need to make sure your SMTP settings (your mail settings) are correct. To review or make changes to your SMTP settings, visit System ➤ Configuration ➤ Advanced ➤ System.

The Administration Interface: Newsletter—Newsletter Templates

Before you can send a newsletter to your customers, you'll need to build a Newsletter Template. Templates contain all required information to send a newsletter to customers. You'll need to enter Template Name, Template Subject, Sender Name, and Sender email. The Template Content Newsletters can be sent as HTML, so you can paste the contents of the email into this section, as shown in Figure 4-33.

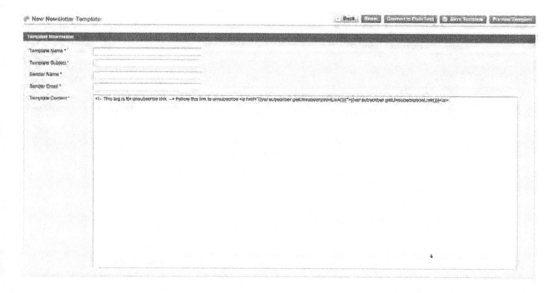

Figure 4-33. Building a new Newsletter Template. Newsletter Templates must be built before newsletters can be sent to customers.

Once you've built a newsletter template, it will be listed under the grid view. To send your newsletter to all current subscribers, you'll need to select Queue Newsletter from the Actions drop down on the right. You will have to assign a date for the Newsletter to be sent out and you also have the ability to modify the Newsletter Template you built before you send it out (see Figure 4-34).

Figure 4-34. *All Newsletter Templates that have been created will be listed on the overview page.*

The Administration Interface: Newsletter—Newsletter Queue

After a Newsletter has been submitted to the Newsletter Queue it will be shown on the Newsletter Queue page. This page allows you to sort newsletters by status, date, and other options. The Newsletter Queue page is not limited to newsletters that are pending, you can also view newsletters which have been previously sent.

After a newsletter has been sent, the number of processed newsletters should be equal to the number of recipients. If this number is different you'll need to visit the Newsletter Problem Reports page.

The Administration Interface: Newsletter—Newsletter Subscribers

The Newsletter Subscribers page provides an overview of all customers that have signed up to receive your newsletters. This page also displays which web site, store, and view the customer is from. You can view and sort customers by the provided fields. The only action that this page provides is the ability to unsubscribe customers in bulk. If you find that a customer is not signed up to received your newsletter you can visit Customer ➤ Manage Customers to add them to the list (see Figure 4-35).

Figure 4-35. *An overview of Newsletter Subscribers*

■ **Note** It's important to know that while you can create as many different types of newsletter as you want when customers sign up to receive a newsletter they are agreeing to receive all newsletters, not just one specific newsletter.

The Administration Interface: Newsletter—Newsletter Problem Reports

If there are any problems during the newsletter being sent to customers, those problems will be listed on this page. The most common problem is if the newsletter is sent to an email address that doesn't exist. This will allow you to remove incorrect email addresses from your records.

The Administration Interface: CMS

The CMS section of the administration interface controls any editable content that your site might require. Static content pages, static content blocks, and polls.

The Administration Interface: CMS—Manage Pages

The Manage Pages area gives you the ability to create and modify non-product content pages. These pages allow you to provide customers with additional information about your store, your policies, or any other information that you feel is relevant to share. Example CMS pages are: About Us, Customer Service, and a 404 error page.

By default, there are five different layouts that static pages can use: Empty, 1 column, 2 columns with left bar, 2 columns with right bar, and 3 columns. Empty pages will be displayed with a blank white background while each of the four other layouts will display the content between the normal page header and footer. Empty pages are ideal to provide quick information that can be displayed in a small external window (see Figure 4-36).

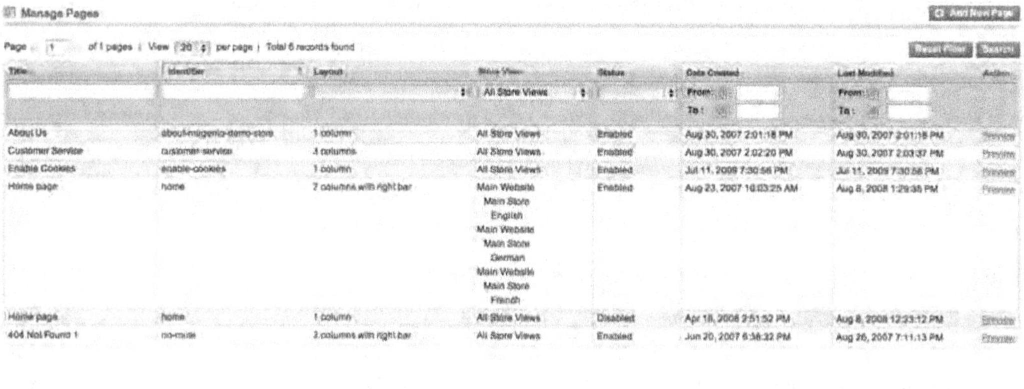

Figure 4-36. *The Manage Pages area controls all non-product related content within your store.*

The Administration Interface: CMS—Static Blocks

Static blocks are small areas within your store used to promote products and provide other features to your customers. Static Blocks can also act as landing pages for product categories. Figure 4-37 is used for an electronics landing page.

Figure 4-37. Editing a static block in the admin interface

Since Magento allows you to build these static blocks as HTML, the possibilities of how static blocks can be designed and laid out are endless. Figure 4-38 is a quick look at what the same static block looks like from the public.

Figure 4-38. *A quicklook at a static block on the public interface*

The Administration Interface: CMS—Poll Manager

Polls are a great informal way of evaluating customer opinions without being obtrusive. Polls can be used to gather information on upcoming products or even how customers feel about their experience using your online store.

You can control which web site store the poll should be viewed from and what information you'd like to poll your customers with. Opening and closing polls lets you control exactly when your polls are viewable on your store. You can also edit the information being asked and the results you've received (see Figure 4-39).

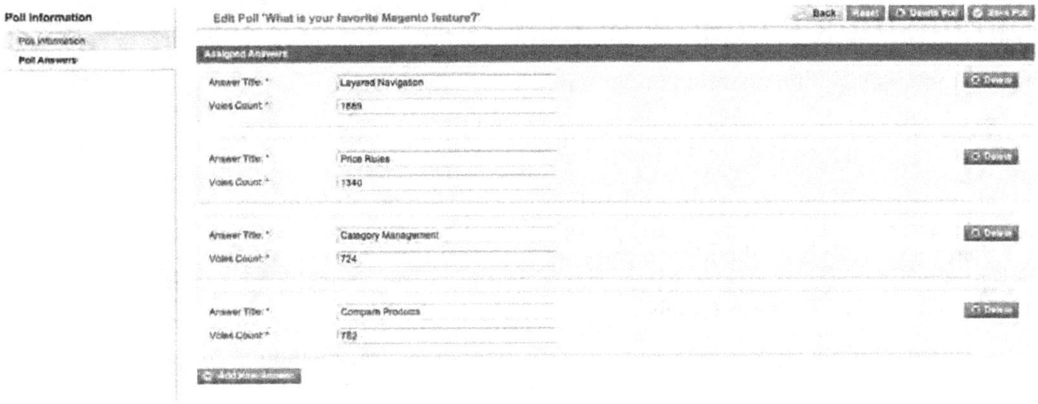

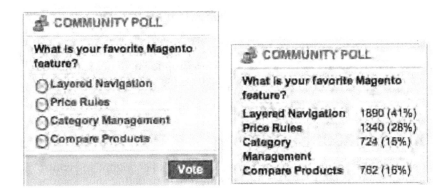

Figure 4-39. *Editing an existing poll*

This is what the same poll looks like from the public interface. Magento keeps a running total of all votes cast for each answer. Answer quantities are listed in both as a number and pecentage (see Figure 4-40).

Figure 4-40. *A before and after of the same poll viewed from the public interface*

The Administration Interface: Reports

The following are the seven different areas under reports.

- *Sales:* Sales offers six different types of reports, which are sales report, tax, shipping, total invoiced, total refunded, and coupons.

- *Shopping cart:* The two reports under shopping cart are products in carts and abandoned carts. Products in carts provide a complete list of items currently in all customer carts. While abandoned carts are carts in which customers began to checkout, but never completed the process. Actions of users who are logged in do count towards these report totals.

- *Products:* Product reports offer four different types of reports, including bestsellers, most viewed, low stock, and downloads.

- *Customers:* The three reports offered about customers are new accounts, customers by orders total, and customers by number of orders.

- *Reviews:* Review reports are organized into two different areas, customer reviews and product reviews. Customer reviews provide a review organized by customer while product reviews are organized by the products themselves.

- *Tags:* Tags offers three different reports, including customers, products, and popular.

- *Search terms:* Although search terms only offer one type of view, this report displays a complete listing of all terms customers have used when searching your site for products.

Magento gives you the ability to view reports by a range of date via a dropdown menu. You can also choose to view the date by a month, week, or day view. All reports can be exported in both excel and csv formats.

The Administration Interface: System

The heart of the administration interface is the system drop down. Here you can configure and control all the different parts of your store, including adding extension to your store to updating your account and contact information to modifying payment and shipping methods.

The Administration Interface: System—My Account

The My Account link allows you to update your information as an administrator. You can update your username, first and last name, email address, and change your password.

The Administration Interface: System—Notifications

Notifications are messages provided by Magento alerting administrators when there is new release or if there are any immediate security issues that you should be aware of. Messages are color coded and labeled by priority from notices, minor issues, major issues, and critical issues (see Figure 4-41).

Figure 4-41. The messages inbox provides a listing of all recent messages sorted by date received.

This area does not need to be checked for new messages. If a new message arrives, it will present itself as not only a horizontal notification bar, but a popup message will also be displayed.

The Administration Interface: System— Tools

By default, there is only one menu item under the tools dropdown: Backups. The backup system allows you to manually generate database backups of your store. These backups can be generated, downloaded, and stored just in case your Magento store is lost or crashes. Magento stores nearly all data inside of its database, including sales orders, customer information, and products. If you need to switch to a new hosting provider or restore a previous state of a store, be sure to make regular backups copies.

If you use the Backup generator, keep backups of your files (via ftp) so if something was to happen to your store, you would be able to restore everything (contained within the backup) within a short amount of time (see Figure 4-42).

Figure 4-42. A list of current database backups. Click the create backup to generate a new database backup.

The Administration Interface: System—Web Services

The Web Services area allows you to provide user web access into your Magento store. Currently, there are two standard protocols available to interface with Magento's web services: SOAP and XML RPC. There are two sections underneath Web Services, Users and Roles. Before you create a new user you'll need to set up specific rolls that the user will have access to. After you've set down some basic rolls, you can set up users. You can also assign unique API Keys to each user.

When setting up Roles you can control which web services commands, known as resources, are allowed. A full list of available web services commands can be found here: `http://www.magentocommerce.com/support/magento_core_api`.

Once a role is configured, you can set up individual users, each with different API keys. For more information about web services, user rolls and API functionality please take a look at Chapter 11.

The Administration Interface: System—Design

In this area, you can preassign changes to the view of each one of your Magento stores. This allows you to create additional views for the different seasons or holidays, for example, and assign specific dates in which the change should take place. You can also assign an end date to when the recent change should be removed.

During the Design assignment process, you'll be asked to pick a new view, labeled as Custom Design on this page. To create a new view, you'll need to visit System ➤ Manage Stores.

The Administration Interface: System—Import/Export

The Import/Export section allows you to import and export Customers and Products for each one of your Magento stores. Labeled as profiles this enables you to quickly duplicate products between two different Magento stores. The Import/Export feature can also act as a secondary backup for your stores (see Figure 4-43).

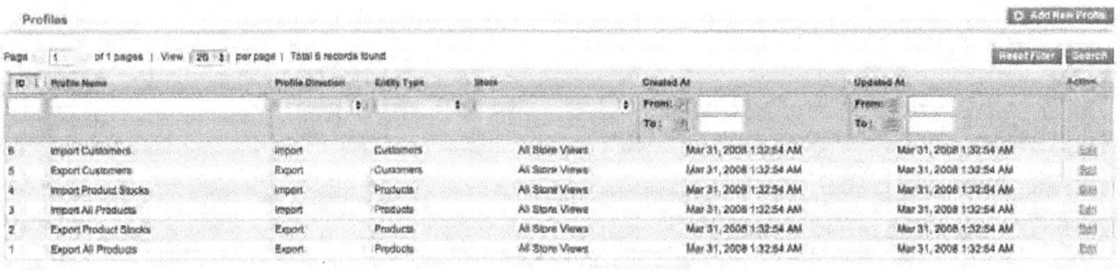

Figure 4-43. *A look at the profiles page underneath Import/Export. This shows a listing of each time something has been imported or exported from your store.*

The Administration Interface: System—Transactional Emails

Transactional emails are emails that notify customers whenever there is an update with their orders or accounts in regard to your store. While Magento includes roughly 35 templates, you will need to configure the email templates to your specific store and purpose. You also have the ablity to insert other dynamic variables like customer names, order details, and other information.

All of the email templates provided by Magento include the Magento logo or the words demo store, so you'll need to update each of these emails before you begin selling products. You can refer to Chapter 8 for additional steps including transactional emails.

The Administration Interface: System—Permissions

The permissions section controls any accounts that have access to the administration interface of Magento. By default, there is only one user, admin, set up as a roll of administrator, but you can create additional roles and create accounts for additional users. When you create a permission role you can restrict access to only specific parts of administration interface. This allows you to create admin type accounts with limited access to protect vital system information or credit card information contained within the orders section. User roles must be created before you create a new user with limited access.

The Administration Interface: System—Magento Connect

Magento describes Magento Connect as a marketplace for the distribution of community and commercial Magento products and services. Magento Connect also has you download plugs, known as extensions, for your Magento store. Extensions provide additional functionality to your Magento Store. Example extensions include additional shipping methods, payment methods, and other administration features. For more information about Magento connect visit the official Magento Connect website at http://www.magentocommerce.com/magento-connect.

You can refer to Chapter 12 for more information about Magento Connect and creating a Magento extension.

The Administration Interface: System—Cache Management

Due to the size and complexity, Magento has it's own caching system. By caching products, content, and other information this allows Magento speed in which pages are loaded. If you are configuring, or modifying Magento inside of a test environment or production server, it might be best to disable the cache system to double-check that your changes have been made. Otherwise, it is recommended that the cache system be enabled to help reduce the load on the server (see Figure 4-44).

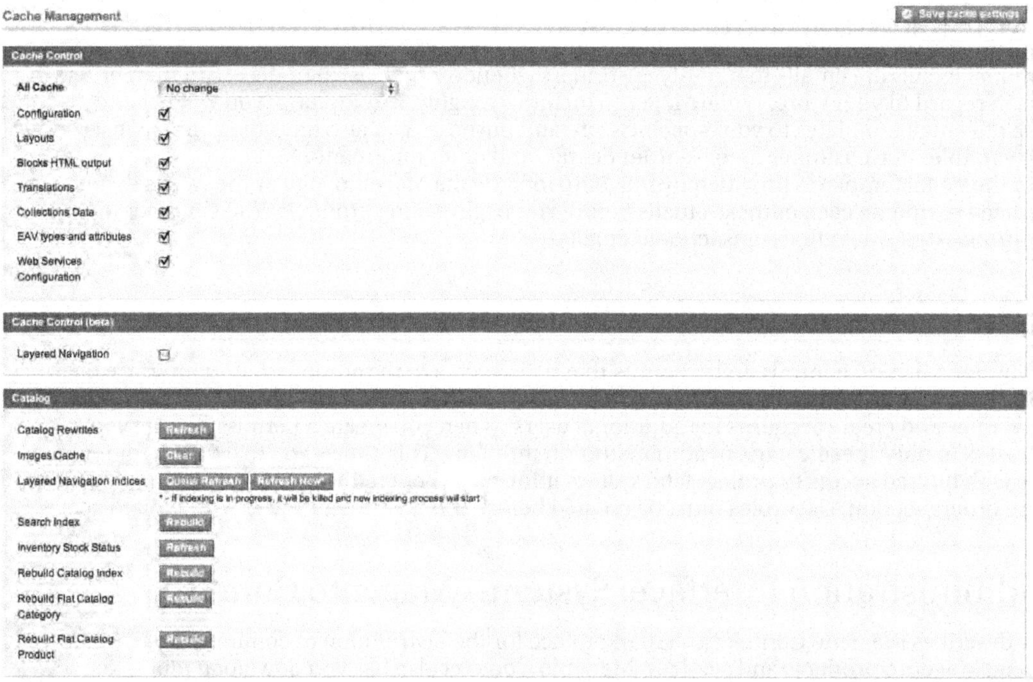

Figure 4-44. *Working with Magento's cache settings*

■ **Tip** If you are making modifications to Magento and you do not see the new changes take effect, make sure that the All Cache option is either set to disabled or refresh after you make your changes.

The Administration Interface: System—Manage Stores

One of the most amazing features about Magento is the ability to access and control multiple stores from one administration interface. The Manage Stores utility allows you to do that. Here you can set up multiple stores that use different domains names as well as multiple views of the same store. Stores also have the ability to share products and other information so this eliminates the need for duplicate information (see Figure 4-45).

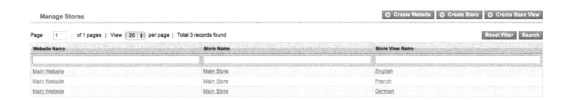

Figure 4-45. *Manage all of your web sites, Magento Stores, and views.*

In Chapter 10, you will be taking an in-depth look at how to set up multiple stores and views.

The Administration Interface: System—Configuration

The name says it all. The Configuration section of Magento controls all of your store settings including email, catalog settings, shipping methods, and payment methods. Notice in the upper left-hand corner the Default Config. Any changes you make while under this option will effect all stores. Alternatively, you can select a store from the dropdown menu and make changes to each store individually. This allows you to create settings and unique situations to each store (see Figure 4-46).

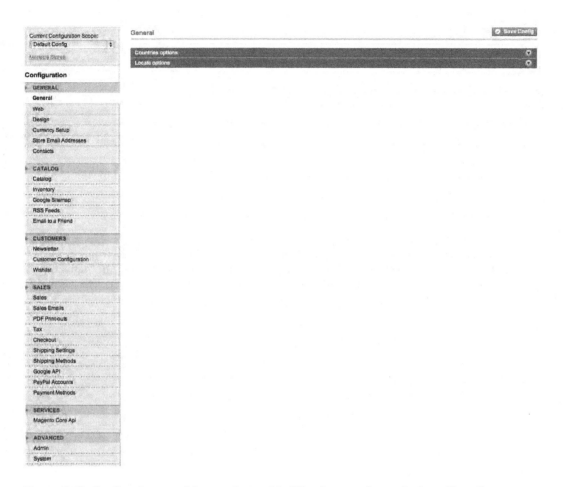

Figure 4-46. *Configuring your Magento Stores. Modifications can be made that affect all stores or individual stores.*

What's Next?

Now that we've covered both the public and administrative interfaces, there are two paths you can continue with this book. Chapters 5 through 7 will take an in-depth look at products, customers, and orders, the heart of your Magento store. If you're comfortable with each of these areas already and you want to start setting up your Magento store for use, I would suggest jumping ahead to Chapter 8.

CHAPTER 5

■■■

Working with Products

Getting Started with Categories

Before you begin working products, you need to set up your store Categories. Categories provide structure and organization to your store. You can use categories to organize products by type, functionality, or even brands. To add new categories or edit existing categories, login to your administrative interface and navigate to Catalog ➤ Manage Categories.

Figure 5-1. The Category administration interface

There are two types of Categories, Root Categories and Subcategories. Think of Root Categories as a big blanket, and while it's not the best practice to assign products to a root category, you are allowed to do this. The best thing to do when building your category structure is to assign products to any of the sub categories listed underneath your Root Category. Magento allows you to have multiple stores and you can assign different root categories to different stores. This allows you to design identical root categories and subcategories, which could contain the same products, but be assigned to different stores.

To change which root categories are assigned to each of your Magento stores, navigate to the System ➤ Manage Stores and select the store you'd like to edit. Even though you can assign multiple subcategories to a root category, you can only have one root category per store at a time.

By default, Magento only requires that you provide a name for a category to save it, but there are specific requirements that categories must meet before they are displayed on the public interface. For Categories to be displayed, they require the following:

- *Root category.* Subcategories must be under the correct root category for the correct store. You can only have one root category per store.

- *Categories must contain products.* Even if you create a category, if you do not have any products assigned to the new category it will not display.

- *Categories must be active.* If you create a new category, you must select yes from the Is Active Drop down; it's underneath the first section called General Information.

- *There must at least one anchor category.* You are allowed to create subcategories of subcategories, but for your categories to be displayed either the category you are working with or the top-level category must be set as an anchor category.

There are four sections under the category management page: General Settings, Display Settings, Custom Design, and Category Products.

Product Categories: General Settings

The general settings section contains the following fields and drop downs: Name, Description, Image, Page Title, Meta Keywords, Meta Description, Is Active, and URL Key. Name, Description, and Image are all items that will be displayed on the category landing page. Page Title gives the category a name. You can turn categories on and off by selecting yes or no from the Is Active dropdown menu. The remaining items, including Page Title, Meta Keywords, Meta Description, and URL Key are all provided by search engine optimization (SEO) for Magento Categories. The URL Key refers to the actual URL. It's recommended to make URLs as friendly as possible by removing any articles, like the words and, to, the, and at.

Product Categories: Display Settings

The display settings section allows you to control the appearance of each category independently from each other. You also have the ability to create CMS Blocks that act as mini landing pages for each one of your categories. This is particularly helpful when customers are interested in a specific product category, but not sure where to navigate to. You can use CMS Blocks to direct uses to different subcategories or pages within your site, as shown in Figure 5-2.

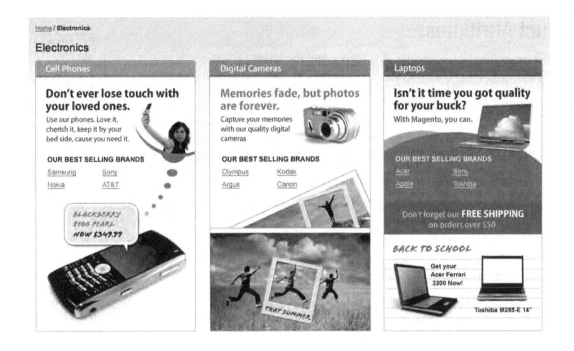

Figure 5-2. A CMS Block that acts a landing page for the Electronics Category

If you want, subcategories are allowed to be anchor links and be displayed as the top-level navigation, but there is limited room in the area provided for anchor links, so you will need to plan out the structure of your site ahead of time.

Product Categories: Custom Design

You are not limited to one design per store. You can set up multiple design variations per store. The custom design section allows you to set a custom design to each category individually. This allows you to create completely unique looks for different categories. Aside from the design of each category, you can select what type of page Layout the category and all its sub categories should use.

For more information about setting up multiple Magento stores and multiple designs, please refer to Chapter 10.

Product Categories: Category Products

Assign pre-existing products to categories under this section. You can search for specific products by Name, Id Number, SKU, Price Range, and Position. Products can be added simply by clicking the checkbox within the row associated with the product.

Product Attributes

Attributes are additional information provided to the clients that enable them to make informed decisions about the products they are looking at. Attributes not only provide customers with additional information about products, but they also provide sorting options as customers browse the category inside the public interface. Attributes are also listed side by side if customers choose to compare two or more products.

Product Attributes: Individual Product Attributes

Attributes are additional information provided to the clients that enable them to make informed decisions about the products they are looking at. Some examples of attributes are: color, size, design, and manufacturer. Product attributes can also contain additional information that is hidden from the customer, including true product cost, manufacturer's name, history, and other internal information. To create a new product attribute set, visit Catalog ➤ Attributes ➤ Manage Attribute.

Product Attributes: Product Attribute Sets

Once you've configured a few individual product attributes, you can build product attribute sets. Sets are huge time savers. Instead of creating attributes, add each attribute individually to a product. When you create a new product you can select an attribute set that already has a predefined assignment of attributes you have set up for your product.

To create a new product attribute set visit, Catalog ➤ Attributes ➤ Manage Attribute Sets and click the Add new set button in the upper left-hand corner. Not only do you control what information is required for different types of products through attributes, you can also control what information is required to gather from the client. Not all attributes are required to fulfill customer orders.

Creating a Simple Product

Once you've created your categories, you'll need to create products to fill those categories. To get started, navigate to Catalog ➤ Manage Products and click add product in the upper right-hand corner. If you set up any attribute sets, you will be presented with two drop down menus before you begin. One asks you to select an Attribute Set and a Product type. To start, let's select Default for Attribute Set and Simple Product for Product Type (see Figure 5-3).

***Figure 5-3.** Selecting an Attribute Set and Product Type to begin the product creation process*

Next is the Product Information screen where you configure all the necessary information about your product. It consists of 13 different areas: General, Prices, Meta Information, Images, Description, Design, Inventory, Web sites, Categories, Related Products, Up-sells, Cross-sells, and Custom options.

Product Information: General

The General section contains much of the core required information for creating a new product. The required fields are: Name, SKU, Weight, Status, Tax Class, and Visibility. With the status drop down, you can quickly enable and disable products.

You can also set products to a new status under the Set Product as New From Date and Set Product as New to Date. This gives you the ability to feature New products as they are added to your store (see Figure 5-4).

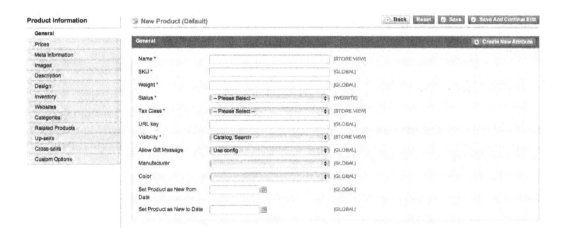

Figure 5-4. *Production Information Page, General tab*

Product Information: Prices

The Prices section contains all pricing information for products. The only required field is the basic Price field. The field called cost is for internal use only, dealing with reporting and is not viewable by customers. Tier Price not only lets you set up quantity base pricing, but quantity-based pricing per customer group. In Chapter 6, you'll be taking an in-depth look at customers, customer groups, and how customer group pricing works.

Products can be given Special Prices in this tab. Special prices are prices which are viable and available to all customers, regardless of their customer group (see Figure 5-5).

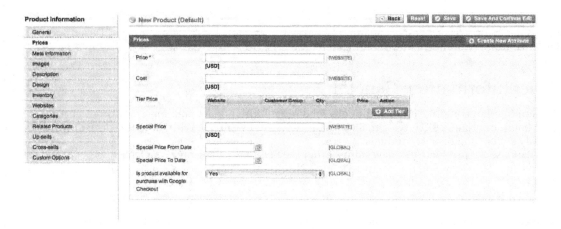

Figure 5-5. *Production Information Page, Prices tab*

Product Information: Meta Information

The Meta Information section contains only three simple fields: Meta Title, Meta Keywords, and Meta Descriptions. All of this information will be displayed in the HTML <HEAD>, and although hidden to the customer it is important for Search Engine Optimization and better search engine results. Information in this tab is not required to create a new product (see Figure 5-6).

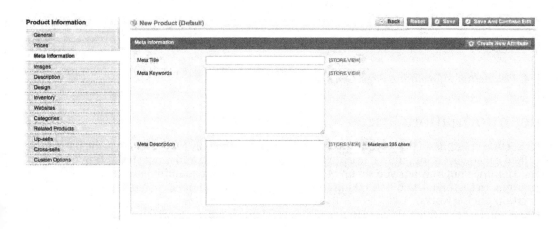

Figure 5-6. *Production Information Page, Meta Information tab*

Product Information: Images

The Images section contains options to upload images for your product. Magento allows you to use different images for each of your different store views. You can also upload different images for thumbnails, small images and base image (full size image). Although recommended, images are not required to create a product (see Figure 5-7).

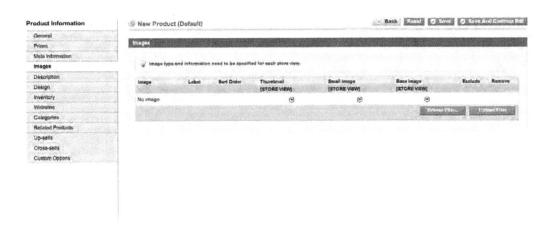

Figure 5-7. *Production Information Page, Images tab*

Product Information: Description

The Description section contains only two fields: Description and Short Description. Both of these fields are required to save a product. The short description will be displayed on the product list view and the Description and short description will be displayed on the product detail page, as shown in Figure 5-8.

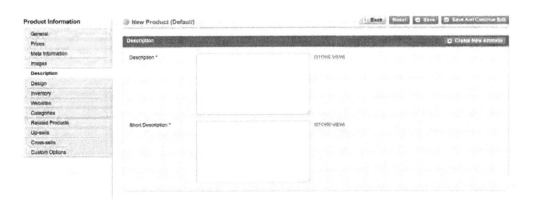

Figure 5-8. *Production Information Page, Description tab*

Product Information: Design

Similar to Category configuration, you can assign unique layouts and designs to individual product pages. There is no required information on this section (see Figure 5-9).

Figure 5-9. *Production Information Page, Design section*

Product Information: Inventory

The Inventory section contains a number of different fields. Most importantly, it is the Qty which is required to save a product. Magento will keep track each time the product is purchased and will adjust the Qty accordingly. You can also set up email notification when product Qty's drop below a specific level. If you do not want to keep track of your inventory in this manner, the Manage Stock drop down can be changed from Yes to No. Aside from basic Qty inventory, you can also control minimum and maximum numbers of the product customers can purchase (see Figure 5-10).

Figure 5-10. *Production Information Page, Inventory section*

> ■ **Tip** Make sure you change the Stock Availability drop down from Out of Stock to In Stock. Although not required, if you do not make this change your product will not display.

Product Information: Web Sites

The web site section controls which web site your product will be displayed on. This is not required to save your product, but it is required if you want your product to be displayed. While you are not limited to displaying products on one web site, you must select the web site you want your product to be displayed in (see Figure 5-11).

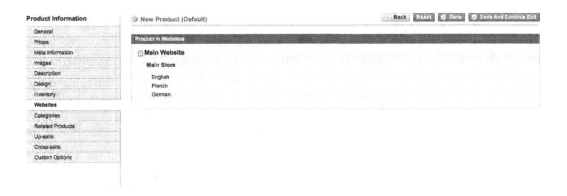

Figure 5-11. Production Information Page, Web sites section

Product Information: Categories

The Categories section brings up a list of all available Categories. Categories must be created before you can assign products to them. Products can be assigned to multiple categories and multiple stores. If you have multiple Magento stores, you will need to assign products to each store and category you want the product to be displayed within (see Figure 5-12).

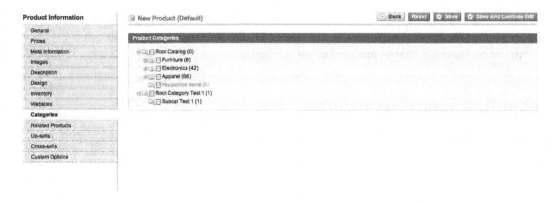

Figure 5-12. Production Information Page, Categories section

Product Information: Related Products, Up-sells and Cross-sells

Related Products, Up-sells, and Cross-sells allow for cross-promotion within your store. You can assign specific related products to the product you are currently making. To assign related products, you'll need to make sure you select the check boxes on the far left column. These products will be displayed on category pages, product details pages, and the customer cart page. Neither Related Products, Up-sells, and Cross-sells are a requirement to create a new product (see Figure 5-13).

Figure 5-13. Production Information Page, Related Products, Up-sells, and Cross-sells section

Product Information: Custom Options

Form elements for custom Forms could include blank fields, drop downs, radio buttons, etc. Custom options differ from product attributes, because they are unique to each individual product. You cannot create sets with custom options. They have to be recreated with every new product. This section is not required to create a new product (see Figure 5-14).

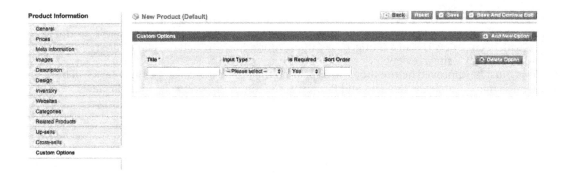

Figure 5-14. *Production Information Page, Related Products section*

Different Types of Products

To review, the following are the six types of products:

- *Single product*: Single products refer to products that can be sold individually or will be sold together as a grouped product.

- *Grouped product*: Grouped products allow you to sell groups of single products that have been grouped together. An example of a group product could be a matching shirt and tie. Any single products that are grouped together must be created first.

- *Configurable product*: Configurable products allow customers the ability to choose attributes when purchasing their product. Attributes can include size, color, and shape.

- *Virtual product:* Virtual products are products which can be purchased, but are typically not physical goods. Virtual Products can include additional product warranties or services. These products do not carry a normal inventory because of their intangible nature.

- *Bundle product*: Bundled products are products that are sold as a single product, but have several possible configurations. Computers are a perfect example of bundled products. Configuration options might include cases, CPUs, hard drives, ram, and monitors.

- *Downloadable product:* Downloadable products are products that can be downloaded once purchased. After customers have purchased the product, they will be emailed a link to download the files they just purchased.

Product Reviews

By now, you should know that customers have the ability to write reviews about your store's products. Associated with each review is also a rating, based upon your criteria, which the clients are required to also submit when they write a review.

Reviews must be approved before they will appear on the public interface. Pending tags will be listed under the menu Catalog ➤ Reviews and Ratings ➤ Customer Reviews ➤ Pending Reviews.

Product tags

Tags are an easy way to associate products with specific keywords. For example, if you are selling a cell phone, some example tags that might be associated with this product would be phone, camera, lcd, sleek, and touchscreen. Tags can be added when the product is first created, but can also be added by customers from the public.

Tags must be approved before they will appear on the public interface. Pending tags will be listed under the menu Catalog ➤ Tags ➤ Pending Tags.

■ **Note** Currently, once a product is created you can only add tags from the public interface. Hopefully, this is an issue that Magento corrects in the future.

What's Next?

That wraps up working with Products. In Chapter 6, you will be taking a look at customers just like you did with products. Chapter 7 includes an in-depth look at orders. If you are looking to jump in and start using your Magento store, take a look at Chapter 8.

■ ■ ■

Working with Customers

Getting Started with Customers

What's an eCommerce store without customers? Customers are an essential part of running an eCommerce-based store. Whether it's updating order information, managing customer groups, creating additional tax classes, or creating new customers, Magento provides the resources that allow you to provide customer interaction and management.

While issues such as conversion rates, discounts, and product promotions are important customer issues, we'll leave those issues up to you and your clients to decide which methods work best for your store.

Guest Checkout Customers

While customers have the ability to register an account before they move to the checkout process, during the checkout process, customers can checkout as guests.

The guest checkout process works exactly the same as a normal checkout process with the exception that customers who check out as a guest will not have their information stored in the Magento database. While this does add an additional level of privacy for customers, it automatically excludes them from receiving your store's newsletter (see Figure 6-1).

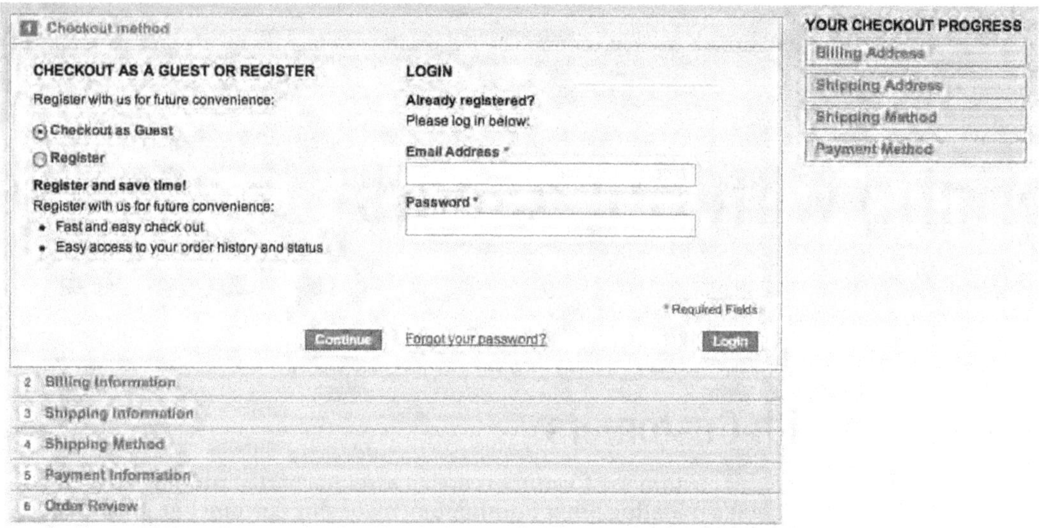

Figure 6-1. Checkout as a guest. This works exactly the same as if a registered customer checkout but guests' information is not saved. Guests will need to either register if they make a second purchase with your store or checkout as a guest again.

If this is not a feature you want to use on your site, you will need to disable customer checkout by navigating to System ➤ Configuration. Once the configuration page has loaded, look for Checkout underneath Sales on the left-hand side. Under the Checkout Options Header, there is a drop down menu called Allow Guest Checkout, select No from the drop down and click save config in the upper-right hand corner (see Figure 6-2).

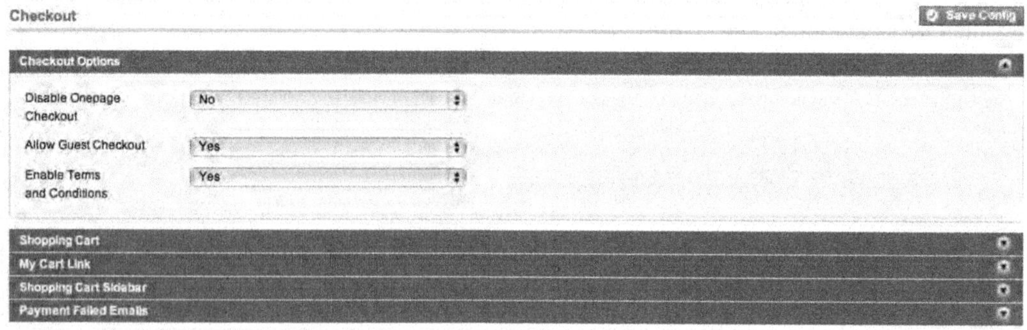

Figure 6-2. Disabling guest checkout from the administrative interface

If you have multiple Magento stores, you adjust this setting under the "Current Configuration Scope" in the upper left-hand corner, for each individual site.

Creating New Customers

Adding new customers are not just unique to new orders, you can add new Customers to your store through the Administration Interface. To do this, navigate to Customers ➤ Manage Customers, then click the Add New Customer button in the upper-right hand corner. Once the create customer page loads it should look like Figure 6-3.

Figure 6-3. *Creating a new customer from the administration interface*

Creating a new customer is divided up into two sections, Account Information and Addresses. The first section, Account Information, includes several required information items that are denoted by the red asterisk. Customer accounts are unique to each web site, and while you can create the same customer for multiple web sites, each one of those accounts must be created separately.

The second section, Addresses, contains address information for the new customer you are creating. While it's not required, if you have their billing and shipping information, it is recommended that when you create a new customer that you enter in this information. It will save the customer time during their checkout process. Customers can add new addresses during the checkout process or manage any of their addresses by clicking the My Account link in the header. Customers must be logged into the public interface to edit their account information.

> ■ **Note** If you have multiple Magento web sites, customers can only be assigned to one web site. This is a permanent assignment that cannot be changed once the customer has been saved.

Importing Customer Information

You can also import existing customers via a csv file in the administrative interface. To import customers you will need to navigate to System ➤ Import/Export ➤ Profiles ➤ Import Customers. You will need to configure your csv file with headers. The easiest thing to do is to create a single customer, and then export that customer list. This will give you an example format to adjust your csv file and import all of your customers. For more information about importing customer profiles, visit this Magento forum thread: http://www.magentocommerce.com/boards/viewthread/22430/.

Detailed Customer Information

Once you've created a new customer, if you navigate back to the customer overview page via Customers ➤ Manage Customers you should see your new customer listed. Like most other areas with the administration interface, you can view, sort, and search for customers. Clicking on any customer will bring up the detailed Customer Information which looks like Figure 6-4.

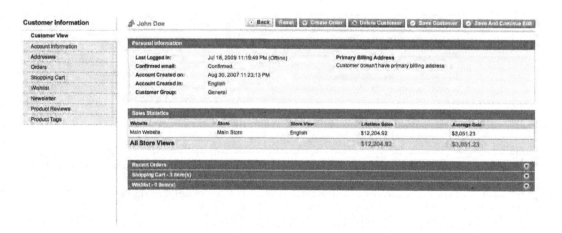

Figure 6-4. *A look at the detailed customer information page*

The detailed customer information page provides a wealth of information and options. You can view an overview of the customer's account, see their past orders, place new orders for the customer, and even modify customer information.

Before we dive into each tab, you'll notice there are six different buttons in the upper-right hand corner.

- *Back*: This returns you to the previous page which should be the customer overview page.

- *Reset*: Reset will reload the page and remove any modifications you might have accidently made to the customer. Once you click save customer or save and continue edit you lose the ability to reset any changes you've made.

- *Create order*: The create order button will begin the order creation process using this specific customer's information.

- *Delete customer*: This will of course delete the customer from the Magento store. Deleting a customer does not delete orders that were placed by the customer. Once a customer has been deleted, they will not be able to login to the web site.

- *Save customer*: This will save any changes you have made to the customer's account. Saving customer changes are permanent and are not reversible once you click either of the save buttons. The save customer button will also return you to the customer overview page once complete.

- *Save and continue edit:* This will save any changes you have made to the customer's account, but will reload the current detailed customer information page.

Detailed Customer Information: Customer View

The customer view tab is the first section that loads when you click on a customer. There are five subsections under the Customer View. The first labeled Personal Information gives a brief summary of the customer, including a primary billing address, which store they are associated with, and which customer group they are a part of. It also shows when their account was created and when the last time they logged in was.

The sales statistics section displays an overview of the customers purchases by web site store and view. It also provides grand totals for all sales this customer was responsible for.

To view the Recent Orders section, you'll need to click on it to expand. The Recent Orders section gives a breakdown of each recent order made by the customer. Attached to each recent order is a reorder button that allows you as an administrator to reorder the same order for the customer.

Expanding the Shopping Cart will reveal any items that the customer current has inside of their shopping cart. It is broken down by Product Id, Product Name, SKU, QTY, Price, and Total.

The wishlist section provides another break down of all items the customer has added to their wishlist, as shown in Figure 6-5. These items are also broken down by Product Id, Product Name, SKU, QTY, Price, and Total.

Personal Information

Last Logged In:	Jul 18, 2009 11:19:49 PM (Offline)	**Primary Billing Address**
Confirmed email:	Confirmed	Customer doesn't have primary billing address
Account Created on:	Aug 30, 2007 11:23:13 PM	
Account Created in:	English	
Customer Group:	General	

Sales Statistics

Website	Store	Store View	Lifetime Sales	Average Sale
Main Website	Main Store	English	$12,204.92	$3,051.23
All Store Views			**$12,204.92**	**$3,051.23**

Recent Orders	
Shopping Cart - 3 Item(s)	
Wishlist - 0 Item(s)	

Figure 6-5. *The first tab under the detailed customer information page: Customer View*

Detailed Customer Information: Account Information

The account information tab has a very similar view to when we created a new account. You can modify basic customer information including first name, last name, email, and which customer group the customer is apart of.

The one new section under Account Information is Password Management. While customers do have the ability to recover forgotten passwords, here you can manually reassign a customer a new password or click the Send Auto-generated password. The Send Auto-generated password will email the customer with a new random password once you click one of the save buttons in the upper-right hand corner. Once they receive their new password, customers have the ability to login and modify their password to whatever they want, as shown in Figure 6-6.

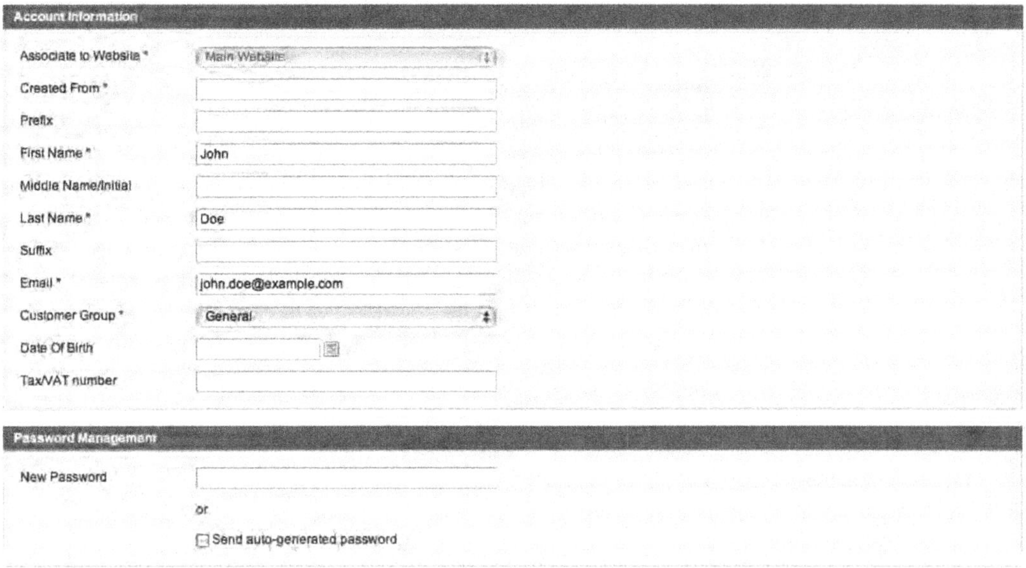

Figure 6-6. *The second tab under the detailed customer information page: Account Information*

Detailed Customer Information: Addresses

Similar to when you created a new customer, the Addresses tab allows you to manually create multiple addresses for each customer. You can also assign a default billing address or a default shipping address. During the checkout process, customers have the ability to select a preexisting address from a drop down list or they can create new addresses on the fly. Adding addresses for customers can be a daunting task, but it greatly speeds up the checkout process. If you choose to import customers instead of manually creating them, you can include customer address as well as any other information you might want to include with your customers, as shown in Figure 6-7.

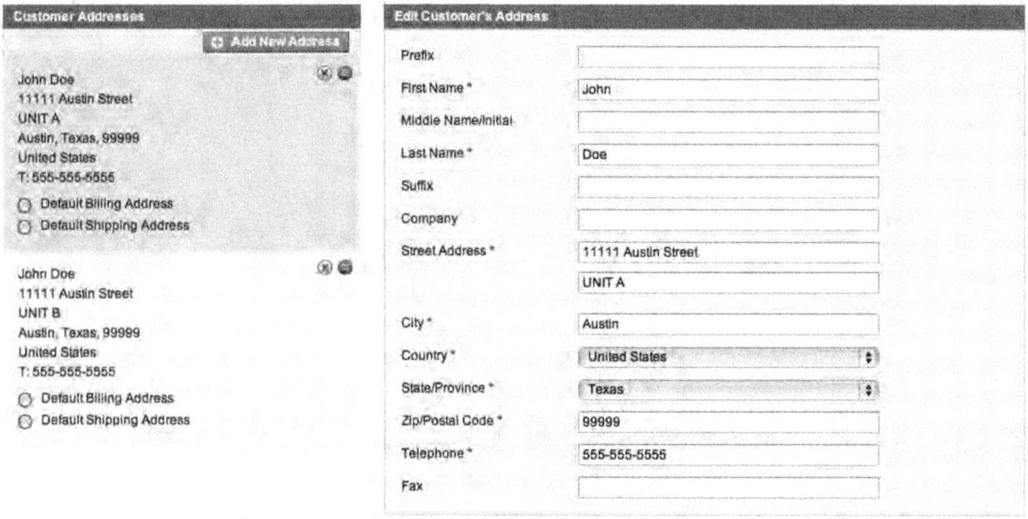

Figure 6-7. The third tab under the detailed customer information page: Addresses

Detailed Customer Information: Orders

Just like the Customer View tab, the Orders tab provides a table listing of each order placed by the customer. Orders are divided up by Order Number, Purchase Date, Bill to Names, Ship to Names, Grand Total and which store the products were purchased from.

Each order also includes the reorder button so you can begin the reorder process for the client. The reorder process does not modify the current order and instead creates an entirely new order, identical to the first, with a new order number (see Figure 6-8).

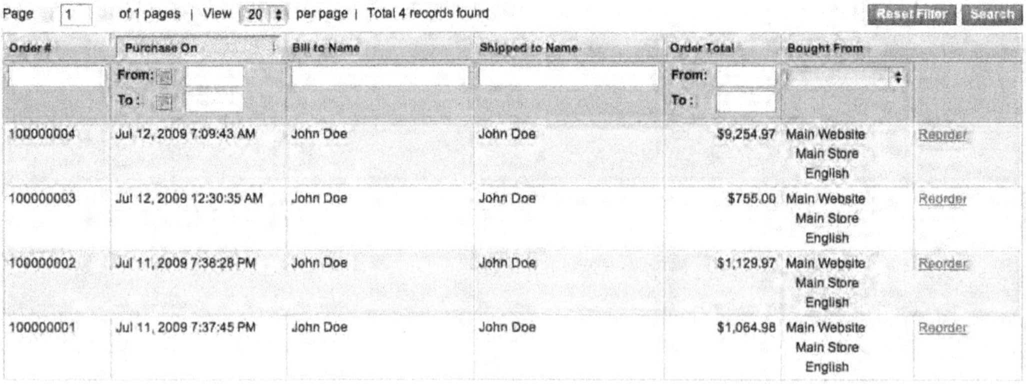

Figure 6-8. The fourth tab under the detailed customer information page: Orders

Detailed Customer Information: Shopping Cart

The Shopping Cart tab provides a table listing of each item currently inside of the customer's shopping cart. This can be used as a good indicator for items that were perhaps too expensive or items that the customer considered purchasing, but then changed their mind. Orders are divided up by Product Id, Product Name, SKU, QTY, Price, and Total. The last column allows you to delete items from a customer's cart (see Figure 6-9).

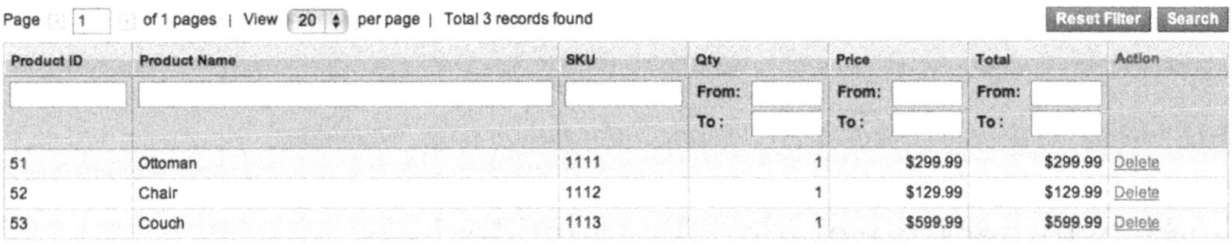

Page [1] of 1 pages | View [20 ▲] per page | Total 3 records found | Reset Filter | Search

Product ID	Product Name	SKU	Qty	Price	Total	Action
			From:	From:	From:	
			To:	To:	To:	
51	Ottoman	1111	1	$299.99	$299.99	Delete
52	Chair	1112	1	$129.99	$129.99	Delete
53	Couch	1113	1	$599.99	$599.99	Delete

Figure 6-9. The fifth tab under the detailed customer information page: Shopping Cart

Detailed Customer Information: Wishlist

The Wishlist tab provides a table listing of each item customers have added to their wishlists. These are typically items customers are interested in purchasing and they either might be waiting for an item to go on sale or they might not be ready to purchse. Wishlist items are divided up by product name, a user provided description, which store the item is from, when the product was added, and how many days it's been in the customers wishlist. There is also a delete button to remove each item from the customer's wishlist (see Figure 6-10).

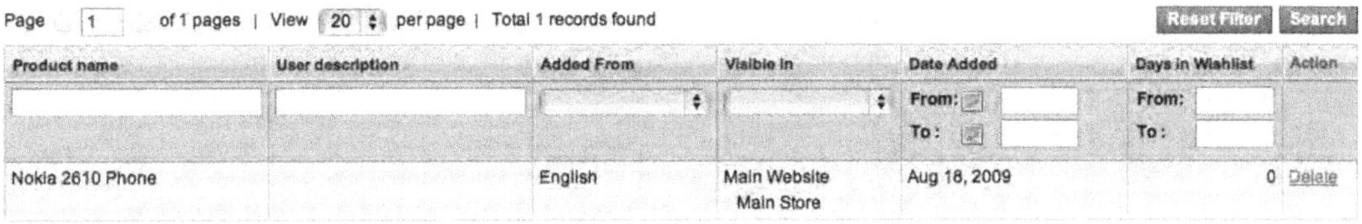

Page [1] of 1 pages | View [20 ▲] per page | Total 1 records found | Reset Filter | Search

Product name	User description	Added From	Visible In	Date Added	Days in Wishlist	Action
				From: ▣	From:	
		▲	▲	To: ▣	To:	
Nokia 2610 Phone		English	Main Website Main Store	Aug 18, 2009	0	Delete

Figure 6-10. The sixth tab under the detailed customer information page: Wishlist

Detailed Customer Information: Newsletter

The Newsletter tab provides two different functions. The first allows you to see if the customer has subscribed to the newsletter and what the date was that the customer subscribed. The second provides a grid view of all newsletters that the customer has received. If you compare products purchased with which newsletters were sent out, this can be a great reference to see how effective each newsletter was per customer, as shown in Figure 6-11.

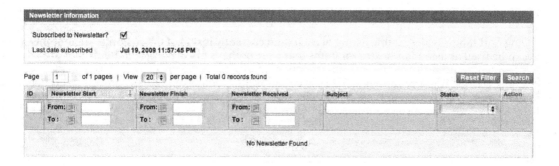

Figure 6-11. The sixth tab under the detailed customer information page: Newsletter

Detailed Customer Information: Product Reviews

The Product Reviews displays a grid view of all product reviews submitted by the customer. Reviews must be approved before they will be displayed in the public interface. To approve a review submitted by a customer, click the edit button. Under the edit page, you also have the ability to edit the review to censor reviews or modify them as you see fit for your store (see Figure 6-12).

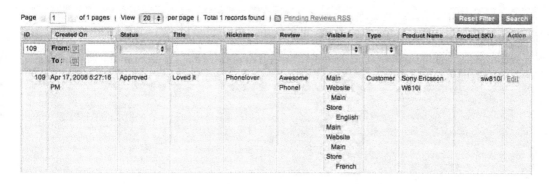

Figure 6-12. The seventh tab under the detailed customer information page: Product Reviews

Detailed Customer Information: Product Tags

The final tab, Product Tags, gives an overview of all product Tags submitted by the customer. Product Tags must be approved before they will appear in the public interface. Unfortunately, you cannot approve product tags from within the customer details page. You'll need to navigate to Catalog ➤ Pending Tags to view a list of tags that are pending approval (see Figure 6-13).

Page 1 ⊕ of 19 pages | View 20 ⬍ per page | Total 369 records found

Tag Name	Status	Product Name	SKU
acer	Approved	Acer Ferrari 3200 Notebook Computer PC	LX.FR206.001
acer	Approved	Apple MacBook Pro MA464LL/A 15.4" Notebook PC	MA464LL/A
amazing	Approved	Acer Ferrari 3200 Notebook Computer PC	LX.FR206.001
Anashria	Approved	Anashria Womens Premier Leather Sandal	ana
and	Disabled	BlackBerry 8100 Pearl	bb8100

Figure 6-13. The eighth tab under the detailed customer information page: Product Tags

Customer Groups

Customer Groups allow you to set up different groups based upon the requirements of your store. Customer groups can be used to differentiate between customers who get discounted or volume-based price and customers who are able to purchase products at wholesale prices with no tax.

Before you add customers to your specific customer groups, you need to navigate to the customer groups page, which is located under Customers ➤ Customer Groups. It should look similar to Figure 6-14.

To add a new customer group click the add new customer group button in the upper-right hand corner. Each group is assigned a name and a specific Tax class and then automatically assigned an id number.

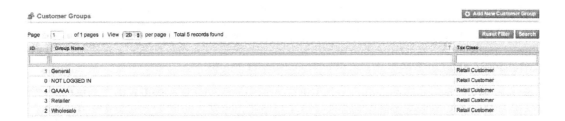

Figure 6-14. The Customer Groups Page

■ **Note** Customers who are not logged in are automatically placed under the NOT LOGGED IN group while customers who have registered and are logged in are automatically grouped under the General group. Outside of these two groups, customers must be manually assigned to different customer groups. To do this, visit Customers ➤ Manage Customers and select the customer you want to edit.

Customer Groups: Group Product Pricing (Tier Pricing)

Magento allows you to specify product pricing based upon a customer's group and a specific quantity amount. To adjust product pricing, navigate to Catalog ➤ Manage Products and select the product you want to adjust, then click on Prices to work with tier pricing. Group product pricing must be assigned to each product individually (see Figure 6-15).

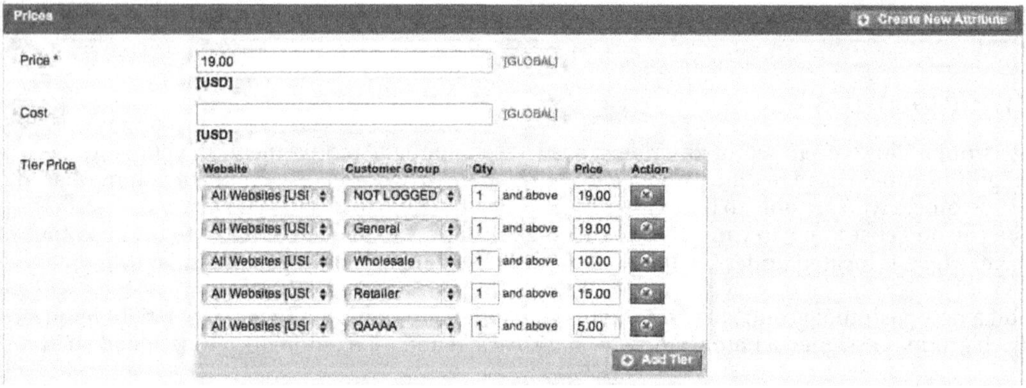

Figure 6-15. *Setting up Tier Pricing for multiple customer groups*

Tier Pricing works twofold. You can assign pricing based on customer groups, but you can also assign volume discounts that are dependent on the specific quantities a customer purchases. You can also assign pricing to different web sites and different customer groups.

In this example, I've created a Tier Pricing setup for each one of our customer groups. If you do not specify a price for your one particular group, they will be presented with the default price. In this example, it's $16.00. Customers must be assigned to their respective groups and be logged in to see the updating pricing. Customers are blind to Tier Pricing and will only be presented with the Tier that they are assigned to.

Alternatively, you can set up a Tier Pricing system aimed at only one customer group. In this example, I set up Tier Pricing for just the Wholesale customer group. This gives anyone inside the wholesale group a discount that increases as they purchase more products. This type of pricing will only affect wholesale customers that are logged in, no other customer groups will receive a discount (see Figure 6-16).

Figure 6-16. *Setting up Tier Pricing for just one customer group*

Online Customers

The online customers menu option takes you to a grid view of all online customers. To view online customers, go to Customers ➤ Online Customers. If the customers are logged in, you will see additional information such as first name, last name, and email, but if they are guests or not logged in they will appear like the example below. Figure 6-17 shows a quick way to review all customers currently using your store and for observing their most recent actions.

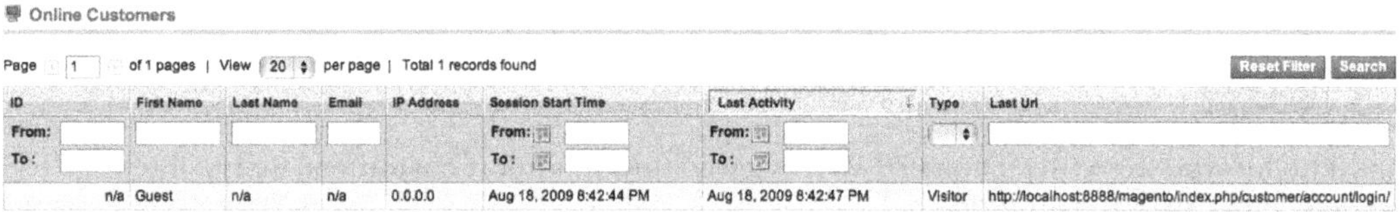

Figure 6-17. *A grid view of all online customers*

Contacting Customers

Currently, the only way to contact customers directly is through orders that have been placed using the customer account. To contact a customer through one of their orders, visit either Sales ➤ Orders and find the specific order you need to contact the customer about or Customers ➤ Manage Customers. Once you find the customer you need to contact under Manage Customers, click on their corresponding order. Either of these links should take you to the order details page. Inside of the order detail page is the Comments History section (see Figure 6-18). Here you can insert your message to the client, check notify customer, and submit comment. If you do not click notify customer, the comment will still be logged in the system, but the customer will not receive notification or be able to view the comment on the order details page. This is also a good place to keep comments for internal use that the customer might not need to be apprised of.

Figure 6-18. Contacting a customer through the use of order comments

What's Next?

That wraps it up for working with customers. We reviewed how to import customers, manually create customers, and view existing customers.

In Chapter 7, you will walk through each status in which an order can be placed. During each of these transitions, you have the ability to notify the customer of the changes that have been made to their order.

PART 2

Advanced Magento Development

In chapters 7-12, you will move beyond the standard Magento site. You will analyze how to manipulate Magento appearance, set up multiple Magento stores, install and build your own extensions, utilize Magento's built-in API, and how to use some unique Magento Tips and tricks.

CHAPTER 7

■■■

Working with Orders

Getting Started with Orders

Once your store starts receiving orders it can be a little overwhelming. Payments need to be received and verified, customers will need updates on orders that have shipped, and you'll need to keep an eye on orders through reports. In this chapter, you'll look at the details of an order, how to process orders, and how to generate reports based upon orders that have been placed. Let's start by taking a look at an order details page. To view the details of an order from the admin panel, navigate to Sales ➤ Orders. Once the grid listing loads, select an order from the provided list to view its details, as shown in Figure 7-1.

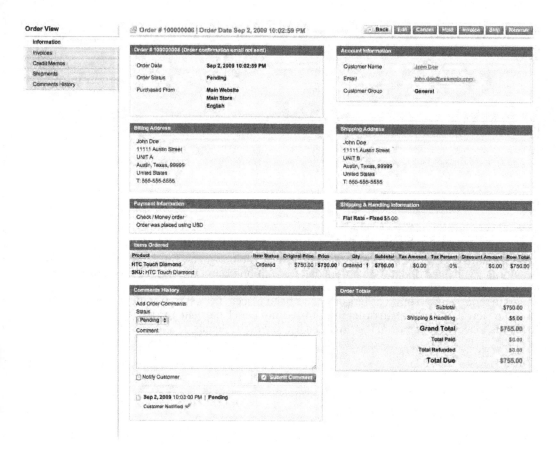

Figure 7-1. *Taking a look at the order details page*

The order details page displays all of the details of the order including order number, customer information, billing and shipping information, payment method, shipping and handling information, an itemized list of each product ordered, a comments area, and an order totals area.

There are two different navigation points on the order details page. Up top are action items that include the following buttons: edit, cancel, hold, invoice, ship, and reorder. You'll be going through each of these actions in this chapter. On the left there are five tabs. The first is the information tab, which is shown in Figure 7-1. It also includes, invoices, credit memos, shipments, and comment history. While no actions can be taken in each of these tabs, once orders have been invoiced and shipped, a record of their respective invoices shipments and credit memos will be listed under each tab.

Since Magento allows you to create multiple stores, it also assigns a unique sequential order number to each store. For example, you placed your order in Figure 7-1 in the first store you created, so it was assigned a 1 in front of the order number of 100000006. If you created a second store and placed an order from that store, the order number would start with 2.

It is important to know that while you can create multiple invoices, shipments, and credit memos each of these items will be contained underneath one order number. The order number in Figure 7-1 is 100000006. Usually, you will only have one invoice, shipment, or credit memo assigned to each order number, but Magento does allow you to create multiples. It can get rather confusing because when you create an invoice or shipment each of these items are assigned a unique number. These numbers are unique to the invoice or shipment that is created. As an example, if I create an invoice for order number 100000006 it could be assigned a sequential invoice number like 100000002. Do not worry if these numbers are not the same, Magento just assigns a unique number to every order, invoice, shipment, and credit memo that is created inside of the system.

The Life Cycle of Orders

Typically orders follow a standard life cycle process which the following outline in order.

1. New orders arrive in the administration interface with a pending status.

2. The next step is creating an invoice for the order. Once an invoice has been created, the order status will change from pending to processing.

3. Finally, orders will need to have a shipment. Creating a shipment for an order will change the status for processing to complete.

■ **Note** You can create a shipment first, but until you complete both steps 2 and 3 the order status will only be reflected as processing. You must create an invoice and a shipment before the order status will be set to complete.

Complete List of Order Status

There are several other order status aside from pending, processing, and complete. Orders can be set to any of the following status:

- *Pending*: Pending orders are brand new orders that have not been processed. Typically, these orders need to be invoiced and shipped.

- *Pending Paypal*: Pending PayPal orders are brand new orders that have not been cleared by PayPal. When using PayPal as a payment method customers are redirected to the PayPal site. If they have not paid for the order, orders will be marked as Pending PayPal. It is not recommended to process these orders without referencing PayPal first to see if payment has been made.

- *Processing*: Processing means that orders have either been invoiced or shipped, but not both.

- *Complete*: Orders marked as complete have been invoiced and have shipped.

- *Cancelled*: Cancelled orders should be used if orders are cancelled or if the orders have not been paid for.

- *Closed*: Closed orders are orders that have had a credit memo assigned to it and the customer has been refunded for their order.

- *On Hold*: Orders placed on hold must be taken off hold before continuing any further actions.

Status Conflicts and Exceptions

While most orders will follow the normal order life cycle, not all systems are the same. For example, if you are using a third party payment gateway for credit card processing, such as authorize.net or PayPal, any new orders could possibly be marked as processing instead of pending. Even if you create an invoice of shipment for this order its status will remain pending. You will need to create both an invoice and shipment for the order status to change to complete.

Contacting Customers

Magento allows you to contact your customers during any part of the transactional processes: when you create an invoice, shipment order, or credit memo. Not only can you send them a template-based email, you can also add custom comments. These comments will be recorded and tracked inside of Magento and will be sent to the customer with the template email. This is a great way to communicate with your customers and keep them updated and informed about their orders.

All customer contacts are stored within an orders comment history. This history can be found on any order details page. To view an order's comment history, navigate to Sales ➤ Orders and click on any of the orders to bring up the order detail page. The comment history section is down and in the middle of the page, as shown in Figure 7-2.

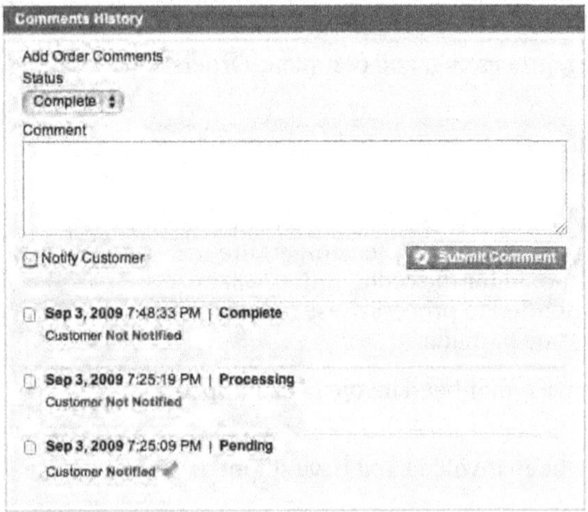

Figure 7-2. Reviewing an order's comment history

For more information about configuring Magento and transitional emails please view Chapter 8.

Creating an Invoice for an Order

Magento allows you to invoice customers for orders that they have placed in your store. While this is a feature that is oftentimes reserved for wholesale and business-to-business transactions it can be quite useful for retail purchases as well. It also can be a huge resource for internal records, because Magento allows you to create multiple invoices if required. This way if someone orders two different products and paid for them separately, you can create two different invoices.

Figure 7-3 is an invoice for your original order 100000006. Notice the items to invoice section. Had this order been placed for multiple products, each of those products would be itemized in this section. This gives you the ability not only to create multiple invoices based upon the quantities that a customer orders, but you could possibly create multiple invoices for different products. In most cases, you will only be creating one invoice per order.

Note the checkboxes labeled: "Append Comments" and "Email Copy of Invoice" next to the submit invoice button. The append Comments will save any comments made in the left-hand Invoice Comments to the invoice. Comments are viewable to the client. The Email Copy of Invoice will send an email copy of the invoice to the customer along with the invoice comments if the Append Comments button is checked (see Figure 7-3).

Figure 7-3. Creating a new customer from the administration interface

Once you've created an invoice for this order, the order status will be changed to processing, as shown in Figure 7-4.

Order Status   Processing

Figure 7-4. *Creating an invoice will change the order status from pending to processing.*

Also, once you created an invoice note that on the product details page the itemized product now has Invoiced 1 below the Qty header. Since Magento gives you the ability to create multiple invoices and shipments per order, you can also get a breakdown view of all invoices, credit memos, and shipments associated with a specific order. To view invoices, credit memos, or shipments associated with your order select one of these three options underneath the information tab on the product details page (see Figure 7-5).

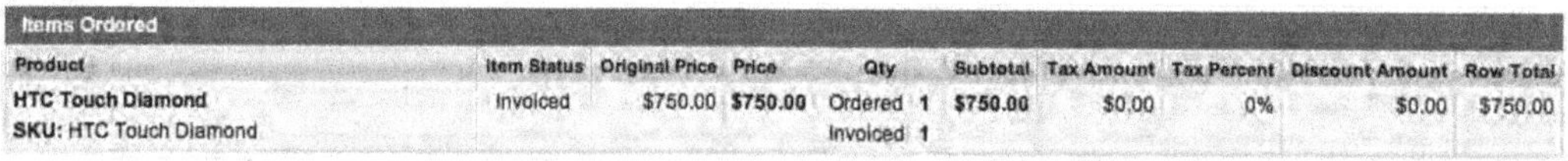

Items Ordered									
Product	**Item Status**	**Original Price**	**Price**	**Qty**	**Subtotal**	**Tax Amount**	**Tax Percent**	**Discount Amount**	**Row Total**
HTC Touch Diamond SKU: HTC Touch Diamond	Invoiced	$750.00	$750.00	Ordered 1 Invoiced 1	$750.00	$0.00	0%	$0.00	$750.00

Figure 7-5. *The order details page lets you know what items have been invoiced.*

Lastly, once an invoice has been created it will be listed in the Invoices tab on the left-hand side of the order details page. You can view the details of an invoice by clicking on the invoice row, as shown in Figure 7-6.

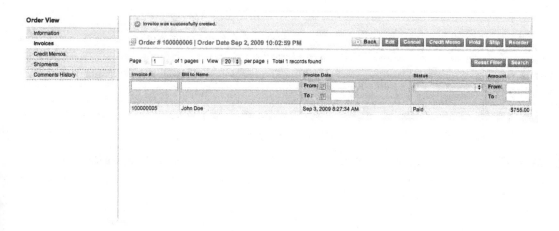

Figure 7-6. *The order details page also shows you invoices associated with your order.*

Bringing up, it provides all the basic invoicing information and looks very similar to the order details page. One important note is that the invoice is marked as paid, but the customer has not been notified. If it is not required to notify a customer when you create an invoice, your store might not need this functionality. Magento is just letting you know that they have not received an email yet (see Figure 7-7).

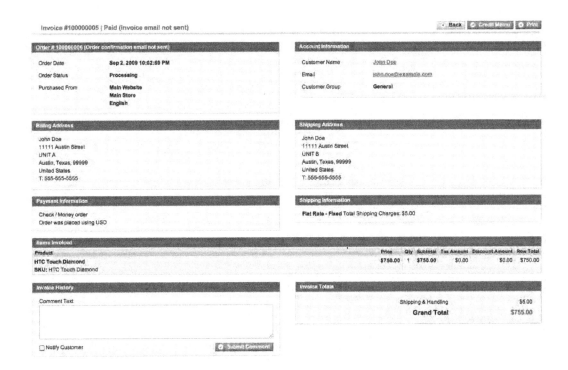

Figure 7-7. *Reviewing an invoice after it has been created.*

Creating a Shipment Order

The next step in processing an order usually includes creating a shipment order. To do this, select the ship button from the order details page (Magento also calls this the Order View page). The new shipment pages should look like the screenshot in Figure 7-8.

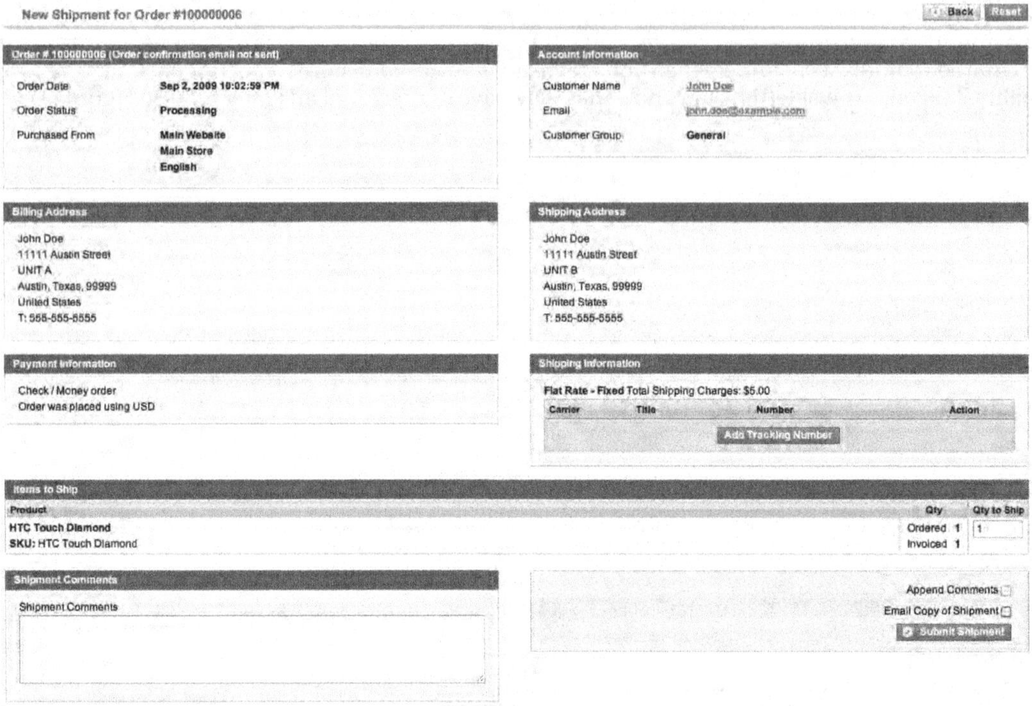

New Shipment for Order #100000006   Back   Reset

Order # 100000006 [Order confirmation email not sent]		Account Information	
Order Date	Sep 2, 2009 10:02:59 PM	Customer Name	John Doe
Order Status	Processing	Email	john.doe@example.com
Purchased From	Main Website	Customer Group	General
	Main Store		
	English		

Billing Address	Shipping Address
John Doe	John Doe
11111 Austin Street	11111 Austin Street
UNIT A	UNIT B
Austin, Texas, 99999	Austin, Texas, 99999
United States	United States
T: 555-555-5555	T: 555-555-5555

Payment Information

Check / Money order
Order was placed using USD

Shipping Information

Flat Rate - Fixed Total Shipping Charges: $5.00

Carrier	Title	Number	Action
		Add Tracking Number	

Items to Ship

Product		Qty	Qty to Ship
HTC Touch Diamond		Ordered 1	1
SKU: HTC Touch Diamond		Invoiced 1	

Shipment Comments

Shipment Comments

Append Comments ☐
Email Copy of Shipment ☐
Submit Shipment

Figure 7-8. Creating a shipment

Just like when you created an invoice there is a field under Qty to Ship that allows you to select a specific qty of items to ship inside of this shipment. This is especially helpful if you ship out products through different carriers or methods.

There is also an area to include shipping information for each shipment that you create. You can select a carrier from the drop down list that includes: DHL, FedEx, UPS, or USPS. You can also enter a custom shipment if it is not one of the ones listed. This information is accessible to customers through the public interface, and if the Email Copy of Shipment button is checked they will also receive the shipping information inside of the email that their order has shipped (see Figure 7-9).

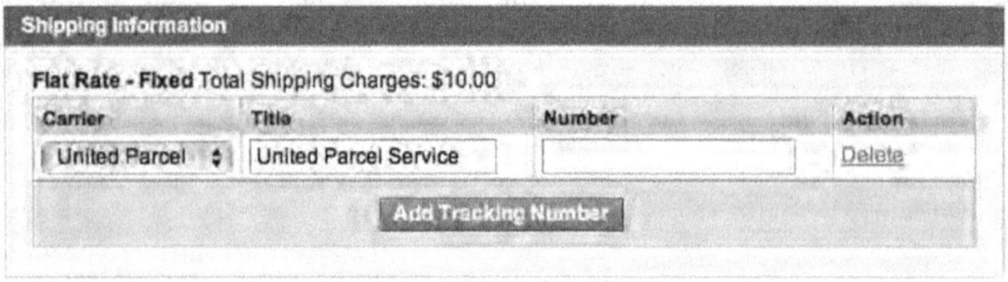

Shipping Information

Flat Rate - Fixed Total Shipping Charges: $10.00

Carrier	Title	Number	Action
United Parcel ⬍	United Parcel Service		Delete
	Add Tracking Number		

Figure 7-9. Adding tracking information to your shipment

■ **Note** If you choose to create multiple shipments for one order until you create a shipment for ALL of your products contained in the order, the order status will remain as processing.

Canceling an Order

Canceling an order halts any further actions that can be taken with that order. Orders that are canceled cannot be invoiced, shipped, or credited. You can reorder cancelled orders, but this will only generate a new order in the system with an unique order number.

An order can be cancelled in one of two ways, the order overview page or the order details page. To cancel an order from the order overview page, navigate to Sales ➤ Orders. When the order overview page loads select the order you wish to cancel by clicking the checkbox located on the same row as the order. Once you have the order selected, select cancel from the actions pulldown and click submit. The page will reload and the order will be cancelled, as shown in Figure 7-10.

Figure 7-10. Cancelling an order from the order overview page. Select cancel from the actions dropdown and click submit.

To cancel an order from the order details page, click on any order from the order overview page to view its details. Once the detail page loads, click the cancel button in the upper right-hand corner. This will cancel the order (see Figure 7-11).

Figure 7-11. Cancelling an order from the order detail page

One problem I've noticed is that if you cancel an order that has either been invoiced or shipped, the order will be cancelled but the status will incorrectly be set to complete instead of cancelled. Only orders marked as pending can be correctly changed to cancelled.

■ **Note** It is important to realize that you cannot un-cancel an order. Orders that are cancelled are permanently cancelled.

Placing an Order on Hold

Orders can be placed on hold during any part of the process and will be given a status of On Hold. Placing orders on hold does not affect an order in any way. The only difference is that you must unhold orders before you can take any further actions with them. If customers view their order details from the public interface they will be able to see that the status of their order has been placed on hold. Similar to how you cancel an order, orders can placed on hold from the order overview page or the order detail page. To place an order on hold from the order overview page, navigate to Sales ➤ Orders. When the order overview page loads, select the order you wish to cancel by clicking the checkbox located on the same row as the order. Once you have the order selected, select hold from the actions pulldown and click submit. The page will reload and the order will be cancelled.

To place an order on hold from the order details page, click on any order from the order overview page to view its details. Once the detail page loads, click the cancel button in the upper-right hand corner. This will place the order on hold.

Once an order is placed on hold to perform any additional actions with an order you must first "unhold" an order.

Credit Memos

Credit Memos allow you to refund customers for orders they have placed in your store. Once you create a credit memo for an order, you can take no further action with the order except to reorder the order. Once you have created a Credit Memo for an order that order status will be changed to Closed, as shown in Figure 7-12.

New Credit Memo for Order #100000008   [Back] [Reset]

Order # 100000008 (Order confirmation email not sent)

Order Date	Sep 3, 2009 7:59:00 AM
Order Status	Processing
Purchased From	Main Website Main Store English

Account Information

Customer Name	John Doe
Email	john.doe@example.com
Customer Group	General

Billing Address

John Doe
11111 Austin Street
UNIT A
Austin, Texas, 99999
United States
T: 555-555-5555

Shipping Address

John Doe
11111 Austin Street
UNIT B
Austin, Texas, 99999
United States
T: 555-555-5555

Payment Information

Check / Money order
Order was placed using USD

Shipping Information

Flat Rate - Fixed Total Shipping Charges: $5.00

Items to Refund

Product	Price	Qty	Return to Stock	Qty to Refund	Subtotal	Tax Amount	Discount Amount	Row Total
HTC Touch Diamond SKU: HTC Touch Diamond	$750.00	Ordered 1 Invoiced 1	☐	1	$750.00	$0.00	$0.00	$750.00

                                                                    [Update Qty's]

Paid Amount	Refund Amount	Shipping Amount	Shipping Refund	Order Grand Total
$755.00	$0.00	$5.00	$0.00	$755.00

Credit Memo Comments

Credit Memo Comments
[   ]

Refund Totals

Subtotal	$750.00
Refund Shipping	5
Adjustment Refund	0
Adjustment Fee	0
Total Refund	**$755.00**

Append Comments ☐
Email Copy of Credit Memo ☐
[Refund]

Figure 7-12. Creating a Credit Memo for an order

Items Ordered

Product	Item Status	Original Price	Price	Qty	Subtotal	Tax Amount	Tax Percent	Discount Amount	Row Total
HTC Touch Diamond SKU: HTC Touch Diamond	Refunded	$750.00	$750.00	Ordered 1 Invoiced 1 Refunded 1	$750.00	$0.00	0%	$0.00	$750.00

Figure 7-13. The order details page now shows that the product has been refunded to the customer.

Deleting Orders

Currently, there is no way to delete orders once they have been created inside of Magento. Magento allows you the ability to cancel an order, but deleting or removing an order is an architectural decision that the Magento team decided to prohibit.

Orders are referenced within multiple tables for optimization of the database. Considering that Magento is still in version 1.0 it is hopeful that they will include this feature in future versions of Magento.

What's Next?

Now that you have taken an in-depth look at how to work with customers, products, and orders it's time to dive into the heart of making modifications to Magento. Coming up in Chapter 8, you will be looking at how to covert Magento from a demo store to a full production store. It's an important chapter with tons of vital information that should not be overlooked.

CHAPTER 8

■■■

Configuring Magento

Why Do I Need to Configure Magento?

Even if you did not install Magento with sample data, every installation of Magento starts off as demo store. What does this mean? This means that there are several different areas of Magento that you need to modify before you are ready for your store's first customers and orders.

Before you dive into configuring Magento, it is my highest recommendation that if you are using Magento for the first time you should set up a test and development environment. Do this before you build any products or categories, so if you run into any problems you can easily start over. In this chapter, you'll be reviewing each area that needs to be modified to convert your Demo Magento store into a fully functional personalized store.

Store Information, Emails, and Meta Data

Sometimes the most important information about your store is the information that most visitors might be unaware of, but help your store with search engine optimization (SEO) and basic functionality. In the following sections, you will be reviewing how to modify the demo store information, store emails, and meta data.

Default Home Page

One of the first things you might notice is the store's default home page. A store that has the sample data installed will have a home page similar to Figure 8-1. It contains three columns with promotional areas on the left and right, and the best selling products in the middle. If your store does not have sample data installed, your default page will be blank.

Figure 8-1. *The default welcome message displayed at the top of your Magento store*

If you current home page is blank or if you want to select a different homepage, you'll need to visit the configuration page. Login to the Administration interface and navigate to System ➤ Configuration. Select the web tab from the left-hand menu. You should see a drop down labeled Default Pages. You can now select a different homepage from the provided CMS Home Page dropdown. For now let's leave Home Page as the default.

Once you've selected a default home page, if you want to make any modifications, you will need to navigate to CMS ➤ Manage Pages. Select the Home Page from the provide table list. You should see an editor page load similar to Figure 8-2. The CMS editor page gives you the ability to individually control each page. You can modify the page title, its URL, which stores the page it is displayed on, and the HTML content used on the page.

For more information about working with CMS pages and the XML driven layout system that Magento uses, please refer to Chapter 9.

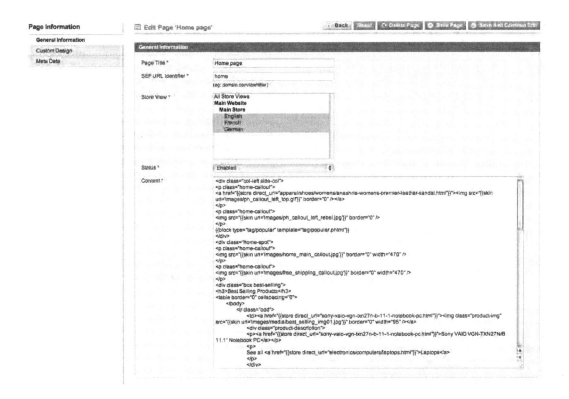

Figure 8-2. *Editing the default homepage*

Page Titles, Meta Keywords, and Meta Descriptions

Meta keywords and meta descriptions are used to accurately describe your store's pages to search engines. While customers might be unaware of most meta keywords and descriptions, properly described pages will help improve search engine results. For more information about meta keywords and meta descriptions, you can read this W3 Schools article: `http://www.w3schools.com/html/html_meta.asp`.

While you can control the use of page titles, meta keywords, and meta descriptions on every CMS page, product category and individual product page, it's a good idea to set up global meta keywords and meta descriptions. To do this, navigate to System ➤ Configuration and then select Design from the right-hand column. Under the HTML Head drop down there are several sections that need to be filled out to set up your global information, including Default Title, Default Description, and Default Keywords.

These settings will only be used in default, so if you do not specify a unique page title, description, or keywords for a particular product, category or content page, these global variables will be used.

Store Emails

Your store emails serve several purposes. When customers place an order in your store, your store email is included as a reply-to email. When a customer sends a message through your contact form, the settings in your store email will be used. Store emails are also used when someone uses a contact form. To configure your store email, navigate to System ➤ Configuration and then select Store Email Addresses from the right-hand column.

There are five drop downs that need to be filled out: General Contact, Sales Representative, Customer Support, Custom Email 1, and Custom Email 2. These can all be set up using the same email address, but it is recommended that they all be filled out because of their use with transactional emails. We will be discussing transactional emails later in this chapter in the section titled "Setting Up Transactional Emails." Proving unique emails for each of these sections allows for an easy way to filter transactional emails versus support emails.

Welcome Message and Page Footer

One of the first things you are going to want to change is the default welcome message that is contained within the header of your Magento store (see Figure 8-3). It currently reads "Default welcome msg!"

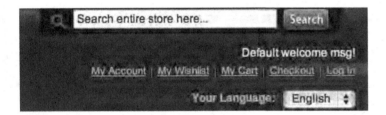

Figure 8-3. The default welcome message displayed at the top of your Magento store

To change the default welcome, login to the Administration interface and navigate to System ➤ Configuration. Once the configuration page loads, click on design tab in the left-hand column. Several menu options will load in the main area, so select the design drop down. You can replace the default welcome message in the Welcome Text area under the header section.

In this same section, you can also change the text used in the store's footer by clicking on the Footer drop down. Editing the Copyright area will change the text shown below. Magento also allows you to insert Miscellaneous HTML in the text area below the copyright field. The Miscellaneous HTML can be used for additional store information, hours, or copyright information (see Figure 8-4).

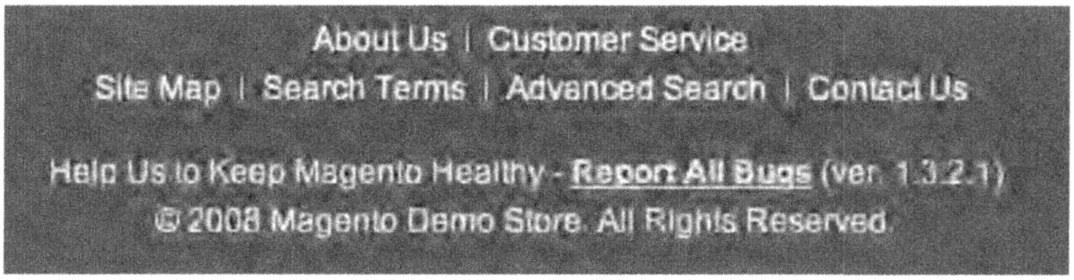

Figure 8-4. *Copyright footer at the bottom of your Magento store*

You might also have noticed the "Help Us to Keep Magento Healthy - Report All Bugs (ver. 1.3.2.1)." This is another section that you are going to want to remove from your store. Unfortunately, this cannot be removed from the administration interface. To remove this, you will need to either comment out or remove the following code found in the following file: .../app/design/frontend/default/default/template/page/html/footer.phtml

```
<?php echo $this->__('Help Us to Keep Magento Healthy') ?> - <a
 href="http://www.magentocommerce.com/bug-tracking" id="bug_tracking_link"><strong><?php
 echo $this->__('Report All Bugs') ?></strong></a> <?php echo $this->__('(ver. %s)',
 Mage::getVersion()) ?><br />
<script type="text/javascript">
$('bug_tracking_link').target = "varien_external";
</script>
```

Setting Up Transactional Emails

Transactional emails refer to any email that is automatically generated from your store. Emails are automatically sent out when a new customer registers, places an order, or receives an update that their orders status has changed. The following list contains a list of all possible emails that your store can send out.

```
New admin password
Currency Update Warnings
New account
New account confirmation key
New account confirmed
New password
New Order
New Order for Guest
Order Update
Order Update for Guest
New Invoice
New Invoice for Guest
Invoice Update
Invoice Update for Guest
New Credit Memo
New Credit Memo for Guest
Credit Memo Update
```

Credit Memo Update for Guest
New Shipment
New Shipment for Guest
Shipment Update
Shipment Update for Guest
Payment Failed
Log cleanup Warnings
Newsletter subscription confirmation
Newsletter subscription success
Newsletter unsubscription success
Share Wishlist
Send product to a friend
Contact Form
Sitemap generate Warnings
Product stock alert
Product price alert
Product alerts Cron error
Amazon Simple Pay notification error

If you do not set up a transactional email for each of the possible store transactions Magento will send out a default email which looks similar to Figure 8-5.

Hello ,
Thank you for your order from . Once your package ships we will send an email with a link to track your order. You can check the status of your order by logging into your account. If you have any questions about your order please contact us at dummyemail@magentocommerce.com or call us at (555) 555-0123 Monday - Friday, 8am - 5pm PST.

Your order confirmation is below. Thank you again for your business.

Your Order # (placed on)

Billing Information:		Payment Method:	

Thank you again,

Figure 8-5. A new order email before it has been modified

To set up your transactional emails, navigate to System ➤ Transactional Emails. Click Add New Template from the upper right-hand corner. Select which transactional email you want to work with from the Template drop down and click load Template.

There are a number of areas you need to modify for this transactional email. Most importantly is the Template Name, Template Subject, and several areas underneath the Template Content. You'll need to update the logo, email address, phone number, and store hours. One cool feature is the "Preview Template" button. This allows you to view your changes before you save your changes.

You will need to repeat this process for each transactional email that your store will be using. Typically that includes the following transactions: new account, new password, new order, new invoice, and new shipment to start (see Figure 8-6).

Figure 8-6. Setting up a transactional email for new orders

Setting Up a Shipping Method

Setting up at least one shipping method is an essential part of running an eCommerce store. Before you set up a shipping method you need to take a look at Shipping Settings. Inside of System ➤ Configuration, select Shipping Settings from the menu on the left.

First up is the Origin configuration, this information is used for both the UPS and FedEx online shipping calculators. This address should be the same as where you will be shipping your products from to give as accurate shipping quotes as possible. The second section called options let's you enable or disable shipping to multiple addresses and control the maximum number of addresses customer can ship to. While customers are allowed to ship to multiple addresses, keep in mind that each unique address is treated as an unique order number and transaction. Customers also have the ability to select different payment methods per each unique address during checkout.

Magento comes pre-installed with several different shipping methods, including table rate shipping, flat rate shipping, UPS, FedEx, and USPS. If any of these shipping methods do not meet the needs of your store, you can visit `http://www.magentocommerce.com/magento-connect` and search for additional shipping method extensions (see Figure 8-7).

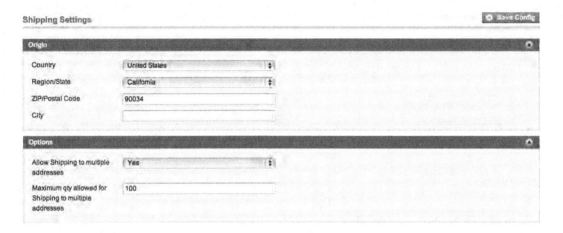

Figure 8-7. *Configing shipping settings*

Once you've got your settings correct for origin and shipping to multiple addresses, you need to set up at least one shipping method for customers to use during checkout. By default, Flat Rate is the only shipping method that is enabled. To view this method and the other shipping methods that are available, select Shipping Methods from the menu on the left (see Figure 8-8).

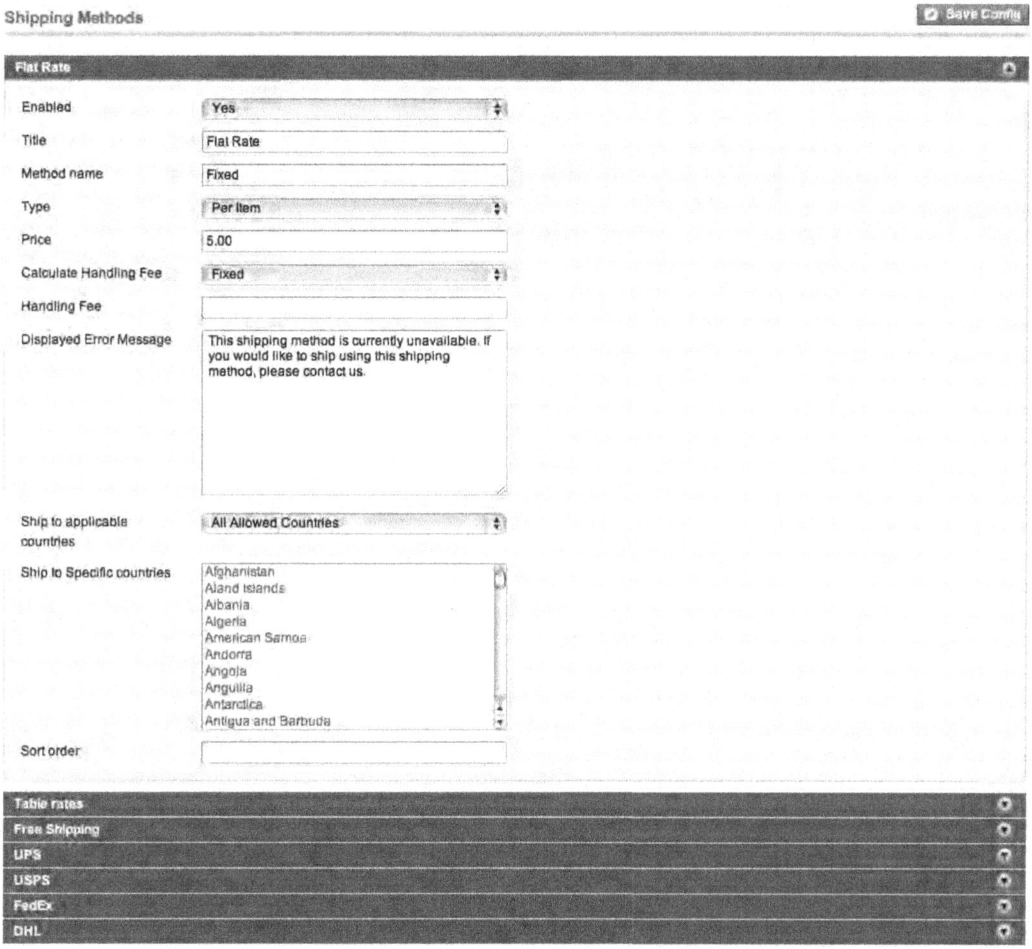

Figure 8-8. *Modifying the default shipping method*

Flat rate is the shipping method that is enabled by default when you install your Magento store. Flat rate basically means that you set a flat rate of shipping either per item or per order. You can change the amount, and even include a handing free. Handling fees are not itemized and are included with the total shipping cost. If you do not want to use Flat rate as your shipping method, you will need to select no from the Enabled drop down and enable another shipping method listed below.

Setting Up a Payment Method

The only payment method that is enabled when Magento is installed is the Check / Money Order payment. You can change the title of this payment method by changing the title field. Orders placed using the Check / Money Order will be given an order status of Pending. You can change this by selecting another status from the New order status drop down. You also have the ability to either disable this payment method or choose any one of the additional payment methods listed, as shown in Figure 8-9.

Figure 8-9. *Modifying the default payment method*

You should also note that by default, Zero Subtotal Checkout is also enabled. This feature does allow for customers to checkout with a cart total of zero dollars. This can be used if your site features downloadable products that are free, but you still require customers to register before they can download the product. To disable this, simply select No from the Enabled drop down under the Zero Subtotal Checkout section.

Similar to shipping methods, payment methods set up under the default Config will affect all stores. You can specify shipping to each store individually by selecting a different store from the Current Configuration Scope drop down.

Deleting Sample Categories

To delete the categories that come pre-installed with the Magento sample data, navigate to Catalog ➤ Manage Categories inside of the administrative interface. Select the categories you want to delete, you'll have to do this one at a time, and click the delete category button in the upper right-hand corner. You must always have a root category, which has been renamed Root Catalog, but you will be able to delete all of the sample Categories which include: Furniture, Electronics, Apparel, and several subcategories under each of these. You will still need to build a new category structure for your own unique site but this remove any sample categories from the Magento installation.

Deleting Sample Products

Removing sample products from your Magento store is even easier than categories. Navigate to Catalog ➤ Manage Products. Once the page loads select 200 from the View drop down. The page should reload to display all of your products. Click the select all button to select all of your products, then select Delete from the Actions drop down. Clicking Submit next to the Actions drop down will remove all products currently listed in your Magento store (see Figure 8-10).

Figure 8-10. Removing sample products from your store

Deleting Test Customers

Customers can be deleted in the same manner that products are removed. Navigate to Customers ➤ Manage Customers. There is only one sample customer: John Doe. To delete John Doe, simply check the box under the far left column, select delete from the actions drop down, and click submit. Alternatively, you can click on John Doe's record and delete a customer from inside the customer details page. Customers who have been deleted will no longer be able to login to the store, as shown in Figure 8-11.

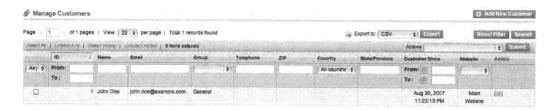

Figure 8-11. Removing sample customers from your store

■ **Note** Deleting customers does not remove orders that the customers have placed within your store. It only delete's the customer account.

Deleting Test Orders

■ **Note** Before you continue with the following script it is important that your Magento database is fully backed up.

Currently, there is no direct method for deleting orders from within the Magento administration interface. To delete any test orders, you will need to go to your MySQL client and run the query that is copied below.

While there are a few Magento extensions that claim to add additional functionality to your store and allow you to delete orders, in my experience I have found these extensions are unable to do what they claim or can cause serious damage to your Magento database.

If this procedure is too advanced I would recommend, simply changing the status of any test orders from pending to canceled. Alternatively, you can do a fresh install of Magento without sample data and you will not have to remove products customers or orders.

■ **Note** Do not run this query if you do not want to delete all orders that are in your store.

```
SET FOREIGN_KEY_CHECKS=0;

TRUNCATE `sales_order`;
TRUNCATE `sales_order_datetime`;
TRUNCATE `sales_order_decimal`;
TRUNCATE `sales_order_entity`;
TRUNCATE `sales_order_entity_datetime`;
TRUNCATE `sales_order_entity_decimal`;
TRUNCATE `sales_order_entity_int`;
TRUNCATE `sales_order_entity_text`;
TRUNCATE `sales_order_entity_varchar`;
TRUNCATE `sales_order_int`;
TRUNCATE `sales_order_text`;
TRUNCATE `sales_order_varchar`;
TRUNCATE `sales_flat_quote`;
TRUNCATE `sales_flat_quote_address`;
TRUNCATE `sales_flat_quote_address_item`;
TRUNCATE `sales_flat_quote_item`;
TRUNCATE `sales_flat_quote_item_option`;
TRUNCATE `sales_flat_order_item`;
TRUNCATE `sendfriend_log`;
TRUNCATE `tag`;
TRUNCATE `tag_relation`;
TRUNCATE `tag_summary`;
TRUNCATE `wishlist`;
TRUNCATE `log_quote`;
TRUNCATE `report_event`;

ALTER TABLE `sales_order` AUTO_INCREMENT=1;
ALTER TABLE `sales_order_datetime` AUTO_INCREMENT=1;
ALTER TABLE `sales_order_decimal` AUTO_INCREMENT=1;
ALTER TABLE `sales_order_entity` AUTO_INCREMENT=1;
ALTER TABLE `sales_order_entity_datetime` AUTO_INCREMENT=1;
ALTER TABLE `sales_order_entity_decimal` AUTO_INCREMENT=1;
ALTER TABLE `sales_order_entity_int` AUTO_INCREMENT=1;
ALTER TABLE `sales_order_entity_text` AUTO_INCREMENT=1;
ALTER TABLE `sales_order_entity_varchar` AUTO_INCREMENT=1;
ALTER TABLE `sales_order_int` AUTO_INCREMENT=1;
ALTER TABLE `sales_order_text` AUTO_INCREMENT=1;
ALTER TABLE `sales_order_varchar` AUTO_INCREMENT=1;
ALTER TABLE `sales_flat_quote` AUTO_INCREMENT=1;
ALTER TABLE `sales_flat_quote_address` AUTO_INCREMENT=1;
ALTER TABLE `sales_flat_quote_address_item` AUTO_INCREMENT=1;
ALTER TABLE `sales_flat_quote_item` AUTO_INCREMENT=1;
ALTER TABLE `sales_flat_quote_item_option` AUTO_INCREMENT=1;
ALTER TABLE `sales_flat_order_item` AUTO_INCREMENT=1;
```

```
ALTER TABLE `sendfriend_log` AUTO_INCREMENT=1;
ALTER TABLE `tag` AUTO_INCREMENT=1;
ALTER TABLE `tag_relation` AUTO_INCREMENT=1;
ALTER TABLE `tag_summary` AUTO_INCREMENT=1;
ALTER TABLE `wishlist` AUTO_INCREMENT=1;
ALTER TABLE `log_quote` AUTO_INCREMENT=1;
ALTER TABLE `report_event` AUTO_INCREMENT=1;

-- reset customers
TRUNCATE `customer_address_entity`;
TRUNCATE `customer_address_entity_datetime`;
TRUNCATE `customer_address_entity_decimal`;
TRUNCATE `customer_address_entity_int`;
TRUNCATE `customer_address_entity_text`;
TRUNCATE `customer_address_entity_varchar`;
TRUNCATE `customer_entity`;
TRUNCATE `customer_entity_datetime`;
TRUNCATE `customer_entity_decimal`;
TRUNCATE `customer_entity_int`;
TRUNCATE `customer_entity_text`;
TRUNCATE `customer_entity_varchar`;
TRUNCATE `log_customer`;
TRUNCATE `log_visitor`;
TRUNCATE `log_visitor_info`;

ALTER TABLE `customer_address_entity` AUTO_INCREMENT=1;
ALTER TABLE `customer_address_entity_datetime` AUTO_INCREMENT=1;
ALTER TABLE `customer_address_entity_decimal` AUTO_INCREMENT=1;
ALTER TABLE `customer_address_entity_int` AUTO_INCREMENT=1;
ALTER TABLE `customer_address_entity_text` AUTO_INCREMENT=1;
ALTER TABLE `customer_address_entity_varchar` AUTO_INCREMENT=1;
ALTER TABLE `customer_entity` AUTO_INCREMENT=1;
ALTER TABLE `customer_entity_datetime` AUTO_INCREMENT=1;
ALTER TABLE `customer_entity_decimal` AUTO_INCREMENT=1;
ALTER TABLE `customer_entity_int` AUTO_INCREMENT=1;
ALTER TABLE `customer_entity_text` AUTO_INCREMENT=1;
ALTER TABLE `customer_entity_varchar` AUTO_INCREMENT=1;
ALTER TABLE `log_customer` AUTO_INCREMENT=1;
ALTER TABLE `log_visitor` AUTO_INCREMENT=1;
ALTER TABLE `log_visitor_info` AUTO_INCREMENT=1;

-- Reset all ID counters
TRUNCATE `eav_entity_store`;
ALTER TABLE `eav_entity_store` AUTO_INCREMENT=1;

SET FOREIGN_KEY_CHECKS=1;
```

What's Next?

In Chapter 8, we covered several different areas including adjusting store information, establishing a shipping method, and email set up. While it's important that each of these areas is adjusted, your work isn't done. In Chapter 9, you are going to take an in-depth look at Magento's use of XML layouts, design, and site structure. Chapter 9 will give you the power to change Magento's default appearance and really make your Magento store your own.

CHAPTER 9

■■■

Customizing Magento's Appearance

A Quick Overview

Magento approaches site layouts and design a little differently than most other platforms. Magento's template architecture has been structured in a way that allows you to update multiple pages at a time, but it is still flexible enough to allow custom modification of certain pages within your eCommerce store.

As you may recall, Magento separates the content from the presentation layer. This chapter will focus on explaining how Magento's themes behave and how to customize the layout.

A Magento theme is broken up into the three following areas.

- *PHTML templates*: PHTML is inherited from Zend's Framework. Similar to HTML, PHTML files provide is the core of Magento themes. The provide structure the basic structure for your store. This structure is defined further by the XML Layouts that Magento uses.

- *XML layouts*: You can use XML layouts to specify which blocks show up on a group of pages. Blocks can be anything from text, images, a customer's mini-cart, or recent items added to cart. For example, you may only want a mini-cart to show up on all of your store's catalog page and not the checkout pages.

- *The skin*: The skin section refers to a folder that contains CSS (cascading style sheets) files, images, and JavaScript files. Basically, any non-structurally related files are placed within this folder.

If you're confused, think of Magento themes like a football game. XML Layouts make up the playbook and define what phtml file to load. PHTML files are the football players, each following their own routes. And, the Skin, well, that's just their jersey colors.

If you are looking at designing a theme for Magento, it's recommended that you be familiar with the basics of HTML, CSS, basic PHP, and XML driven layouts.

Why This Structure Is Good

To be fair you are going to take a look at both the positive and negative sides of working with a framework that is structured like this. First, the reasons why this type of structure is good:

- *Global changes are easy*. Many of the changes you can make to any of Magento's files will affect multiple views. This allows you to quickly update graphics, logos, and other items used within your theme by editing one file.

- *Distinct file separation*: Although Magento's file structure can be a little excessive at times, since each of the different sections is separate, it enables you to update the files you need. For example, all of the checkout pages contact pages and catalog pages are all grouped respectively. If you are updating images and colors for your site, those files are grouped together in the skin folder.

- *Rapid theme development*: Since Magento employs a MVC structure it allows you to develop, import, and export themes easily without ever having to affect Magento's core files.

Potential Problems with This Type of Structure

With good intentions, Magento does its best to separate the different pieces of a theme, but there are some reasons to why this type of structure hurts more than helps. The following are a few reasons why:

- *Steep learning curve*: Magento was approached from a development standpoint and has an objected-oriented coding structure. Magento's unique file structure contains many inherit elements. It is a huge system with thousands of different pieces and can take a while to understand and debug.

- *Deep file structure*: One of the biggest complaints about Magento is the deep file structure. Files are often separated and organized several levels deep. While Magento's structure gives performance benefits, its set up file organization leaves a little to be desired. You'll take a look at Magento's file structure in the next section.

- *Multiple languages*: Working with Magento's themes require an understanding of multiple languages, including HTML, XML, PHP, and CSS. It is not for the faint of heart beginning designer.

Beyond This Chapter

If you are looking at designing a theme for Magento, it's recommended that you start by either modifying the default Magento theme or first downloading and installing the Magento blank theme (http://www.magentocommerce.com/extension/reviews/module/518). Getting familiar with not only the file structure, but theme components and phtml files will allow you to gain a better understanding of how Magento works.

Understanding a Magento Theme

In Chapter 3, we gave a pretty in-depth walk-through of the Public Interface. In this section, you'll be taking a look at everything that powers a Magento theme. First up is the important areas to keep in mind when you start modifying an existing theme or building one from scratch.

Important Theme Areas to Keep in Mind

- *Logo*: A logo is an important feature on your site that lets customers know exactly what kind of a store they are viewing. The default Magento logo is placed in the upper left-hand corner.

- *Shopping cart*: The shopping cart is an important feature for any eCommerce store. It should have prominent placement within your store and allows customers to view the products currently in their cart as well as offer the ability to proceed to checkout at any time.

- *Login and account management*: Customers will also need the ability to not only log into their accounts, but be able to manage their accounts and view previous orders. Magento provides both a login and account management sections, but you'll need to make sure these links are included if you modify your Magento theme.

- *Organization, planning, and workflow*: It's important to think about the best way to structure your store. Your products need to be organized into categories, and customers will need easy access to their account information to check out once they've added products to their account. There are a lot of items to keep in mind when you are planning how to modify a Magento theme or create a new one.

Default and NonDefault Magento Themes

By now, you know that Magento allows you to set up multiple stores. Not only can you have multiple stores, you can have multiple themes within one store. This is useful because you can create multiple themes to use for different categories, products and seasonal themes, to use throughout the year. Default themes refer to themes that contain non-default themes and only contain the elements you want to change. For example, you might want to use a different style sheet on one particular product page, a nondefault theme would allow you to do that. For the purpose of this chapter, you will only be working with default themes.

The Default Magento Theme

Let's take a look at the default Magento theme. This theme is the default theme that is included when you install Magento. The default Magento theme does a great job of showing you all the versatility of a Magento theme, although you might not need to use all of the same elements in your Magento store. Magento theme's can be customized to meet even the most complex eCommerce stores (see Figure 9-1).

Figure 9-1. *The default Magento theme*

Default Theme Layouts

Diving further into the default theme, you discover layouts. The default Magento theme includes five different layouts. Each of these layouts are shown in Figures 9-2 to 9-6.

- *Empty.* An empty page displays the content of a specific page on a white background that is not within the framework of your theme. Empty pages can be used as landing or single pages, not regularly used with your store. Empty pages are often referred to as blank pages, because they contain no background or images.

- *One column.* This is the simplest type of layout. A one column layout will only display a page's content without a column on either side of the content.

- *Two columns with right bar.* Page content is displayed on the left and a sidebar column is displayed on the right.

- *Two columns with left bar*: Page content is displayed on the right and a sidebar column is displayed on the left.

- *Three columns*: This layout displays the page content in the middle with sidebar column on both the left and right-hand side.

Figure 9-2. *The empty default theme layout. The empty theme layout has no background and does not include the Magento header or footer. This layout is perfect for landing pages that are custom designed.*

Figure 9-3. *The one column default theme layout. This layout is the most basic layout. It includes the Magento header and footer, but no left or right columns.*

Figure 9-4. *The two column with left bar default theme layout. This layout features a left sidebar with the main page content displayed on the right.*

Figure 9-5. *The two column with right bar default theme layout. This layout features a right sidebar with the main page content displayed on the left.*

Figure 9-6. *The three column default theme layout. This layout features both sidebars with the main page content in the middle.*

These layouts are used throughout your entire Magento store. You can specify unique layouts for different categories, product pages, and content management system (CMS) pages.

Magento File Structure

Before you dive into how to do some simple modifications with your Magento theme, you need to take a look at how Magento theme file structure is set up. Earlier, we talked about the three different components of a Magento theme: PHTML Templates, XML Layouts, and the Skin. These three different areas are divided into two different folders.

PHTML Templates and XML Layouts are contained under the app directory, while The Skin files and folders are all contained within the skin directory. Let's take a quick look at these files from an FTP perspective (see Figure 9-7).

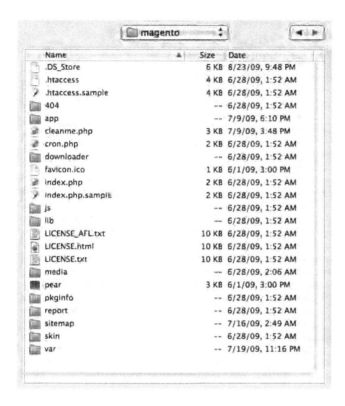

Figure 9-7. Highlighting the app and skin directory that house all of the major components of a Magento theme.

Inside the App Directory

To navigate to the default theme folder, you will need to navigate inside the app directory to app ➤ design ➤ frontend ➤ default ➤ default. All of the PHTML template files are contained within the template folder, while all of the XML Layouts are contained within the layout folder (see Figures 9-8 and 9-9).

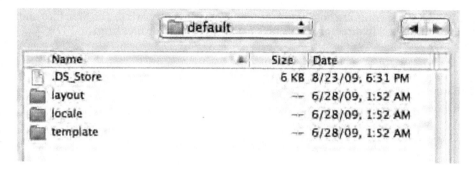

Figure 9-8. *Inside the app directory*

Name	Size	Date
amazonpayments.xml	2 KB	6/28/09, 1:52 AM
bundle.xml	14 KB	6/28/09, 1:52 AM
catalog.xml	21 KB	6/28/09, 1:52 AM
catalogsearch.xml	5 KB	6/28/09, 1:52 AM
checkout.xml	19 KB	6/28/09, 1:52 AM
cms.xml	3 KB	6/28/09, 1:52 AM
contacts.xml	2 KB	6/28/09, 1:52 AM
core.xml	1 KB	6/28/09, 1:52 AM
customer.xml	10 KB	6/28/09, 1:52 AM
directory.xml	2 KB	6/28/09, 1:52 AM
downloadable.xml	8 KB	6/28/09, 1:52 AM
giftmessage.xml	2 KB	6/28/09, 1:52 AM
googleanalytics.xml	1 KB	6/28/09, 1:52 AM
googlecheckout.xml	2 KB	6/28/09, 1:52 AM
googleoptimizer.xml	7 KB	6/28/09, 1:52 AM
newsletter.xml	2 KB	6/28/09, 1:52 AM
page.xml	8 KB	6/28/09, 1:52 AM
paypal.xml	2 KB	6/28/09, 1:52 AM
paypaluk.xml	2 KB	6/28/09, 1:52 AM
poll.xml	2 KB	6/28/09, 1:52 AM
productalert.xml	2 KB	6/28/09, 1:52 AM
reports.xml	1 KB	6/28/09, 1:52 AM
review.xml	5 KB	6/28/09, 1:52 AM
rss.xml	3 KB	6/28/09, 1:52 AM
sales.xml	13 KB	6/28/09, 1:52 AM
sendfriend.xml	2 KB	6/28/09, 1:52 AM
shipping.xml	2 KB	6/28/09, 1:52 AM
tag.xml	5 KB	6/28/09, 1:52 AM
weee.xml	2 KB	6/28/09, 1:52 AM
wishlist.xml	3 KB	6/28/09, 1:52 AM

Figure 9-9. *Inside the XML layout directory contained within the app directory*

Figure 9-10. *Inside the PHTML Template directory contained within the app directory*

Inside the Skin Directory

To navigate to the default theme skin directory, you will need to navigate inside the app directory to skin ➤ frontend ➤ default ➤ default. All of the CSS files, images, and javascript files are contained within this directory (see Figure 9-11).

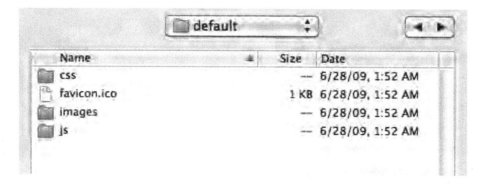

Figure 9-11. Inside the Skin directory. This folder contains css files, images, and javascript files.

Performing Some Simple Modifications

Now that you have a basic understanding of where each of the different elements of a theme are contained, let's look at making a few quick changes to each one of these sections.

Turn on Developer Hints

When you are working with Magento themes, one of the best things you can do is to turn on template path hints. Template path hints allow you to easily identify file paths for each part of your Magento site. To turn on developer hints, login to your administrative interface and navigate to System ➤ Configuration. Once the configuration page loads, select your store from the drop downmenu from the list under Current Configuration Scope. Then, click on developer at the bottom of the page under Advance select Developer located in the bottom left, which will bring up the Developer configuration. Click on debug and make sure Template Path Hints is changed to Yes. Click Save Config in the upper right-hand corner. This one tip will save you many sleepless nights (see Figures 9-12 and 9-13).

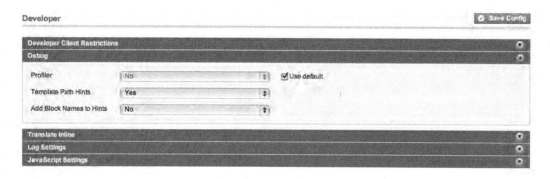

Figure 9-12. Turning on template path hints from the admin panel

Figure 9-13. Viewng a category with template path hints turned on.

As you can see in Figure 9-13, each area is highlighted with its respective file path in red and white. When template path hints are turned on you are able to view the file paths for each of the different elements on your site. All of these file references are contained within the app ➤ design directory. For example, you would find the newsletter (shown in the lower-left hand corner) at app ➤ design ➤ frontend ➤ default ➤ default ➤ template ➤ newsletter ➤ subscribe.phtml.

Modifying a XML Layout File

Let's take a look at Figure 9-14. For this example, you are going to remove the "Did you know?" box with the image of the dog by editing its related XML Layout file.

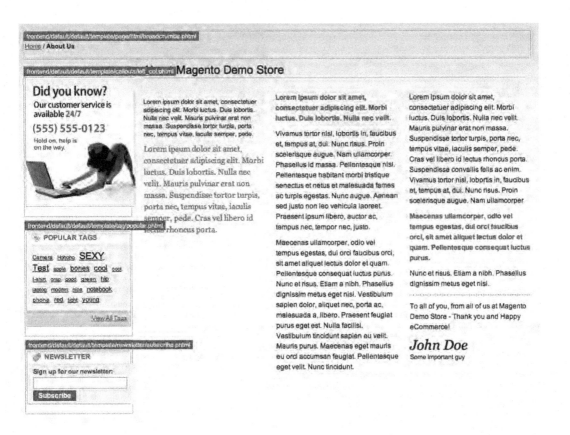

Figure 9-14. Showing the about us page, using a 2 column left bar layout. This is before you remove the "Did you know?" block.

This particular block you are working with is referred to as a callout, both the left and right columns contain callouts. These callouts are specific blocks that are used on any page of your store that has a left or right column. Typically, callouts are placed at the top of each column, but the position can also be adjusted by the use of xml.

There are 30 xml layout files contained within the default theme: amazonpayments.xml, bundle.xml, catalog.xml, catalogsearch.xml, checkout.xml, cms.xml, contacts.xml, core.xml, customer.xml, directory.xml, downloadable.xml, giftmessage.xml, googleanalytics.xml, googlecheckout.xml, googleoptimizer.xml, newsletter.xml,page.xml, paypal.xml, paypaluk.xml, poll.xml, productalert.xml, reports.xml, review.xml, rss.xml, sales.xml, sendfriend.xml, shipping.xml, tag.xml, weee.xml, wishlist.xml. These xml files are labeled by the area in which they control. For example, checkout.xml covers all of the blocks that are used within Magento's checkout process.

For our example, since you are working with the catalog part of Magento the xml references for the left callout is located within the catalog.xml. To edit this file, navigate to app ➤ design ➤ frontend ➤ default ➤ default ➤ layout ➤ catalog.xml. Do a search and find the following snippet:

```
<block type="core/template" name="left.permanent.callout" template=↵
"callouts/left_col.phtml">
    <action method="setImgSrc"><src>images/media/col_left_callout.jpg</src></action>
            <action method="setImgAlt" translate="alt" module="catalog"><alt>↵
Our customer service is available 24/7. Call us at (555) 555-0123.</alt></action>
            <action method="setLinkUrl"><url>checkout/cart</url></action>
</block>
```

While you could easily remove the "Did you know?" block, simply delete or comment out the entire code snippet shown above this would not be consider a best practice when working with Magento files. The correct way to edit this file is actually to copy /app/design/frontend/default/default to a new template folder set up name like /app/design/frontend/default/mytemplate/. Once you have set up, this folder structure and copied over the above file, from within the administrative interface, navigate to system ➤ Design ➤ Add Design Change ➤ then select "mytemplate." This way the default Magento template remains intact.

Once you've followed the above steps and deleted the above code snippet from within the new file and folder structure, refresh the page and your about us page should now look like Figure 9-15.

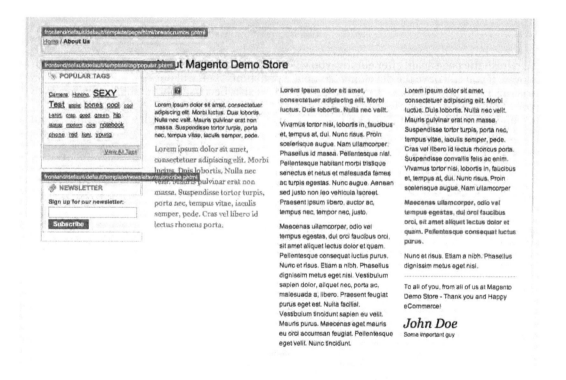

Figure 9-15. *Showing the about us page, using a two column left bar layout. This is after you have removed the "Did you know?" block.*

Modifying a PHTML Template File

For the second example, you are going to remove the "Did you know?" block again, but this time you are only going to edit a phtml file. Callouts for both the left and right column can be found in the same location. To edit either the left or right callouts, navigate to app ➤ design ➤ frontend ➤ default ➤ default ➤ template ➤ callouts. For this example, you will be editing the left_col.phtml since you are working with the left column. To remove the "Did you know?" simply delete the following code snippet:

```
<div class="box">
    <?php if (strtolower(substr($this->getLinkUrl(),0,4))==='http'): ?>
        <a href="<?php echo $this->getLinkUrl() ?>">
    <?php elseif($this->getLinkUrl()): ?>
        <a href="<?php echo $this->getUrl($this->getLinkUrl()) ?>">
    <?php endif ?>
    <img src="<?php echo $this->getSkinUrl($this->getImgSrc()) ?>" width="195" alt="<?php
echo $this->__($this->getImgAlt()) ?>" style="display:block;" />
    <?php if ($this->getLinkUrl()): ?>
    </a>
    <?php endif ?>
</div>
```

If you refresh the page again after editing, you will notice that the "Did you know?" block has again been removed. If you still have the developer "template path hints" you will notice that the block is gone, but there is still a template reference to the left callout. This exists because there is still a reference in the catalog.xml file you were working with in the previous section. Even though this shows up with the template path hints still turned on, the next block "Popular Tags" will appear flush with the title "About Magento Demo Store."

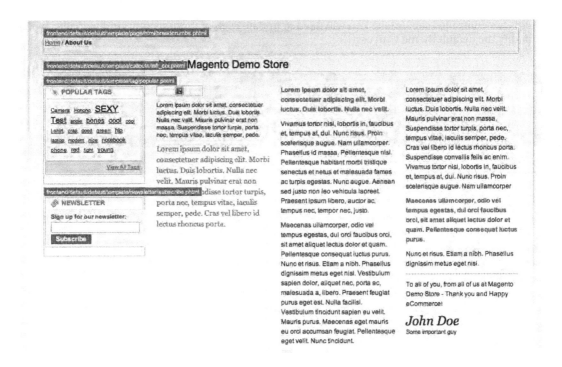

Figure 9-16. *Viewing the about us page after we removed the "Did you know?" block by editing the left_col.phtml template file. Notice the template path hints still show the block.*

Modifying a CSS file

Modifying the CSS (cascading style sheet) of a Magento theme is really no different than any other CSS you've worked with before. The only difference is that in Magento, stylesheets are divided up into several different files including boxes.css, clears.css, ie7minus.css, iestyles.css, menu.css, print.css, and reset.css. The majority of the default Magento theme style is contained within the boxes.css and reset.css files.

As a quick example, you are going to change the default theme background to a solid block color or #000000. To do this, navigate to the reset.css file. It can be found within the skin ➤ frontend ➤ default ➤ default ➤ css directory. Find the body section that looks like the snippet below:

```
body { background:#496778 url(../images/body_bg.gif) 50% 0 repeat-y; color:#2f2f2f;↵
  font:12px/1.55em arial, helvetica, sans-serif; text-align:center; }
```
Change the snippet to the following:
```
body { background:#000000; color:#2f2f2f; font:12px/1.55em arial, helvetica, sans-serif;↵
  text-align:center; }
```

If you refresh your store, you will notice that the background at the bottom of the page has changed to black. It should look similar to Figure 9-17. In the default theme, the header, menu and footer backgrounds are controlled separately. You will need to update each of these sections individually if you want to modify the default theme with css.

Figure 9-17. *Updating the default magento theme using css. Notice the black in the background at the bottom of the image?*

The Blank Theme for Magento

If you feel that using the default Magento is not going to give you enough freedom to customize your store then I would suggest installing the blank theme for Magento. Functionally, this theme is exactly the same as Magento's default theme, but it includes a minimal design and a simplified CSS (cascading style sheet) for rapid modification and theme development.

Download the Blank Theme

Before we go continue, I would like to stress the fact that you should back up your system. There is no rollback option for extensions. You can uninstall an extension, but that doesn't guarantee the extension was able to undo any database changes or file structure modification.

■ **Note** Each extension listed on Magento Connect contains a unique extension key. This key is what Magento uses to identify the correct PEAR package to download and install.

To download the blank theme visit http://www.magentocommerce.com/magento-connect and click on the core link on the right-hand side of the page. Click on the Blank Interface extension. This page can also be accessed directly by visiting: http://www.magentocommerce.com/extension/612/blank-interface. Once this page loads, locate the "Get extension key" button (See Figure 9-18).

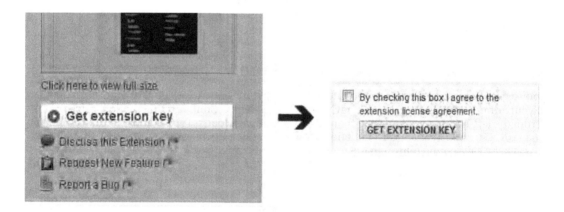

Figure 9-18. Magento Connect—Get Extension Key

You'll be asked to accept their license agreement. Check the box to agree and you'll be given an extension key. Copy this key into your Magento Connect Manager (see Figure 9-19).

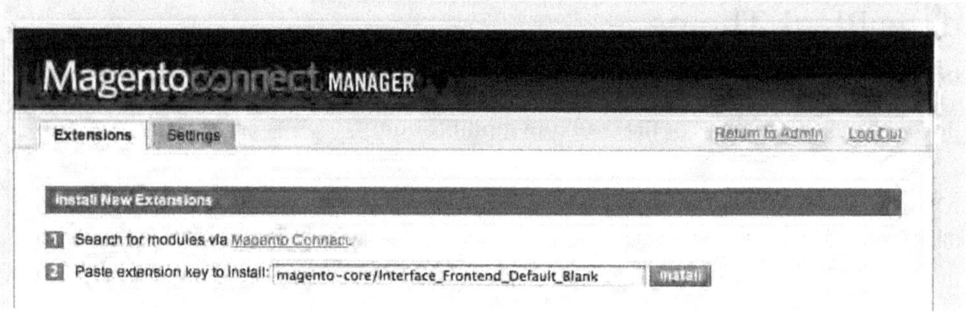

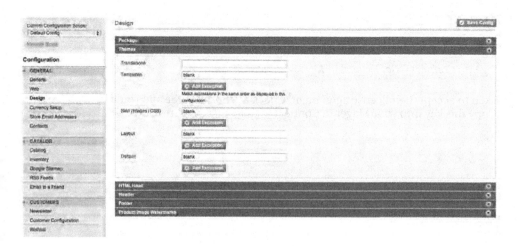

Figure 9-19. *Magento Connect Manager —Pasting in the blank theme Extension Key Install*

Click the Install button. A dialog will appear to begin the automated install. If the output displays "install ok," then you've installed an extension! Click the Refresh button and you can view the installed package.

From this window you can reinstall, uninstall, and check for upgrades on extensions installed on your system. For more information about downloading and installing the blank theme and other extensions please refer to Chapter 10.

Assigning the Blank Theme to Your Store

Once you've got the blank the downloaded into your store, you'll need to assign it to a store. To do this, login to your administrative interface and navigate to the System ➤ Configuration section. Click on design from the left-hand menu and then themes when that page loads. Type blank into the Templates, Skin (Images/CSS), and Layout and Default fields. This will assign the blank theme to your store. Make sure you click the save config button in the upper-right hand corner (see Figure 9-20).

Figure 9-20. *Examining the file structure for adding a second theme to your Magento store*

■ **Note** Changing the settings shown in Figure 9-20 will affect all of your Magento stores. If you do not want to change the theme used on all of your stores, you will need to select your store from the drop down menu and make the necessary adjustments per store.

In case you are wondering, the name blank refers to the folder "blank" which contains the same files used in the default Magento theme discussed earlier in this chapter. Blank theme files can be found in two different places: app ➤ design ➤ frontend ➤ default ➤ blank and skin ➤ frontend ➤ default ➤ blank. Themes are always pared in this way. One directory contained within app and the other within skin (see Figure 9-21).

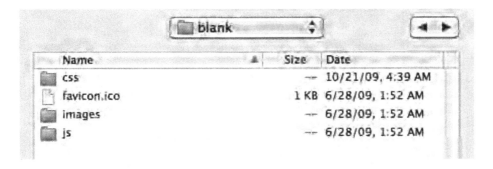

Figure 9-21. Examining the file structure for adding a second theme to your Magento store

After you have assigned the blank theme to your store, refresh your public interface. It should look something like Figure 9-22. The blank theme includes only the most basic styling so you can easily modify it to suit the needs of your store.

Figure 9-22. *The blank Magento theme*

What's Next?

Designing and developing themes for Magento can be hard work, but with a little patience and study of some preexisting themes you can begin creating Magento themes in no time. Coming up in Chapter 10, you will be taking an in-depth look at how to download, install, and write your own modules and extensions.

CHAPTER 10

■ ■ ■

Magento Extensions

Overview

Magento designed its architecture in a flexible format that encourages users and communities to build and extend the core application. What does this mean? Simply put, if a feature is missing, you can build it yourself.

And if you want to contribute, you can post your home brew extension through Magento Connect (`www.magentocommerce.com/magento-connect`), which is a growing community that consists of open source and commercial extensions. There's even a section of goodies built by the Magento's internal team.

You'll begin this chapter by exploring Magento Connect Manager, installing a third-party module, moving into building a simple Hello World module, extending that into a random product module, and finally deploying the custom module into an extension.

■ **Note** Extensions, modules, and plug-ins are used interchangeably. The naming can get confusing, but the important thing to note is that extensions are packaged modules. You can build many modules for your Magento shop, but it only becomes an extension once you have packaged it using Magento's built-in function. (We'll explain more near the end of this chapter.)

Magento Connect Manager

Let's become familiar with the way Magento handles extensions. Log in through the Admin Panel: choose System, Magento Connect, Magento Connect Manager. The Magento Connect Manager page is displayed (see Figure 10-1).

Figure 10-1. *Magento Connect Manager*

This is your extension portal page. From here, you can browse, view, remove, or upgrade extensions installed on your system. If you receive warning messages, check your folder permissions. Magento Connect Manager is an auto installer that uses PEAR to handle installs and upgrades of Magento modules. (For more information on PEAR, visit http://pear.php.net.)

Under the Settings tab, you can set your preferences for which type of release your Magento server will accept (see Figure 10-2). This is useful because your Magento server will not accept or install any extensions that are below your preferred state; e.g. if you have your preferred state set to Stable, you will receive a warning message when you try to download and install an extension that is classified Alpha or Beta.

■ **Note** Release info—such as stability settings of Alpha, Beta, and Stable—are set by extension owners and developers.

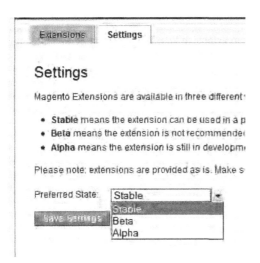

Figure 10-2. Magento Connect Manager settings

Finding an Extension

The Magento Connect Manager has a convenient link to its public Magneto Connect site (www.magentocommerce.com/magento-connect).

As of this writing, Magento Connect is broken up into three types of extensions: Community, Commercial, and Core.

- *Community extension*: This extension is free to the masses, built by the open source community, and released under the Open Source License 3.0. All extensions are labeled "Provided as is".

- *Commercial extension*: This is a paid extension that will link to external sites. Be sure to read the reviews before purchasing to make sure it meets your needs and works in your environment and version.

- *Core extension*: This extension has been blessed by the Magento team (built by the same set of developers). It is also released under the Open Source License.

Browse the huge repository of extensions, read their reviews and ratings, and follow the forum discussions. There's a lot to see and do in Magento Connect.

Installing an Extension

Before you continue, we want to remind you to back up your system. There is no rollback option for extensions. Although you can uninstall an extension, it might not undo any database changes or file structure modifications.

■ **Note** Each extension listed on Magento Connect contains a unique extension key. This key is what Magento uses to identify the correct PEAR package to download and install.

Once you find an extension you like to install, locate the Get Extension Key button (see Figure 10-3).

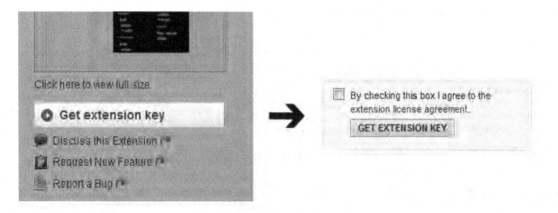

Figure 10-3. Magento Connect—Get extension key

You'll be asked to accept the license agreement. Check the box to agree and you'll be given an extension key. Copy this key into your Magento Connect Manager (see Figure 10-4).

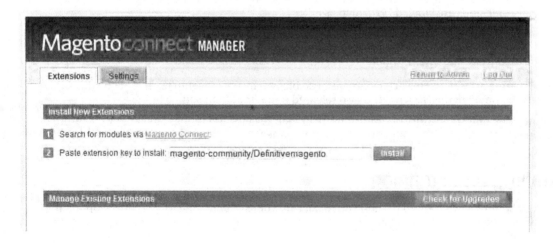

Figure 10-4. Magento Connect Manager—Extension key install

Click the Install button. A dialog will appear to begin the automated install. If the output displays Install Ok, you've installed an extension! Click the Refresh button and you can view the installed package (see Figure 10-5).

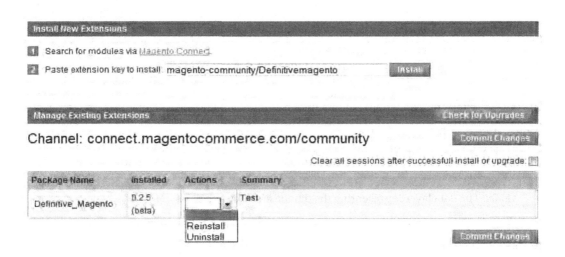

Figure 10-5. *Manage Existing Extensions*

From this window you can reinstall, uninstall, and check for upgrades on extensions installed on your system.

Uninstalling an Extension

From the window shown in Figure 10-5, you can select Uninstall from the Actions column and click the Commit Changes button. A dialog will display the result of the removal.

Once completed, you can click the Refresh button to return back to your Magento Connect Manager extension page.

Building a Module

In this section, you will get your hands dirty with some code. The process is very technical, but don't worry—we will hold your hand throughout the whole process.

The goal of this section is to build a simple Hello World extension. It's the foundation of every programming language tutorial and it serves as a wonderful stepping stone into understanding Magento's extension architecture.

Before you begin, let's go through a set of rules.

Rules

Magento is unforgiving when it comes to errors. All file names and attributes must be exact or else Magento's extensions will throw errors or (worse) do nothing.

When developing, it's recommended to disabled your cache. If you make a code change, and refreshing the page does not reflect any updates, it's most likely due to Magento's cache. To disable Magento's cache, log on on to the Admin Panel and go to System, Cache Management. Select Disable under Cache Control, All Cache. Click Save Cache Settings.

Class names and methods follow Zend's namespace architecture. You will see long class names chained with underscore characters. This is how Zend determines the location of each file. The underscore characters represent the file path separator. While this can be confusing at first, you'll get the hang of it. As a side effect, names cannot contain underscores. Even making a file name camel case will throw errors, so it's best to avoid it. (For more information on Zend's rule sets, visit `http://framework.zend.com/manual/en/coding-standard.html`.)

Because Magento is built on top of Zend's framework, it strictly follows the Model-View-Controller (MVC) pattern. This segregates the business logic from presentation, allowing standard structure and defined roles to each layer:

- *Model*: The data layer representing the database structure.

- *View*: The presentation layer rendering the template files to the audience.

- *Controller*: The conductor between Model and View. This layer handles the logic and processing of data from the Model layer to the View layer.

More information can be found here: `http://en.wikipedia.org/wiki/Model%E2%80%93view%E2%80%93controller`

Directory Structure

You won't need all these directories for the sample extension, but we'll list them here as references:

```
\app
        \code
            \local
                \Definitivemagento
                    \appname
                            \Block
                            \controllers
                            \etc
                            \Helper
                            \Model
                            \sql
\etc
        \modules
```

Notice that you're storing the module under `\app\local\`. This is considered best practice to avoid conflict and overwriting during software upgrades that modifies Magento's core files, which is located under `\app\code\core\Mage\`. If you do need to overwrite Magento's core file, there is a clean approach to tackle this situation (see Chapter 12).

■ **Tip** You can view great examples of various file structures by browsing the core Magento (\app\code\core\Mage*) or any third-party modules installed in your system (\app\code\community*).

\app\code\local\Definitivemagento: This is the main root directory for your project. If you have a company name, this is where you would rename Definitivemagento to your company name.

\app\code\local\Definitivemagento\appname: It is useful to create subdirectories that match the name of your application or module. That way, if you plan to create multiple modules under the same company, it can all live in its own directory name.

\app\code\local\Definitivemagento\appname\Block: From an MVC perspective, this is the View layer. It contains the data that will be displayed into HTML through Magento's CMS Blocks or within .phtml files.

\app\code\local\Definitivemagento\appname\controllers: This contains the actions of your module. It handles all logic and passes data between your Models and Blocks. A controller is not required for building the Helloworld module, but if you plan to access the module through a URL such as www.demosite.com/Definitivemagento/Helloworld/, you need a controller to handle the event and process actions.

\app\code\local\Definitivemagento\appname\etc: This directory gives Magento detailed information about your module and how each piece is connected.

\app\code\local\Definitivemagento\appname\Helper: Helper files are essential for building applications that may contain repeatable routines or simple procedural methods.

■ **Note** Even if you don't use helper files in your custom module, it's required to exist in your package if you plan to add UI components into the Admin Panel. This is an oversight in Magento's architecture, and all the Magento core files have Helper files with two lines of code (e.g., \app\code\core\Mage\Poll\Helper\Data.php).

\app\code\local\Definitivemagento\appname\Model: This model interfaces with your business logic, the database. Here is where you define custom method and function calls to fetch, save, and modify data.

\app\code\local\Definitivemagento\appname\sql: This directory name can be misleading. Its purpose is twofold: to define custom database tables and process any upgrades to your extension.

\etc\modules: This is a stepchild directory, located outside the confines of the package. Files located here register your module into Magento's system.

Simple Hello World Module

Now you'll dive deeper and build a simple Hello World module. You'll start small and use only the directories needed. Once you have a basic understanding, reading the core complex modules won't be a shot in the dark.

Files for Hello World Module

```
\app
        \code
                \local
                        \Definitivemagento
                                \Helloworld
                                        \Block
                                                \Hi.php
                                        \etc
                                                \config.xml
\etc
        \modules
                \Definitivemagento_All.xml
```

As you can see, this is very bare bones. But it's important to start small and build up from there.

```
\app\code\local\Definitivemagento\Helloworld\Block\Hi.php:
<?php
class Definitivemagento_Helloworld_Block_Hi extends Mage_Core_Block_Template
{
    rotected function _toHtml()
    {
        return "Hello World";
    }
}
```

Notice the naming convention used here. The class name is Definitivemagento_Helloworld_Block_Hi. Each underscore represents the directory structure. This is Magento/Zend's way of handling namespaces. This knowledge is good to know, especially if you'll be reading Magento's core files and figuring out which file is being accessed.

This method extends Magento's Block class so you can call it within a CMS block element. For simplicity's sake, you'll be using the _toHtml() method to output the data. If you don't use the _toHtml() method and define your own, you need to call it directly: $this->methodName().

```
\app\code\local\Definitivemagento\Helloworld\etc\config.xml
<?xml version="1.0"?>
<config>
    <modules>
        <Definitivemagento_Helloworld>
            <version>1.0</version>
        </Definitivemagento_Helloworld>
    </modules>
```

```
    <global>
        <blocks>
            <Definitivemagento_Helloworld>
                <class>Definitivemagento_Helloworld_Block</class>
            </Definitivemagento_Helloworld>
        </blocks>
    </global>
</config>
```

This is the configuration file. The first set of tags, <modules>, defines the name/path and version of your custom module.

Everything else will go under the <global> tag, which defines the resources, classes, and blocks. Because you're building a Hello World block, you'll define the <blocks> tag and define the class name here. If you were building a Model, they would link in here.

Note Unfortunately, Magento's documentation is lacking. But by viewing the core Magento files, you can get a sense of which other parameters can exist within this file. Take a look at the Catalog core file (\app\code\core\Mage\Catalog\etc\config.xml). You can see how <admin> defines the input text fields for the Admin Panel, <adminhtml> creates the drop down menu of the Admin Panel, and <frontend> allows you to access catalog through the URL.

```
\app\etc\modules\Definitivemagento_All.xml
<?xml version="1.0"?>
<config>
    <modules>
        <Definitivemagento_Helloworld>
            <active>true</active>
            <codePool>local</codePool>
        </Definitivemagento_Helloworld>
    </modules>
</config>
```

Creating this file under \app\etc\modules\ will register your custom module into your Magento site. Notice that all the Mage core files are listed here, too.

The <codePool> represents the directory structure \app\code\local\. If you didn't place your custom module package under \local, you would need to update this value.

Tip The naming convention must be exact. For example, <codepool> is not the same as <codePool>. This will save you hours of debugging if you create a working template such as Helloworld, and keep it extending it for future modules.

Verify that the Module Is Registered

After all the files are in place, it's best to verify whether your module has been registered correctly with Magento.

From the Admin Panel, choose System, Configuration, Advanced, Advanced. Expand the Disable Modules Output row. You should see your module listed, as shown in Figure 10-6.

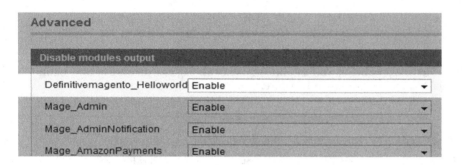

Figure 10-6. Verifying modules

Displaying Hello World in Blocks

Now that Magento knows about the new modules, let's inject the code into a Block and test it out.

From the Admin Panel, choose CMS, Manage Pages. Let's display the Helloworld module in the Home page. Select the row labeled Home page. From the General Information tab, under Content, you can add the following line of code:

```
<h1>  {{block type="Definitivemagento_Helloworld/hi"}}  </h1>
```

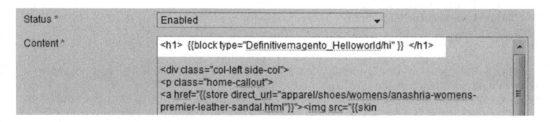

Figure 10-7. Calling Helloworld

■ **Note** Pay close attention to which letter requires capitalization and which should be lowercase. The namespace starts with capital letters, but the block action, in this case "hi", is lowercase.

Refresh your Magento site and see the results, as shown in Figure 10-8.

Figure 10-8. *Results of Hello World*

Okay, now give yourself a pat on the back. You have just created a Magento module! Now let's do some real-world stuff.

Random Products Module

Let's extend the Helloworld module to query a random list of products and display them to the user. You will build your own customize models as well as use Magento's core models.

Files for Random Products Module

```
\app
        \code
                \local
                        \Definitivemagento
                                \Helloworld
                                        \Block
                                                \Hi.php
                                                \Randomproducts.php
                                        \Model
                                                \Randomproducts.php
                                        \etc
                                                \config.xml
\etc
        \modules
                \Definitivemagento_All.xml
```

You added a new Model directory. It will do the heavy lifting, but you need the Block to handle the view component.

```
\app\code\local\Definitivemagento\Helloworld\Model\Randomproducts.php
<?php
class Definitivemagento_Helloworld_Model_Randomproducts
            extends Mage_Core_Model_Abstract
{
    public function getRandomProducts($maxCount = 5)
    {
        $randProducts = array();
        $allProducts = array();
        $productCollection = Mage::getModel('catalog/product')
            ->getCollection()
            ->addAttributeToSelect('*')
            ->getItems();
        foreach ($productCollection as $id => $data)
        {
            $allProducts[] = $data;
        }
        $productIds = array_keys($allProducts);
        $totalProductIds = count($productIds);
        for ($i=0; $i<$maxCount; $i++)
        {
            $randIndex = rand(0,$totalProductIds);
            $randProductId = $productIds[$randIndex];
              $randProducts[] = $allProducts[$randProductId];
        }
        return $randProducts;
    }
}
```

There's a lot going on here. Similar to the Block class, you go ahead and extend the base core Model. The purpose of this model is to fetch the random set of products and return that data to the Block.

There are numerous ways to pull a list of products from your store. If you're old school, you can go straight SQL by reviewing its open schema (www.magentocommerce.com/wiki/development/magento_database_diagram). But the most flexible way is to use Magento's models:

```
$productCollection = Mage::getModel('catalog/product')
```

This line of code allows you to ask Magento for its catalog product model. A full list of available models and methods can be found on its massive documentation page (http://docs.magentocommerce.com/). Be warned; this is not for the faint of heart.

Once you have obtained the model, go ahead and grab the collection:

```
->getCollection()
```

Then set the MySQL Select query to return all columns:

```
->addAttributeToSelect('*')
```

And finally return it as an array of items:

```
->getItems();
```

■ **Note** The quickest way to view what type of data is being returned is to reverse engineer the methods. Perform var_export or var_dump within PHP. Then you can see how the data is set up within the objects.

Now that you have all the products in the store, let's clean up the result set. We performed a simple loop to extract only the product objects:

```
foreach ($productCollection as $id => $data)
{
    $allProducts[] = $data;
}
```

Within each product objects are key value arrays:

```
$productIds = array_keys($allProducts);
```

This will return all the product ids so you can perform a random draw. You'll use the rand() method from PHP to extract five products from the collection (www.php.net/manual/en/function.rand.php). To use the rand() method, give PHP a start number and an ending number. Because an array index starts at 0, you need to obtain only the end value, which is the total size of the array:

```
$totalProductIds = count($productIds);
```

Now you loop five times:

```
for ($i=0; $i<$maxCount; $i++)
```

Draw a random number between 0 and the total size of the array:

```
$randIndex = rand(0,$totalProductIds);
```

Extract the random productId from the array:

```
$randProductId = $productIds[$randIndex];
```

Then store the product object into the result set:

```
$randProducts[] = $allProducts[$randProductId];
```

The model is complete. Let's move into the Block layer.

```
\app\code\local\Definitivemagento\Helloworld\Block\Randomproducts.php:
class Definitivemagento_Helloworld_Block_Randomproducts extends Mage_Core_Block_Template
{
    protected function _toHtml()
    {
        $randProdModel = Mage::getModel('Definitivemagento_Helloworld/Randomproducts');
        $randProducts = $randProdModel->getRandomProducts();
        $html = "<ul>";
        foreach ($randProducts as $product)
        {
            $name = $product->getName();
            $price = number_format($product->getPrice(), 2);
            $imageLink = $this->helper('catalog/image')
                ->init($product, 'thumbnail')->resize(100,100);
            $productLink = $this->helper('catalog/product')->getProductUrl($product);
            $html .= "
                <p>
                    <a href='$productLink'><img src='$imageLink' alt='$name'/></a><br/>
                    $name <br/>
                    $price
                </p>";
        }
        $html .= "<ul>";

        return $html;
    }
}
```

You'll continue to use the _toHtml() method to initialize the block. Does the code look familiar? Similar to the previous code, you'll perform another getModel call:

```
$randProdModel = Mage::getModel('Definitivemagento_Helloworld/Randomproducts');
```

Now you're using the model you just built. Let's activate the random code:

```
$randProducts = $randProdModel->getRandomProducts();
```

Because you'll be outputting HTML, use a variable to store all the results and output them when you're done:

```
$html = "<ul>";
```

The next set of code will extract the random array and prepare the data into HTML:

```
foreach ($randProducts as $product)
```

Using Magento's documentation, you can use methods such as getName() and getPrice(). There are also helper methods that will aid in performing image resize and product URLs.

```
$name = $product->getName();
$price = number_format($product->getPrice(), 2);
$imageLink = $this->helper('catalog/image')
    ->init($product, 'thumbnail')
    ->resize(100,100);
$productLink = $this->helper('catalog/product')->getProductUrl($product);
```

Note If Magento's documentation is too confusing, use PHP's get_class_methods to see what available methods you can use: http://us2.php.net/manual/en/function.get-class-methods.php.

Next, take the formatted data and create the HTML:

```
$html .= "
    <p>
        <a href='$productLink'><img src='$imageLink' alt='$name'/></a><br/>
        $name <br/>
        $price
    </p>";
```

You have one more step to connect everything.

\app\code\local\Definitivemagento\Helloworld\etc\config.xml:

```
<?xml version="1.0"?>
<config>
    <modules>
        <Definitivemagento_Helloworld>
            <version>1.0</version>
        </Definitivemagento_Helloworld>
    </modules>
    <global>
        <blocks>
            <Definitivemagento_Helloworld>
                <class>Definitivemagento_Helloworld_Block</class>
            </Definitivemagento_Helloworld>
        </blocks>
        <models>
            <Definitivemagento_Helloworld>
                <class>Definitivemagento_Helloworld_Model</class>
            </Definitivemagento_Helloworld>
        </models>
    </global>
</config>
```

Because you created the new Model, you have to add it to the config.xml file. And you're done.

Displaying Random Products in Blocks

Let's repeat the procedure from Hello World. From the Admin Panel, choose CMS, Manage Pages. Select the row labeled Home page. From the General Information tab, under Content, you can add the following line of code (see Figure 10-9):

```
{{block type="Definitivemagento_Helloword/randomproducts"}}
```

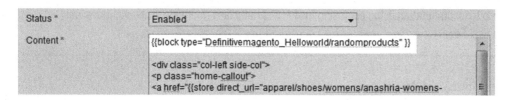

Figure 10-9. Adding random product module

Refresh your Magento site and see the results. This is very bare bones, but with a little CSS styling you can incorporate this output to match the flow of your template and design (see Figure 10-10).

Figure 10-10. Results of random product module

Displaying Random Products in Template files

Not a fan of the CMS Block? Would you rather place this element within your template page? The modification is simple. The default template for the demo site is 2columns-right.phtml:

`\app\design\frontend\default\default\template\page\2columns-right.phtml`

To add the block, open up the page.xml from the layout directory:

`\app\design\frontend\default\default\layout\page.xml`

Look for the template tag page_two_columns_right and inject the random products block in there:

```
<page_two_columns_right>
      <reference name="root">
          <action method="setTemplate">
              <template>page/2columns-right.phtml</template>
          </action>
          <!-- Mark root page block that template is applied -->
          <action method="setIsHandle"><applied>1</applied></action>
      </reference>
      <reference name="right">
          <block type="Definitivemagento_Helloworld/randomproducts"/>
      </reference>
</page_two_columns_right>
```

Refresh the index page and you'll now see the random products block displayed on the right panel.

Turning a Module into an Extension

Now let's take the creation and turn it into a real extension.

■ **Note** Before you begin, make sure that your /var/pear/ path exists and that it has writable permission.

From the Admin Panel, choose System, Magento Connect, Package Extensions.

Package Info

The Package Info section contains the following fields (see Figure 10-11):

Name: Enter the package name

Channel:

- For Core packages: connect.magentocommerce.com/core
- For Community packages: connect.magentocommerce.com/community

Summary: A short title name for your package

Description: A detailed explanation about your package

License: Your preferred license, such as OSL v3.0

License URI: URL to the above license

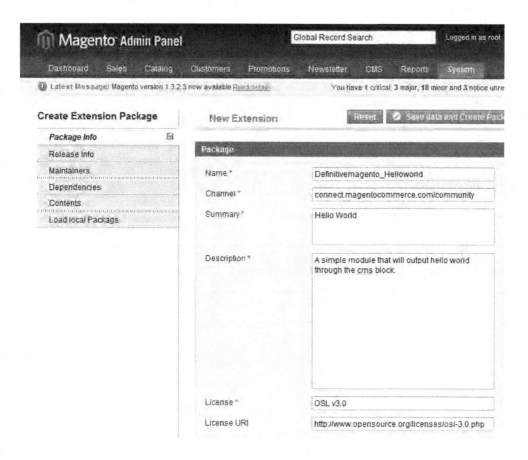

Figure 10-11. Package Info

Release Info

The Release Info section contains the following fields (see Figure 10-12):

> *Release Version*: Numeric value representing your current version
>
> *API Version*: Also separate version info for your API
>
> *Release Stability*: State of your module; Development, Alpha, Beta, Stable
>
> *API Stability*: State of the API
>
> *Notes*: Any additional information for your users

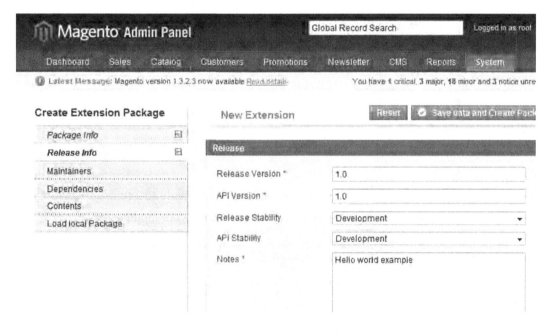

Figure 10-12. *Release Info*

Maintainers

This section lists the members involved (see Figure 10-13). Click Add Maintainer.

■ **Note** The information input here should match the Magento Connect account. If you have not done so, please register and create an account on Magento Connect (www.magentocommerce.com/boards/member/register/).

Level: Each maintainer listed is defined under one of four roles: Lead, Developer, Contributor, or Helper. Only the Lead member can upload new releases of your extension.

Name: Your full name.

User: This field should match your username (not your screen name) in Magento Connect. Go to www.magentocommerce.com/boards/member/profile/, Personal Settings, Username, Password.

Email: Your e-mail address. This will be listed in the package file.

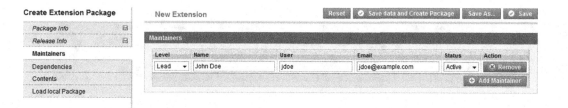

Figure 10-13. *Maintainers*

Dependencies

If the module contains any dependencies, they must be listed here (see Figure 10-14):

PHP Version: List the min/max version of PHP required to run your module. You can specify a recommended version, which will be used even if a newer version is available. An exclude option is also available if there are known issues with your code executing with specific PHP versions.

Packages: List any Magento packages required (e.g., Mage_Core_Modules) and their channel info. This information can be gathered from the package info section when you use the Load Local Package option (discussed in the next few pages).

Subpackages: This is required only if your new package has been split into two or more packages and they are dependent on the same set of files.

Extensions: These are PHP and PECL extensions. If your source code uses PDO or curl, for example, they must be selected here.

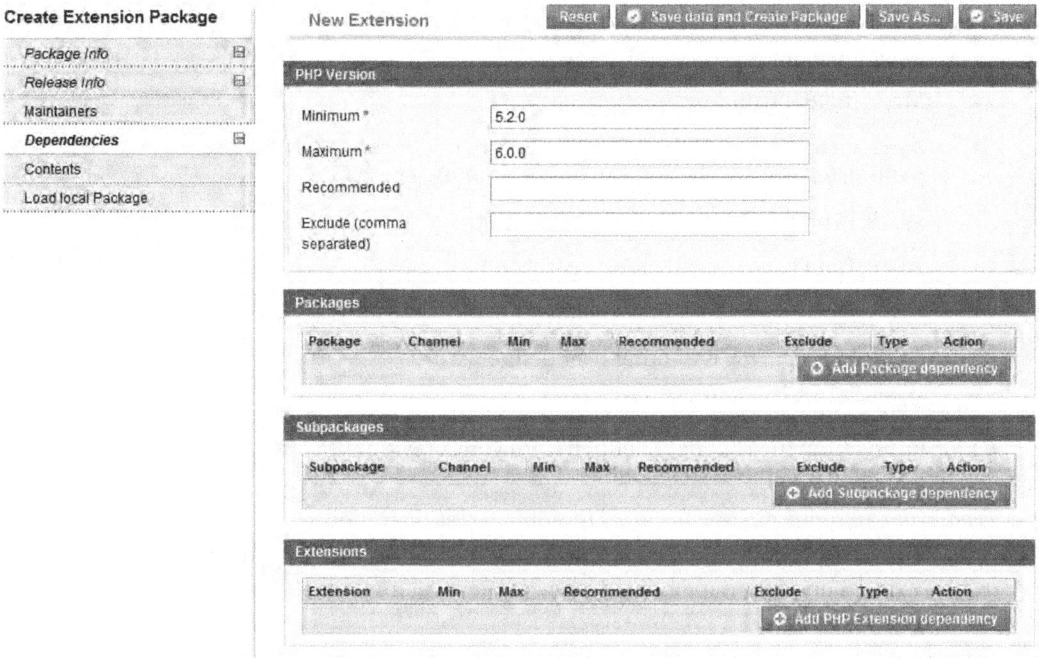

Figure 10-14. *Dependencies*

Contents

This is the section in which you add all your module files (see Figure 10-15).

> *Role*: The roles here are mapped to their root path that will be used in conjunction with the Path field.

- *Magento Local module file:* The Helloworld module is under the \app\code\local\ directory, so select this choice.

- *Magento Community module file:* These are files located under \app\code\community\.

- Magento Core team module file: \app\code\core\.

- Magento User Interface (layouts, templates): \app\design\.

- Magento Global Configuration: \app\etc\.

- Magento PHP Library file: \lib\.

- Magento Locale language file: \app\locale\.

- Magento Media library: \media\.

- Magento Theme Skin (Images, CSS, JS): \skin\.

- Magento Other web accessible file: \.

- Magento PHPUnit test: \test\.

- *Magento other:* This is the user define path. If it doesn't fit in any of the paths listed previously, you can define your own path here.

- *PEAR:* PHP files: \downloader\pearlib\php\.

- *PEAR:* Data files: \downloader\pearlib\data\.

- *PEAR:* Documentation: \downloader\pearlib\docs\.

- *PEAR:* Scripts: This is another user define path.

- *PEAR:* Tests: \downloader\pearlib\tests\.

Path: Starting from the root path defined from your previous selection of Roles, fill in the directory name of the module.

Type: This can represent one file or all files under this directory.

Include: This tells the engine to include files using * for wildcard matching, or regular expression pattern matching if you denote a deliminator such as #^Definitive.*#.

Ignore: Used to not include file(s). Uses wildcard and regular expressions.

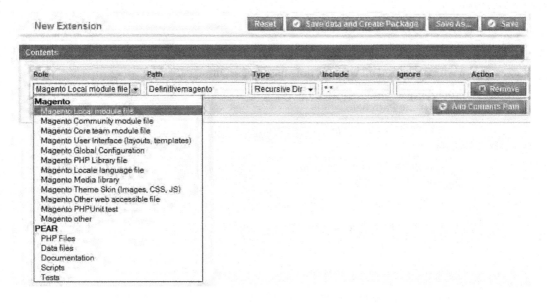

Figure 10-15. *Creating Extension Package – Contents*

That's all the information you need. Click the Save button and then the Save Data and Create Package, which will generate the extension.

■ **Note** The interface is confusing here. One would assume the next step is to proceed downward and click Load Local Package. But this would clear out all the information you just typed.

Extension Completed

Once Magento has completed the auto packaging, you should see the window shown in Figure 10-16.

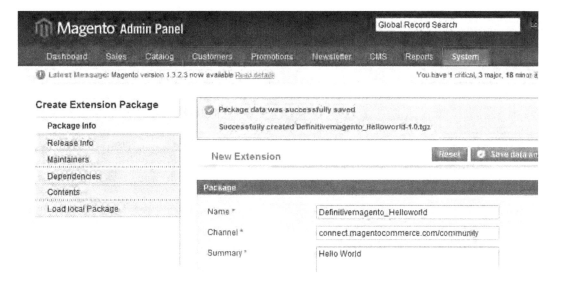

Figure 10-16. Creating Extension Package completed

You will see your package file stored under \var\pear\. If you want to upload your custom extension to the Magento Connect, either for open source or commercial deployment, follow the steps from the web site (www.magentocommerce.com/wiki/how_to_use_magentoconnect#creating_a_magento_ community_extension.

Load Local Package

If you want to review your created package(s), you can click the last section labeled Load Local Package. You newly created extension will be displayed on the first row. Click the row and it will reload all your information for viewing.

Summary

This chapter showed you how to browse and install extensions through Magento Connect, build your own module, and package it into an extension. There still many more options to explore. Browsing through the documentation and looking at all the core modules (`http://docs.magentocommerce.com/`) can make your head spin. But that also means that there are endless possibilities of how to extract and create your own module.

Magento Connect is filled with enthusiasts who have built wonderful extensions for the open community. We encourage you to install a handful and look at their source code. That will give you an idea of how others are building their extensions and maybe foster new ideas.

What's Next?

Check out the next chapter to learn how to configure and set up Magento's API to allow external web apps to communicate with your store.

CHAPTER 11

■ ■ ■

API

What is an *application programming interface (API)*? It is a component that allows execution of system methods through a standard protocol. In the case of Magento, it is often referred to as a *web API* or as *web services*.

The power of web services is not in the technology, but in the third-party innovation that evolves by accessing and extracting the application's core services. Successful companies such as IBM, Google, Yahoo, Twitter, and Facebook have APIs in their applications. APIs enable your applications to use services such as Google Maps, and allow users to sign in through their Facebook login. API access opens up the door to an array of third-party applications, fostering innovation and behavior that extends your current features.

Magento allows access into its API through two standard protocols: XML-RPC and SOAP. This chapter discusses numerous examples of each available API method, switching from both protocols. Magento is still in its infancy stage, so there are existing bugs. This chapter provides solutions and workarounds so that your first journey into Magento's API will be less of a headache.

XML-RPC

RPC stands for *remote procedure call*. Prepend the word "XML" and you have a remote procedure call through XML syntax. XML-RPC has a very simple design. Within <methodCall> and <params>, it has enough structure to communicate with the server and process the request.

XML-RPC has been around since 1998, so nearly all programming languages have libraries to construct an XML-RPC call. We won't dive into too many details because this is a book about Magento, not XML-RPC. For more information, please visit www.xmlrpc.com/.

SOAP

SOAP stands for *simple object access protocol.* It also uses XML syntax, very similar to XML-RPC, but more advanced and complex. It is the predecessor to XML-RPC, allowing developers to extend and customize data types. But these types of features increase the overhead, which deters most performance enthusiastic.

Why use SOAP? It has the stamp of approval from the World Wide Web Consortium (W3C). As an open standard, the adoption and support for SOAP are increasing. SOAP also runs on both SMTP and HTTP to transport easily through firewalls, guaranteeing access.

PHP with XML-RPC or SOAP?

For the examples in this chapter, you will be using the de facto language of Magento: PHP. Programming languages from C to .NET can connect into Magento and execute procedural calls through XML-RPC or SOAP protocol. But for the sake of simplicity, you will focus only on displaying PHP snippets.

Now, do you choose XML-RPC or SOAP? We won't make that decision for you, but will provide examples of both.

■ **Note** If your Magento store is installed on a hosting server, it's best to check which types of protocols are installed. Performing a basic phpinfo may be enough to know.

If you are going with XML-RPC, we recommend using a client. You don't want to perform repetitive xmlrpc_decode and encode for each call. The client will handle all the heavy lifting of creating, packaging, and sending an HTTP request to the XML-RPC server. But picking an XML-RPC client can be confusing. There are a gazillion XML-RPC libraries out there, and each web server or hosting server installs a handful or none. We will go through the widely adopted PEAR's XML-RPC client and also the Zend's XML-RPC.

■ **Note** If you plan to use XML-RPC, please note that it isn't installed by default. Access `http://us.php.net/manual/en/xmlrpc.installation.php`.

If you plan to use SOAP, there is a standard SOAP client that comes with PHP 5. You can verify SOAP installation through phpinfo or you'll need to configure your PHP: `http://us3.php.net/manual/en/soap.installation.php`. Examples of PHP's SOAP clients are shown throughout this chapter.

Setting Up Magento for Web Services

By default, Magento has web services disabled. This is a good thing because there's no need to open ports or services if they won't be used. Web services within Magento are handled through a role-based authorization. You will create roles with specific permissions and then map them to your web services users.

■ **Note** Users created for web services are not the same as normal Magento users or customers. They are users with a single purpose: to access and execute API methods.

To enable web services on your Magento shop, you have to first define roles and users.

Roles

First, log in through the Admin Panel by choosing System, Web Services, Roles. Click the Add New Role button.

There are two sections to fill out: Role Info and Role Resources.

Role Info

Under Role Info, create a role name. You should create four sets of roles:

- *Read Only*: Users under this role have only read access to the system. They can't create, edit, delete, or modify the system in any way.

- *Restricted*: You should allow a handful of methods for the restricted role. For example, you can allow the Account team access to only the sales_order methods. (This is discussed in more detail in the next section.)

- *Custom*: This role can be special set in which you can allow the public to see a listing of all your products. They can't view customer data, but inventory and catalogs are accessible.

- *All Access*: Users under this group can perform all API methods. Be careful about giving access to this role.

Role Resources

Once you click Role Resources on the left panel, you will see the list shown in Figure 11-1.

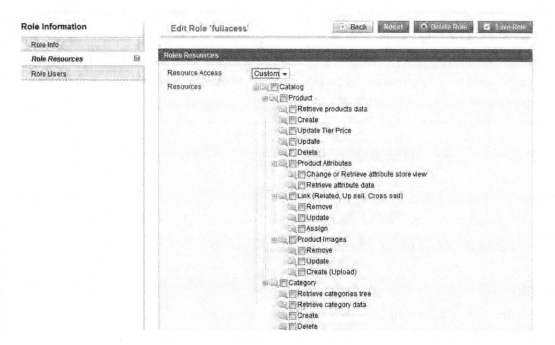

Figure 11-1. *Role Resources*

Select the check box to give this role the specific resources. Click Save Role after you finish.

Each environment and setup is different, but you should not give the All Access role to all your web services users. Magento has given you the ability to control access, so use it wisely.

Users

After you set up roles and resources, you can create a user.

From the Admin Panel, choose System, Web Services, Users. Click the Add New User button. Similar to roles, there are two sections to fill out: User Info and User Role.

User Info

Note the User Name and New Api Key (see Figure 11.2). They are used to authenticate with your Magento server before you can send commands.

Figure 11-2. *User Info*

■ **Note** You should be a tad paranoid and use a very complex Api Key that is hard to crack. Security is a big issue, so take it into account if you allow users to access sensitive data from the server. Use at least 10–15 characters, nondictionary words, an uppercase and lowercase mix, and even symbols.

User Role

Select the role for this user. If you defined multiple roles previously, you should see a list of roles to choose from. Click the radio button to assign the role to your user and then click Save User.

After is all set and complete, you can proceed with API coding.

API Coding

This section shows you some basic code snippets to access Magento's API. You have two types of protocols at your disposal: XML-RPC and SOAP. But within those protocols, you also have multiple PHP libraries to choose from. You will see examples from two main libraries: Zend's XML-RPC client and PHP's SOAP client.

■ **Note** You can use any programming language that has XML-RPC or SOAP protocol to perform web services into Magento. Because Magento was built in PHP, you will see code snippets in PHP.

You are writing test scripts, so they can be placed on any web server; they do not have to be located on the same server as your Magento install. The purpose for API usage is that these scripts are executed by third-party applications.

Using XML-RPC (PEAR Client)

To use the XML-RPC client, you have to set up your environment. Follow these steps:

1. Let's assume that you plan to run your custom API scripts from /www/. Make a directory for the XML-RPC client (for example: /www/XML_RPC-1.5.2/).

2. Download the XML-RPC client from http://pear.php.net/package/XML_RPC/.

3. Extract the files to a /tmp directory.

4. Once extracted, copy the RPC.php to your script location (for example: cp/tmp/XML-RPC-1.5.2/XML-RPC-1.5.2/RPC.php /www/XML_RPC-1.5.2/).

5. Test the setup. Create a test PHP file under /www/:

```php
<?php
// This file is /www/test.php
// include your PEAR XML_RPC library (change path if needed)
require_once 'XML_RPC-1.5.2/RPC.php';

// start the client (change myserver.com to your webserver
// and if you are using SSL, then change the port to 443)
$client = new XML_RPC_Client('/api/xmlrpc', 'myserver.com', 80);

// fill in your webservice_username and passwd from Magento
$arguments = array(
    new XML_RPC_Value('webservice_username', 'string'),
    new XML_RPC_Value('webservice_passwd', 'string')
);

// create the login command
$message = new XML_RPC_Message('login', $arguments);

// send the command
$resp = $client->send($message);

// verify connection
if (!$resp) {
    echo 'Communication error: ' . $client->errstr;
    exit;
}

// check for command result
if (!$resp->faultCode()) {
    $session_id = $resp->value()->getVal();
    echo 'Connection complete: session id = ' . $session_id;
```

```
} else {
    echo 'Fault Code: ' . $resp->faultCode() . '<br/>';
    echo 'Fault Reason: ' . $resp->faultString();
}
```

6. If the script completed successfully, you see this message: Connection complete: session id = *xxxxxx*.

■ **Tip** If you run into problems, enable the debug mode to investigate: `$client->setDebug(1);`.

■ **Tip** We had some problems running with XML-RPC. Magento kept returning this error: Calling parameters do not match signature. It turns out that we had to disable the warning because PHP native objects and Magento's Zend XML-RPC objects have conflicts during validation checking. If you get the same message, try this solution:

1. From the Magento folder, edit this file: /lib/Zend/XmlRpc/Server.php.
2. Find this line of code:

```
throw new Zend_XmlRpc_Server_Exception(
    'Calling parameters do not match signature', 623);
```

3. Comment it out:

```
// throw new Zend_XmlRpc_Server_Exception(
    'Calling parameters do not match signature', 623);
```

4. Save the file; this should fix the signature problem.

Using XML-RPC (Zend Library)

Another solution is to use the XML-RPC library that comes with the Zend library. Zend is a bulky install, so it is recommended if you are already using Zend in your project.

> **Note** If you are running the API scripts on the same web server as your Magento install, you can use the same Zend library that comes with the Magento install. Depending on the location of your API script, you can set the path to the Zend library or use the same path set from the app directory:

```php
require_once('../app/Mage.php');
```

```php
<?php

// include your Zend XMLRPC library (change path if needed)
require_once 'Zend/XmlRpc/Client.php';

// start the client (change myserver.com to your webserver)
$client = new Zend_XmlRpc_Client('http://myserver.com/api/xmlrpc/');

// send the login command
try {
    // fill in your webservice_username and passwd from Magento
    $session_id = $client->call('login', array(
        'webservice_username',
        'webservice_passwd'
    ));
    echo 'Connection complete: session id = ' . $session_id;
} catch (Zend_XmlRpc_Client_FaultException $e) {
    echo 'Fault Code: ' . $e->getCode() . '<br/>';
    echo 'Fault Reason: ' . $e->getMessage();
}
```

The Zend library is shorter because it automatically converts the type. In the PEAR library, you had to define the arguments as string, but Zend will check the native PHP object and handle the conversion. More information can be found from Zend: `http://framework.zend.com/manual/en/zend.xmlrpc.client.html`.

Using SOAP (PHP Standard Library)

We're fans of SOAP because we had very few problems when using SOAP to connect into Magento's web services:

```php
<?php

// start the client (change myserver.com to your webserver)
$client = new SoapClient(
    'http://myserver.com/api/soap/?wsdl'
);

try {
```

```
    // fill in your webservice_username and passwd from Magento
    $session_id = $client->login(
        'webservice_username',
        'webservice_passwd'
    );
    echo 'Connection complete: session id = ' . $session_id;
} catch (SoapFault $fault) {
    echo 'Fault Code: ' . $fault->faultcode . '<br/>';
    echo 'Fault Reason: ' . $fault->faultstring;
}
```

▓ **Tip** We don't read documentation; we use it as a last resort. We like extracting all my available types/methods from SOAP calls and start coding from there. Here's a handy snippet to hack your way through SOAP methods:

```
$functions = $client->__getFunctions();
echo "<h1>Functions</h1><br><br><pre>";
print_r($functions);
echo "</pre><h1>Types</h1><br><br><pre>";
$types = $client->__getTypes();
print_r($types);
echo "</pre>";
```

There is no right or wrong solution here. It comes down to a matter of favorites. So pick your weapon of choice and away you go!

Code Comparison

Depending on your hosting server, you might not have SOAP enabled. So you have to use XML-RPC. If you are curious about the syntax for the other protocols, you will see examples for you to compare and contrast.

One example of each protocol is listed so you can view them side by side. They are great for references if you have to switch protocols because of a limitation on the hosting server.

PEAR XML-RPC Example

```
// search for all customer data created after 2007-08-29.
$filters = array(
    new XML_RPC_Value(
        array('created_at' =>
            new XML_RPC_Value('2007-08-29, 'string')),
        'struct'
    ),
    'array'
);
// create the params
$params = array(
    new XML_RPC_Value($session_id, 'string'),
    new XML_RPC_Value('customer.list', 'string'),
    new XML_RPC_Value($filters, 'array')
);
// create the call
$msg = new XML_RPC_Message('call', $params);
// send the PEAR XML-RPC call
$resp = $client->send($msg);
// decode the results
$results = XML_RPC_decode($resp->value());
// view results
    var_dump($results);
```

Zend XML-RPC Example

```
// search for all customer data created after 2007-08-29.
$filters = array(
    'created_at' => '2007-08-29'
);
// using SOAP method
    $results = $client->call(
'call',
array($session_id, 'customer.list', array($filters))
);
    // view results
    var_dump($results);
```

SOAP Example

```
// search for all customer data created after 2007-08-29.
$filters = array(
    'created_at' => '2007-08-29'
);
// using SOAP method
$results = $client->call($session_id, 'customer.list',
array($filters));
// view results
var_dump($results);
```

▨ **Note** These examples include the variable $session_id, so you have to include the previous login snippet before executing this code. You can omit them to save space.

Slice and Dice with or without the Operators

Magento allows great flexibility when it comes to API coding. You can use the direct key to value mappings, multiple sets of filters, or advance operators to slice and dice your methods.

Following are a few more examples that achieve the same results. It comes down to a matter of favorites, but they are noted here in case you are reading other code and aren't aware of them.

Example without Operators (Direct Key/Values)

```
// search for all customer data created after 2007-08-29 and are within
// store id 1.
$filters = array(
    'created_at' => '2007-08-29',
    'store_id' => '1'
);
// using SOAP method
$results = $client->call($session_id, 'customer.list',
    array($filters));
// view results
var_dump($results);
```

Example with Operators

```
// search for all customer data created after 2007-08-29 and are within
// store id 1.
$filters = array(
    'created_at' => array('gt' => '2007-08-29'),
    'store_id' => array('eq' => '1')
);
// using SOAP method
```

```
$results = $client->call($session_id, 'customer.list',
    array($filters));
// view results
var_dump($results);
```

If you have used any database languages before, notice that the operators are simple mappings to the standard DB conditions. Please see the Appendix for a full list of common operators to use in your API methods.

Summary

Magento provides a robust set of APIs out of the box. Although there is online documentation, it is very sparse: `www.magentocommerce.com/support/magento_core_api`. An API reference in the Appendix of this book is furnished with various examples and fixes to bridge the gap from the missing documentation. And if you run into problems or need more examples, always check with the forums (`www.magentocommerce.com/boards`) or even the bug tracker (`www.magentocommerce.com/bug-tracking/search/`).

What's Next?

Now turn to the last chapter to learn about common problems and solutions you may experience when working with Magento.

CHAPTER 12

■■■

Tips and Tricks

This is the fun part. This chapter shows examples of tips and tricks for Magento that we have acquired during our freelance/contract work with Magento. As the number of projects increases, we start to notice that the requirements start to repeat and overlap. Clients want to import/export their products, the accounting team needs invoices ported to QuickBooks, or the fulfillment department needs orders in CSV/XML format. Within the next few sections, you'll see how Magento is used in the real world.

We'll also share some subtle tips that will help you debug the system. They are various pain points that we have endured but don't wish on our readers. So relax, sit back, and pour a cup of coffee. Let's venture into some real-world examples.

Importing Products

There are numerous ways to import multiple products. The simple approach is to use a comma-separated-value (CSV) text file. It's fast, effective, and gets the job done. The other is a programmatic solution that would be more complex, but you gain flexibility in how the data is inputted.

Importing Products Through a CSV File

When importing through a CSV file, the best method is to actually perform an export, open the exported CSV file, and then populate it with your new data. If your Magento installation contains the sample data set, you can proceed to the export feature. If not, go ahead and create one product with all the information filled out (refer to Chapter 5).

After you have one product in your inventory, you can start the export. First, log in through the Admin Panel by choosing System, Import/Export, Profiles. Select the Export All Products profile (see Figure 12-1).

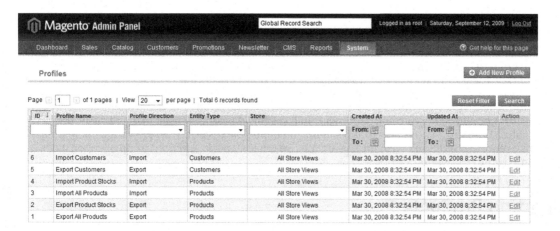

Figure 12-1. *Import/Export profiles*

Within the Profile Wizard, you can set up exporting path, file name, and custom filters (see Figure 12-2). If you made changes, make sure that you click the Save and Continue Editing button.

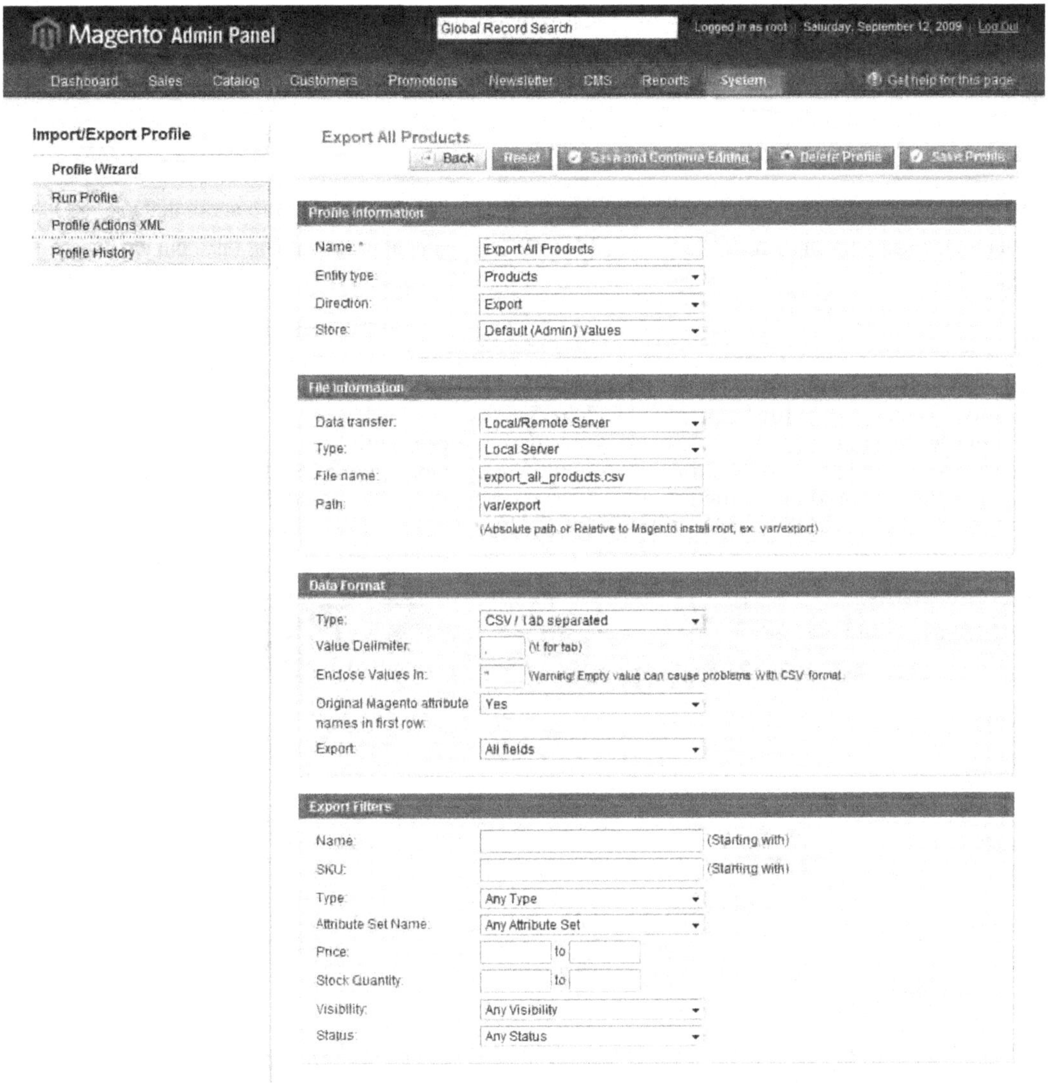

Figure 12-2. Profile Wizard

When you are ready to create the CSV file, click the Run Profile link located on the left navigation bar. Click Run Profile in Popup to start the exporting, which creates a pop-up window that displays debug messages for you to view. When that is complete, navigate to the /var/export/ directory (unless you changed the export path in the Profile Wizard) and you'll see the newly created CSV file.

Open the file up in your favorite editor or spreadsheet application. All the columns should be labeled. From this point on, it's pretty self-explanatory. Add a new row with your new products and repeat. If you use a spreadsheet application, make sure that you select Save As… CSV when you are complete.

■ **Note** If your client already has a CSV file with product information, you have to create a script that will read the file and map it to the same columns as Magento's CSV file. (This is a simple programming task, but we won't cover it here.)

After you have the CSV file filled out with your new products, from the top menu go to System, Import/Export, Profiles. Select the Import All Products profile.

The Profile Wizard has an array of choices. Running the import with default settings is fine. Select Update File from the left subnav. Click the Browse button and choose your CSV file. Before you can run the profile, click the Save and Continue Editing button to upload the file. Select Run Profile from the left subnav and the drop down menu should contain the CSV file you just uploaded (see Figure 12-3).

Figure 12-3. *Run Profile*

Click Run Profile in Popup and the importing will start. Once completed, you can go to Catalog, Manage Products and verify that all the new products have been imported.

▓ **Note** Because the Import/Export tool runs in the web browser, you may receive errors such as PHP Max Execution timeout or Upload file exceeds Max File Size.

max_execution_time (`http://us2.php.net/manual/en/function.set-time-limit.php`)
upload_max_size (`http://us2.php.net/manual/en/ini.core.php#ini.upload-max-filesize`) post_max_size
- (`http://us2.php.net/manual/en/ini.core.php#ini.post-max-size`)

When this occurs, you'll want to start using the Import/Export filters shown in Figure 12-2 to limit the data processed. You can also change your PHP's variables within the php.ini or through .htaccess file. Check with your hosting provider for a valid solution.

Importing Products through Scripts

Sometimes you will have a client that already has all the products in a CSV file. The best approach is to customize a script that will take in the CSV file and use the Magento's API to create the products.

For the extent of this example, you use a basic set of columns, but you are welcome to extend this functionality to custom attributes, separate stores, tier pricing, and so on.

To get started, you'll need an example of the client's CSV product file. Let's assume the following:
Content of CSV file (import_products.csv):

```
Name, SKU, Description, Short Description, price, image_path
Red Truck, 12345, "A small plastic truck", "The Classic Red Truck", 19.99, redtruck.jpg
Blue Truck, 67890, "A small plastic truck", "The Classic Blue Truck", 19.99, bluetruck.jpg
Yellow Truck, 24680, "A small plastic truck", "The Classic Yellow Truck", 19.99, ↵
 yellowtruck.jpg
```

Content of PHP script file (import_script.php):

```php
<?php
// =====================
// setup vars
// =====================
$magento_webserver = 'www.myDomain.com';
$magento_webservices_username = 'xxxx';
$magento_webservices_passwd = 'xxxx';
$csv_file = 'import_products.csv';

// =====================
// no maximum execution time
// =====================
set_time_limit(0);
echo "===================== \n";
echo "Begin product importing... \n";
```

```php
// =======================
// verify login to magento web services
// =======================
try
{
    $client =
        new SoapClient(
            "http://$magento_webserver/index.php/api/soap/?wsdl");
    $session_id= $client->login(
        $magento_webservices_username,
$magento_webservices_passwd);
    echo "Soap login complete! \n";
}
catch (SoapFault $fault)
{
    die("\n\n SOAP Fault: (fault code: {$fault->faultcode},
        fault string: {$fault->faultstring}) \n\n");
}

// =======================
echo "Opening csv file: $csv_file \n";
$fp = fopen($csv_file,'r');

// =======================
// before we start, let's fetch the product_attribute_set
$product_attribute_set = $client->call(
    $session_id, 'product_attribute_set.list');
foreach ($product_attribute_set as $set)
{
    // we're only fetching the Default set, if you
    // have a custom set, please change the name here.
    if ($set['name'] == 'Default')
        $default_attribute_set_id = $set['set_id'];
}

if (empty($default_attribute_set_id))
    die('At least one attribute set must be set to continue');

while (($data = fgetcsv($fp, 1000, ",")) !== false)
{
    // make sure we all 6 columns and it isn't the header
    if (count($data) == 6 && $data[0] != 'Name')
    {
        // extract the data
        $name = trim($data[0]);
        $sku = trim($data[1]);
        $desc = trim($data[2]);
        $short_desc = trim($data[3]);
        $price = trim($data[4]);
        $image_path = trim($data[5]);
```

```php
        // build the data array
        $data = array(
            'name' => $name,
            'description' => $desc,
            'short_description' => $short_desc,
            'price' => $price
        );

        // create the product
        $new_product_id = $client->call($session_id, 'product.create',
            array(
                'simple',
                $default_attribute_set_id,
                $sku,
                $data
            )
        );
        echo "Created product name: $name \n";

        // now we create the data for product image
        $data = array(
            'file' => array(
                'content' => base64_encode(file_get_contents($image_path)),
                'mime' => 'image/jpeg'
            ),
            'label' => $name
        );
        // create the product image
        $results = $client->call(
            $session_id,
            'catalog_product_attribute_media.create',
            array($new_product_id, $data
            )
        );
        echo "Created product image for: $image_path \n";
    }
}

fclose($fp);

echo "======================== \n";
echo "End of product importing \n";
```

To execute the following script, use the shell prompt:

```
> php -f import_script.php
```

You're welcome to place this file on a web server and execute it through a web browser, but remember that the script might time out if the execution is too long. Running it within the shell prompt will avoid this problem.

■ **Note** The script assumes that the image_path gathered from the CSV file exists in the same location as the PHP script.

The following example is very basic, and modification will be needed if you're not using the default attribute set and/or custom attributes. But the point is to give you a simple example of what can be achieved with about 100 lines of code.

■ **Note** Some people are comfortable with using Magento's model approach, which can be found in the community (www.magentocommerce.com/boards/viewthread/30888/), but we prefer the API methods. It's a matter of preference, so feel free to choose a solution that you are comfortable with.

Export Orders and Build QuickBooks Invoices

Another common work request we receive from clients involves the ability to hook Magento's data into QuickBooks. This is useful for the accounting team if they are keeping all billing records through QuickBooks.

The biggest hurdle was figuring out how QuickBooks IIF file format works. It's very particular and exact, and the mathematical logic had to match up correctly, or else QuickBooks' importing would fail. More information on IIF format can be found here:
http://support.quickbooks.intuit.com/support/Pages/KnowledgeBaseArticle/bde7b06f.

In this script, you will pull all orders that contain shipping invoices, extract the billing and shipping info, and create an IIF file for QuickBooks to import.

Content of PHP script file (create_iif_file.php):

```php
<?php
// =====================
// setup vars
// =====================
$magento_webserver = 'www.myDomain.com';
$magento_webservices_username = 'xxxx';
$magento_webservices_passwd = 'xxxx';
$iif_file = 'exported_orders.iif';

// =====================
// helper function
// =====================
function quickbooksDateFix($x)
{
    $x = array_shift(split(' ', $x));
    list($y, $m, $d) = split("[-]", $x);
    $m = intval($m); // remove leading zeros
```

```php
    $d = intval($d); // remove leading zeros
    return "$m/$d/$y";
}
function removeCommas(&$x)
{
    foreach ($x as $key => $val)
    {
        $x[$key] = str_replace(',', '', trim($val));
        $x[$key] = str_replace(array("\r","\n"), ' ', $x[$key]);
    }
}


// =====================
// no maximum execution time
// =====================
set_time_limit(0);
echo "======================= \n";
echo "Begin IIF file creation... \n";


// =====================
// verify login to magento web services
// =====================
try
{
    $client = new
        SoapClient("http://$magento_webserver/index.php/api/soap/?wsdl");
    $session_id= $client->login($magento_webservices_username,
        $magento_webservices_passwd);
    echo "Soap login complete! \n";
}
catch (SoapFault $fault)
{
    die("\n\n SOAP Fault:
        (fault code: {$fault->faultcode},
        fault string: {$fault->faultstring}) \n\n");
}


// ======================================
// STEP 1: FETCH ALL SHIPMENT ORDERS
// ======================================
echo "Fetching all shipment orders created between now and yesterday... \n";
$orders = $client->call($session_id, 'sales_order_shipment.list',
    array(
        array('created_at'=>array('gt'=>
            date('Y-m-d h:i:s',
            strtotime('yesterday'));
            )
        ))
    )
);
```

```php
if (is_array($orders) && count($orders) > 0)
{
    // output file header
    $csvFile = "!TRNS\t" .
                "TRNSID\t" .
                "TRNSTYPE\t" .
                "DATE\t" .
                "ACCNT\t" .
                "NAME\t" .
                "AMOUNT\t" .
                "ADDR1\t" .
                "ADDR2\t" .
                "ADDR3\t" .
                "ADDR4\t" .
                "ADDR5\t" .
                "SADDR1\t" .
                "SADDR2\t" .
                "SADDR3\t" .
                "SADDR4\t" .
                "SADDR5\t" .
                "PONUM\t" .
                "DOCNUM\t" .
                "SHIPDATE\t" .
                "TERMS\r\n";
    $csvFile .= "!SPL\t" .
                "SPLID\t" .
                "TRNSTYPE\t" .
                "ACCNT\t" .
                "QNTY\t" .
                "PRICE\t" .
                "AMOUNT\t" .
                "INVITEM\t" .
                "MEMO\r\n";
    $csvFile .= "!ENDTRNS\r\n";

    // loop through the orders
    foreach ($orders as $orderInfo)
    {
        // this will store all the data before creating the CSV
        $orderInfoShipping = '';
        $orderInfoBilling = '';
        $orderInfoItems = array();
        $salesCompletedDate = '';
        $detailedInfo = array();

        $orderId = (isset($orderInfo['order_increment_id']) ?
        $orderInfo['order_increment_id'] : '');

        // =======================================
        // STEP 2: extract more info (sales_order.info)
        // =======================================
        if ($orderId)
```

```php
{
   try
   {
      $detailedInfo = $client->
         call($session_id, 'sales_order.info', $orderId);
   }
   catch (SoapFault $fault)
   {
      die("SOAP Fault: (fault code: {$fault->faultcode},
      fault string: {$fault->faultstring})");
   }

 // =====================================
 // extract data - items
 // =====================================
 $orderInfoItems = (isset($detailedInfo['items']) ?
    $detailedInfo['items'] : '');

 // =====================================
 // extract data - shipping_address
 // =====================================
 $orderInfoShipping = (isset($detailedInfo['shipping_address']) ?
    $detailedInfo['shipping_address'] : '');

 // =====================================
 // extract data - billing_address
 // =====================================
 $orderInfoBilling = (isset($detailedInfo['billing_address']) ?
    $detailedInfo['billing_address'] : '');

 // =====================================
 // extract data - status_history
 // =====================================
 if (isset($detailedInfo['status_history']))
 {
    foreach ($detailedInfo['status_history'] as $valArray)
      {
      if (isset($valArray['status']) && $valArray['status'] == 'complete')
         $salesCompletedDate = quickbooksDateFix($valArray['created_at']);
    }
 }

}

// =====================================
// remove all commas, just in case
// =====================================
removeCommas($orderInfo);
removeCommas($orderInfoShipping);
```

```php
// **special: payment type
$specialPayment = '';
$term = 'PAID';


// =========================================
// STEP 3: Build the TRNS section
// =========================================
$deliminator = "\t";
$csvFile .=
    "TRNS" . $deliminator .
    $deliminator .
    "INVOICE" . $deliminator .
    quickbooksDateFix($orderInfo['created_at']) . $deliminator .
    "Accounts Receivable" . $deliminator .
    $orderInfoBilling['firstname'] . " " .
        $orderInfoBilling['lastname'] . $deliminator .
    $detailedInfo['grand_total'] . $deliminator .
    $orderInfoBilling['firstname'] . " " .
        $orderInfoBilling['lastname'] . $deliminator .
    $orderInfoBilling['company'] . $deliminator .
    $orderInfoBilling['street'] . $deliminator .
    $orderInfoBilling['city'] . ", " .
        $orderInfoBilling['region'] . " " .
        $orderInfoBilling['postcode'] . $deliminator .
    $orderInfoBilling['telephone'] . $deliminator .
    $orderInfoShipping['firstname'] . " " .
        $orderInfoShipping['lastname'] . $deliminator .
    $orderInfoShipping['company'] . $deliminator .
    $orderInfoShipping['street'] . $deliminator .
    $orderInfoShipping['city'] . ", " .
        $orderInfoShipping['region'] . " " .
        $orderInfoShipping['postcode'] . $deliminator .
    $orderInfoShipping['telephone'] . $deliminator .
    $specialPayment . $deliminator .
    $orderInfo['increment_id'] . $deliminator .
    $salesCompletedDate . $deliminator .
    $term . $deliminator .
    "\r\n";


// =========================================
// each item(s) that the customer purchased will need to be a new line
// in the CSV file. So let's loop through all items
// =========================================
foreach ($orderInfoItems as $orderInfoItem)
{
    // =========================================
    // STEP 4: Build the SPL section
    // =========================================
    $csvFile .=
        "SPL" . $deliminator .
        $deliminator .
        "INVOICE" . $deliminator .
```

```
            "ITEMS" . $deliminator .
            "-" . intval($orderInfoItem['qty_ordered']) . $deliminator .
            floatval($orderInfoItem['price']) . $deliminator .
            "-" . floatval(intval($orderInfoItem['qty_ordered']) *
                    floatval($orderInfoItem['price'])) . $deliminator .
            $orderInfoItem['sku'] . $deliminator .
            $orderInfoItem['name'] .
            "\r\n";
    }

    // =======================================
    // Add discount section
    // =======================================
    if (floatval($detailedInfo['discount_amount']) > 0)
    {
        $csvFile .=
            "SPL" . $deliminator .
            $deliminator .
            "INVOICE" . $deliminator .
            "ITEMS" . $deliminator .
            "-1" . $deliminator .
            floatval($detailedInfo['discount_amount']) . $deliminator .
            floatval($detailedInfo['discount_amount']) . $deliminator .
            "Discount" . $deliminator .
            "Discount" .
            "\r\n";
    }

    // =======================================
    // Add shipping section
    // =======================================
if (floatval($detailedInfo['shipping_amount']) > 0)
    {
        $csvFile .=
        "SPL" . $deliminator .
        $deliminator .
        "INVOICE" . $deliminator .
        "ITEMS" . $deliminator .
        "-1" . $deliminator .
        floatval($detailedInfo['shipping_amount']) . $deliminator .
        "-" . floatval($detailedInfo['shipping_amount']) . $deliminator .
        "SHIPPING" . $deliminator .
        "SHIPPING" .
        "\r\n";
    }
    // =======================================
    // Add tax section
    // =======================================
    if (floatval($detailedInfo['tax_amount']) > 0)
    {
        $csvFile .=
            "SPL" . $deliminator .
```

```
                    $deliminator .
                    "INVOICE" . $deliminator .
                    "ITEMS" . $deliminator .
                    "-1" . $deliminator .
                    floatval($detailedInfo['tax_amount']) . $deliminator .
                    "-" . floatval($detailedInfo['tax_amount']) . $deliminator .
                    "TAX" . $deliminator .
                    "TAX" .
                    "\r\n";
        }

        // ========================================
        // End the TRNS section
        // ========================================
        $csvFile .= "ENDTRNS\r\n";
    }

    // ========================================
    // STEP 5: create file and store it on server
    // ========================================
    $fp = fopen($iif_file,'w');
    echo "Creating local file: $iif_file ... ";
    $re = fputs($fp, $csvFile);
    if (!$re) die("FAILED! \n");
    echo "Done! \n";
    fclose($fp);
}

echo "======================== \n";
echo "End of IIF file creation \n";
```

There's a lot going on in this script. It starts by grabbing all shipment orders dated from midnight yesterday to now. Assume that if a shipment order has been created, it's safe to import into QuickBooks for invoice creation and recordkeeping. Once you have a list of order IDs, you can start extracting the detailed information such as the individual items ordered, shipping address, billing address, and when the sales transaction was completed. Next, purge all that info into QuickBooks' IIF format. And you're done.

Figure 12-4 shows a sample output.

```
1  !TRNS    TRNSID   TRNSTYPE   DATE     ACCNT    NAME    AMOUNT   ADDR1    ADDR2   ADDR3     ADDR4       ADDR5     SADI
2  !SPL     SPLID    TRNSTYPE   ACCNT    QNTY     PRICE   AMOUNT   INVITEM  MEMO
3  !ENDTRNS
4  TRNS     INVOICE  9/17/2009  Accounts Receivable jay lee 704.9900    jay lee     123 congress     austin,
5  SPL      INVOICE  ITEMS      -1   699.99  -699.99 M9179LL 30" Flat-Panel TFT-LCD Cinema HD Monitor
6  SPL      INVOICE  ITEMS      -1   5    -5  SHIPPING    SHIPPING
7  ENDTRNS
8
```

Figure 12-4. Sample output of IIF file

You can also run this script through the command line, but we set up this script to run daily using the linux cron command. To find more information on cron, go to `http://en.wikipedia.org/wiki/Cron`.

From the preceding examples, you can see how to extract sales order information from Magento and customize the output into any format. QuickBooks' IIF file format requires tab delineation, but you can easily change it to commas or even XML tags. All the customized scripts have been a variation of the preceding sample. XML creation isn't discussed because each company has its own XML attributes, and there are plenty of examples online. But we hope you saw how the API can be used in the real world to extract useful information for your purposes.

Localhost Install for Windows

When working on any project, it's wise to have a test or development environment. Magento was built originally for Linux, so there are plenty of instructions online, and the install process goes pretty smoothly. We'll be showing you tips on how we set up a Windows environment and the various hacks involved. We don't recommend setting up your production with hacks, but it serves a good purpose for a test or dev environment.

We come from an old school background. Before WAMP Server (`www.wampserver.com/`) and XAMP (`www.apachefriends.org/en/xampp.html`), there was something called Uniform Server (`www.uniformserver.com/`). These are packaged applications that come with Apache, MySQL, and PHP. We recommend using one of these packages for Windows to create an internal sandbox environment.

Here are some quick-and-dirty steps to get Magento v.1.3.2.3 installed quickly on Windows:

1. Open up C:\Windows\System32\drivers\etc\hosts and add the following:

   ```
   127.0.0.1   localhost
   127.0.0.1   www.localhost.com
   ```

■ **Note** Depending on your version of Windows, your host file might be in a different location: `http://en.wikipedia.org/wiki/Hosts_file`

---

2. Install WAMP or Uniform Server.

3. Start up Apache web server.

4. Download Magento's sample data and unzip.

5. Under WAMP or Uniform Server, go to phpMyAdmin, create a new database, and import Magento's sample data sql file.

6. Download Magento Full Release; unzip into the web path.

7. Move the media directory in Magento's sample data zip file into your web path.

8. From the web path, open up \app\code\core\Mage\Install\Model\Installer\Db.php.

■ **Note** We commented out the three lines of code that start with "check MySQL Server version" and also the three lines of code "check InnoDB support". Both sections always seem to fail when we perform Windows installations.

---

9. From the web path, open up \app\code\core\Mage\Core\Model\Session\ Abstract\Varien.php.

10. Under the set session cookie params, comment out the last three lines:

```
session_set_cookie_params(
    $this->getCookie()->getLifetime(),
    $this->getCookie()->getPath()
 // $this->getCookie()->getDomain(),
    // $this->getCookie()->isSecure(),
    // $this->getCookie()->getHttponly()
 );
```

11. Now you're ready to start the Magento install. Open up a web browser and navigate to your Magento web path to perform the install.

More information on localhost install can be found here: http://magentocommerce.com/wiki/ general/installing_on_windows_with_xampp_and_wamp

Debug Tricks: Turning on Template Path

When modifying Magento's templates and pages, it's always good to turn on template path hints:

1. Log in through the Admin Panel: System, Configuration.

2. From the left nav, in the Current Configuration Scope drop down menu, select the Main Website.

3. Then from the left nav, click Developer under Advance.

4. Under Debug, you'll see Template Path Hints. Select Yes and click the Save Config button (see Figure 12-5).

5. If you navigate to the web site, you can see the file paths to each block (see Figure 12-6).

Figure 12-5. *Template Path Hints*

Figure 12-6. *Web site shows file paths*

Modifying Core Files

You'll often need to add a customized PHP snippet within a model file or to inject something into the view.phtml files to work with your template. This would require changing files within /app/code/core/. You want to avoid making changes in those directories because when you perform a Magento upgrade, these files will be overwritten. But never fear; there is a clean approach to modifying Magento's core files.

Let's take an example. Suppose that you need to modify this file:

`\app\code\core\Mage\Shipping\Model\Shipping.php`

It's best to copy/paste the Shipping.php file into this new path:

`\app\code\local\Mage\Shipping\Model\Shipping.php`

Notice the local directory. This works because Magento will look for files in a local directory before loading the core directory. So you don't edit the core files, but you can still make the necessary changes. If you're curious, open up /app/Mage.php; you'll see the included path ordering of /local, /community, and /core.

Modifying Template Files

Similar to the core files, if you need to update the theme or template files, just copy the necessary files into another theme directory.

Suppose that you need to edit this file:

`\app\design\frontend\default\default\template\email\order\items.phtml`

Copy/paste the items.phtml into this new path:

`\app\design\frontend\default\mytemplate\template\email\order\items.phtml`

Clearing the Database of Test Orders

Before you deploy to production, you may have been creating a handful of sample orders to make sure that the system is working as designed. But Magento doesn't have an option to clear all test data from the database.

■ **Caution** Before you begin, please back up all your database data. You don't want to clear an important table that might be needed by Magento to function correctly.

To perform this purge, you need to use MySQL commands. We found this snippet online through Inchoo (`http://inchoo.net`), which is a wonderful team that's been blogging about Magento for more than a year now. Definitely a valuable resource for the Magento community!

You can cut/paste these commands into phpMyAdmin or any MySQL client:

```
SET FOREIGN_KEY_CHECKS=0;

TRUNCATE `sales_order`;
TRUNCATE `sales_order_datetime`;
TRUNCATE `sales_order_decimal`;
```

```
TRUNCATE `sales_order_entity`;
TRUNCATE `sales_order_entity_datetime`;
TRUNCATE `sales_order_entity_decimal`;
TRUNCATE `sales_order_entity_int`;
TRUNCATE `sales_order_entity_text`;
TRUNCATE `sales_order_entity_varchar`;
TRUNCATE `sales_order_int`;
TRUNCATE `sales_order_text`;
TRUNCATE `sales_order_varchar`;
TRUNCATE `sales_flat_quote`;
TRUNCATE `sales_flat_quote_address`;
TRUNCATE `sales_flat_quote_address_item`;
TRUNCATE `sales_flat_quote_item`;
TRUNCATE `sales_flat_quote_item_option`;
TRUNCATE `sales_flat_order_item`;
TRUNCATE `sendfriend_log`;
TRUNCATE `tag`;
TRUNCATE `tag_relation`;
TRUNCATE `tag_summary`;
TRUNCATE `wishlist`;
TRUNCATE `log_quote`;
TRUNCATE `report_event`;

ALTER TABLE `sales_order` AUTO_INCREMENT=1;
ALTER TABLE `sales_order_datetime` AUTO_INCREMENT=1;
ALTER TABLE `sales_order_decimal` AUTO_INCREMENT=1;
ALTER TABLE `sales_order_entity` AUTO_INCREMENT=1;
ALTER TABLE `sales_order_entity_datetime` AUTO_INCREMENT=1;
ALTER TABLE `sales_order_entity_decimal` AUTO_INCREMENT=1;
ALTER TABLE `sales_order_entity_int` AUTO_INCREMENT=1;
ALTER TABLE `sales_order_entity_text` AUTO_INCREMENT=1;
ALTER TABLE `sales_order_entity_varchar` AUTO_INCREMENT=1;
ALTER TABLE `sales_order_int` AUTO_INCREMENT=1;
ALTER TABLE `sales_order_text` AUTO_INCREMENT=1;
ALTER TABLE `sales_order_varchar` AUTO_INCREMENT=1;
ALTER TABLE `sales_flat_quote` AUTO_INCREMENT=1;
ALTER TABLE `sales_flat_quote_address` AUTO_INCREMENT=1;
ALTER TABLE `sales_flat_quote_address_item` AUTO_INCREMENT=1;
ALTER TABLE `sales_flat_quote_item` AUTO_INCREMENT=1;
ALTER TABLE `sales_flat_quote_item_option` AUTO_INCREMENT=1;
ALTER TABLE `sales_flat_order_item` AUTO_INCREMENT=1;
ALTER TABLE `sendfriend_log` AUTO_INCREMENT=1;
ALTER TABLE `tag` AUTO_INCREMENT=1;
ALTER TABLE `tag_relation` AUTO_INCREMENT=1;
ALTER TABLE `tag_summary` AUTO_INCREMENT=1;
ALTER TABLE `wishlist` AUTO_INCREMENT=1;
ALTER TABLE `log_quote` AUTO_INCREMENT=1;
ALTER TABLE `report_event` AUTO_INCREMENT=1;
```

```
-- reset customers
TRUNCATE `customer_address_entity`;
TRUNCATE `customer_address_entity_datetime`;
TRUNCATE `customer_address_entity_decimal`;
TRUNCATE `customer_address_entity_int`;
TRUNCATE `customer_address_entity_text`;
TRUNCATE `customer_address_entity_varchar`;
TRUNCATE `customer_entity`;
TRUNCATE `customer_entity_datetime`;
TRUNCATE `customer_entity_decimal`;
TRUNCATE `customer_entity_int`;
TRUNCATE `customer_entity_text`;
TRUNCATE `customer_entity_varchar`;
TRUNCATE `log_customer`;
TRUNCATE `log_visitor`;
TRUNCATE `log_visitor_info`;

ALTER TABLE `customer_address_entity` AUTO_INCREMENT=1;
ALTER TABLE `customer_address_entity_datetime` AUTO_INCREMENT=1;
ALTER TABLE `customer_address_entity_decimal` AUTO_INCREMENT=1;
ALTER TABLE `customer_address_entity_int` AUTO_INCREMENT=1;
ALTER TABLE `customer_address_entity_text` AUTO_INCREMENT=1;
ALTER TABLE `customer_address_entity_varchar` AUTO_INCREMENT=1;
ALTER TABLE `customer_entity` AUTO_INCREMENT=1;
ALTER TABLE `customer_entity_datetime` AUTO_INCREMENT=1;
ALTER TABLE `customer_entity_decimal` AUTO_INCREMENT=1;
ALTER TABLE `customer_entity_int` AUTO_INCREMENT=1;
ALTER TABLE `customer_entity_text` AUTO_INCREMENT=1;
ALTER TABLE `customer_entity_varchar` AUTO_INCREMENT=1;
ALTER TABLE `log_customer` AUTO_INCREMENT=1;
ALTER TABLE `log_visitor` AUTO_INCREMENT=1;
ALTER TABLE `log_visitor_info` AUTO_INCREMENT=1;

-- Reset all ID counters
TRUNCATE `eav_entity_store`;
ALTER TABLE  `eav_entity_store` AUTO_INCREMENT=1;

SET FOREIGN_KEY_CHECKS=1;
```

*Original source found here: http://inchoo.net/ecommerce/magento/delete-test-orders-in-magento/.

Special Thanks to Branko Ajzele and the Inchoo Team

Because we're on the topic of wonderful people who have aided the Magento community, we wanted to list the awesome apps and tutorials created by Branko and the Inchoo team. Magento's documentation is far from complete, and we owe a great deal of knowledge to these guys. As a prime example, we include links to two admin modules that are great skeleton templates to help you build customized modules:

- *CoolDash*: Blank Magento extension for building admin system configuration area: `http://inchoo.net/ecommerce/magento/cooldash-blank-magento-extension-for-building-admin-system-configuration-area/`

- *CoffeeFreak*: Blank Magento extension for building main admin menu with sidebar and tabs: `http://inchoo.net/ecommerce/magento/coffeefreak-blank-magento-extension-for-building-main-admin-menu-with-sidebar-and-tabs/`

There's also another site started by Branko that allows users to post their Magento snippets: `http://snippi.net/`. It's a valuable resource if you're looking for tips and tricks for Magento. A couple of other cool sites are as follows:

- *Inchoo's site*: These guys focus on designing and building Magento sites. The site offers valuable tips and tricks for all things Magento: `http://inchoo.net`.

- *Branko Ajzele's site*: Branko lives and breathes Magento full time. He shares his tips and even frustration with Magento's quarks on his blog. Definitely a guy that knows his stuff: `http://activecodeline.com/`

Searching the BugTracker

The last thing we want to mention is Magento's Bug Tracker: `www.magentocommerce.com/bug-tracking`
If you run into an error, and there isn't any information in the community, the last place to check is its Bug Tracker.

Summary

This book covered the fundamental topics that allow you to start using Magento as your e-commerce solution. We started with a chapter on installation; moved into the admin interface; dove into products, customers, and orders; and then discussed full customization of UI and Core features.

What's Next?

As you can see, there are many ways you can slice and dice Magento to fit your needs. We hope this book helps you jump start your Magento adventure and we encourage you to continue playing with all the features and options available. You can be a 100% satisfied customer configuring Magento through the Admin Panel and not touch any coding. Or you can customize, modify, and tailor Magento into your ultimate e-commerce solution. It's an open source application, and you are in control.

We hope this book has been helpful to you. We had a blast writing it, but alas, it is the end and we must depart. If you do have questions or run into Magento problems, please post on the forums (`www.magentocommerce.com/boards`). Both of us are active participants. Who knows? Maybe our paths will cross. Bye!

APPENDIX

■■■

API References

API Operators

These are common operators that are used in API methods.

Operator	SQL Translation
eq	Equal to…
neq	Not equal to…
gt	Greater than…
lt	Less than…
gteq	Greater than or equal to…
lteq	Less than or equal to…
in	In… (can accept Array)
nin	Not in… (can accept Array)
like	Like… (can accept % as wildcard)
nlike	Not like… (can accept % as wildcard)
is	Is…
from	From… (also known as "after the date")
to	To… (also known as "before the date")

null	Is null…
notnull	Is not null…
finest	Filter in the set (used to extract values within keys such as category_ids)

API Faults

Faults will happen when you start to program. If you do receive faults, the following table will aid in your investigation.

Fault Code	Fault Reason
0	Unknown Error.
1	Internal Error. Please see log for details.
2	Access denied.
3	Invalid API path.
4	Resource path is not callable.

Magento APIs

Magento has broken up its API methods into five sections: customer, directory, catalog, sales, and inventory. We'll explore each one of these in detail so you can understand how they are connected.

Customer API

The customer API allows standard access into customer information, such as addresses, purchase order numbers, and associated groups. There are three subsets: customer, customer group, and customer address.

Customer Set

The customer set gives you the basic list, create, update, and delete methods:

- `customer.list()`
- `customer.info()`
- `customer.create()`

- customer.update()
- customer.delete()

Method: customer.list ($filters)

Description: Obtains a list of customer information, depending on your filters.

Return: Arrays of key/values.

Argument:

- $filters (optional). Uses an array of key/value pairs to set filters.

Available filter keys:

- increment_id
- customer_id
- created_at
- updated_at
- website_id
- store_id
- email
- lastname
- firstname
- middlename
- prefix
- suffix
- taxvat
- password_hash
- group_id
- default_billing
- default_shipping
- created_in

Sample Return Set

```
array (
  0 =>
array (
    'customer_id' => '123',
```

```
    'created_at' => '2009-09-01 17:10:09',
    'updated_at' => '2009-09-01 17:12:56',
    'increment_id' => '000000358',
    'store_id' => '0',
    'website_id' => '2',
    'created_in' => 'Admin',
    'default_billing' => '87',
    'default_shipping' => '87',
    'email' => john@test.com',
    'firstname' => 'John',
    'group_id' => '3',
    'lastname' => 'Doe',
    'middlename' => '',
    'password_hash' => *****:**',
    'prefix' => '',
    'suffix' => '',
    'taxvat' => '',
  )
)
```

SOAP Example

```
// search for all customer data created after 2009-02-24.
$filters = array(
    'created_at' => '2009-02-24'
);
// using SOAP method
$results = $client->call($session_id, 'customer.list',
    array($filters));
// view results
var_dump($results);
```

Method: customer.info ($customer_id)

Description: Obtains detail information given a customer_id.

Return: Key/values array

Argument:

- $customer_id (required). ID can be found through previous customer.list()
  method.

Sample Return Set

```
array (
  'customer_id' => '123',
  'created_at' => '2009-09-01 17:10:09',
  'updated_at' => '2009-09-01 17:12:56',
  'increment_id' => '000000358',
  'store_id' => '0',
  'website_id' => '2',
```

```
'confirmation' => NULL,
'created_in' => 'Admin',
'default_billing' => '87',
'default_shipping' => '87',
'dob' => NULL,
'email' => 'john@test.com',
'firstname' => 'John',
'group_id' => '3',
'lastname' => 'Doe',
'middlename' => '',
'password_hash' => '*****:**',
'prefix' => '',
'suffix' => '',
'taxvat' => '',
)
```

SOAP Example

```
// view customer info for customer id '34'.
$customer_id = '34';
// using SOAP method
$results = $client->call($session_id, 'customer.info', $customer_id);
// view results
var_dump($results);
```

■ **Note** Magento's API documentation, which is very sparse, states that you can pass an "attribute" array as another argument. We did not witness this behavior so it isn't included in the API reference. More info can be found here: www.magentocommerce.com/wiki/doc/webservices-api/api/customer#customer.info.

Method: customer.create ($data)

Description: Creates new customers. Magento lets you create a customer with all NULL data. The only requirement is that the e-mail address must not match any current e-mail within the same website_id.

Return: Int value representing the new customer_id is created.

Argument:

- $data (required). Uses an array of key/value pairs to set data.

Available data keys:

- increment_id
- created_at
- updated_at
- website_id
- store_id
- email (*email must be unique, or exception will be thrown)
- lastname
- firstname
- middlename
- prefix
- suffix
- dob
- taxvat
- password_hash
- group_id
- default_billing
- default_shipping
- created_in

Zend XML-RPC Example

```
// Prepare information
$data = array(
    'firstname' => 'John',
    'lastname' => 'Doe',
    'website_id' => '1',
    'email' => 'john@test.com'
);
// using Zend XML-RPC method
$customer_id = $client->call('call', array($session_id,
    'customer.create', array($data)));
// display new customer id
echo $customer_id;
```

Note There are two ways to create a password_hash through the API. You can set a basic md5 hash such as the following:

```
$data = array(
    'firstname' => 'John',
    'lastname' => 'Doe',
    'password_hash' => md5('secret')
);
```

You can also include a salt through the following method:

```
$salt = 'super_secret1234';
$data = array(
    'firstname' => 'John',
    'lastname' => 'Doe',
    'password_hash' => md5($salt.'secret').':'.$salt
);
```

Method: customer.update ($customer_id, $data)

Description: Updates customer information given the customer_id and a key/value array of data.

Return: Boolean; true if update was successful.

Argument:

- $data (required). Uses an array of key/value pairs to set data.

Available data keys:

- increment_id
- created_at
- updated_at
- website_id
- store_id
- email (*email must be unique, or exception will be thrown)
- lastname
- firstname

- middlename

- prefix

- suffix

- dob

- taxvat

- password_hash

- group_id

- default_billing

- default_shipping

- created_in

Zend XML-RPC Example

```
// Prepare information to update
$customer_id = '324';
$data = array(
    'dob' => '1990-12-30'
);
// using Zend XML-RPC method
$result = $client->call('call', array($session_id, 'customer.update',
    array($customer_id, $data)));
// return true if update was successful
var_dump($result);
```

Method: customer.delete ($customer_id)

Description: Deletes a customer given a customer_id.

Return: Boolean; true if delete was successful.

Argument:

- $customer_id (required). ID can be found through previous customer.list() method.

Zend XML-RPC Example

```
// Customer to delete
$customer_id = '324';
// using Zend XML-RPC method
$result = $client->call('call', array($session_id, 'customer.delete',
    array($customer_id)));
// return true if delete was successful
var_dump($result);
```

Customer Group Set

The customer group set includes one method:

- customer_group.list()

Method: customer_group.list ()

Description: Obtains a list of customer groups.

Return: Arrays of key/values.

Argument: N/A.

Sample Return Set

```
array (
  0 =>
  array (
    'customer_group_id' => '0',
    'customer_group_code' => 'NOT LOGGED IN',
  ),
  1 =>
  array (
    'customer_group_id' => '1',
    'customer_group_code' => 'General',
  ),
  2 =>
  array (
    'customer_group_id' => '2',
    'customer_group_code' => 'Custom_Tier_Bronze',
  ),
  3 =>
  array (
    'customer_group_id' => '3',
    'customer_group_code' => 'Custom_Tier_Silver',
  )
)
```

SOAP Example

```
// using SOAP method
        $results = $client->call($session_id, 'customer_group.list');
        // view results
        var_dump($results);
```

Customer Address Set

Similar to the normal customer set, the customer address set allows you to list, create, update, and delete addresses. One customer can have many addresses (for example, billing and shipping addresses).

- customer_address.list()
- customer_address.info()
- customer_address.create()
- customer_address.update()
- customer_address.delete()

Method: customer_address.list ($customer_id)

Description: Obtains a list of customer addresses.

▓ **Caution** Please note there are errors in this API output. See following message.

Return: Arrays of key/values.

Argument:

- $customer_id (required). Can be obtained through the customer set.

Sample Return Set

```
array (
  0 =>
  array (
    'customer_id' => '465',
    'created_at' => '2009-05-31 16:51:38',
    'updated_at' => '2009-06-04 03:31:46',
    'increment_id' => '',
    'city' => 'Austin',
    'company' => 'Test Company',
    'country_id' => 'US',
    'fax' => '',
    'firstname' => 'John',
    'lastname' => 'Doe',
    'middlename' => '',
    'postcode' => '78704',
    'prefix' => '',
    'region' => 'Texas',
    'region_id' => '57',
    'street' => '123 W. 29th Street',
    'suffix' => '',
    'telephone' => '5555555555',
    'is_default_billing' => false,
    'is_default_shipping' => false,
  ),
)
```

Zend XML-RPC Example

```
// Customer to view addresses
$customer_id = '324';
// using Zend XML-RPC method
$results = $client->call('call', array($session_id,
    'customer_address.list', array($customer_id)));
// view results
var_dump($results);
```

■ **Caution** Tested on Magento's version 1.3.2.3, the output for this API returns the following incorrect data (shown in bold in previous sample return set:

> 'customer_id' should be 'address_id'.
> 'is_default_billing' always returns false.
> 'is_default_shipping' always return false.

Because we ran across this bug during one of my projects, we provide the fix here.
To change 'customer_id' to 'address_id':
Open up this file:

```
\app\code\core\Mage\Customer\Model\Address\Api.php
```

Replace line 37

```
'customer_id' => 'entity_id'
```

with this:

```
'address_id' => 'entity_id'
```

To fix the 'is_default_billing' and 'is_default_shipping' bug:
Open up this file:

```
\app\code\core\Mage\Customer\Model\Address\Api.php
```

Replace line 77 and 78 with this:

```
$row['is_default_billing'] =
$customer->getDefaultBillingAddress()->entity_id == $address->getId();
$row['is_default_shipping'] =
$customer->getDefaultShippingAddress()->entity_id == $address->getId();
```

Method: customer_address.info ($address_id)

Description: Obtains detail information given an address_id.

▓ **Caution** Please note there are errors in this API output. See previous note.

Return: Key/values array.

Argument:

- $address_id (required). ID can be found through the previous customer_address.list() method.

Sample Return Set

```
array (
  'customer_id' => '465',
  'created_at' => '2009-07-31 16:51:38',
  'updated_at' => '2009-08-04 03:31:46',
  'increment_id' => '',
  'city' => 'Austin',
  'company' => 'Test Company',
  'country_id' => 'US',
  'fax' => '',
  'firstname' => 'John',
  'lastname' => 'Doe',
  'middlename' => '',
  'postcode' => '78704',
  'prefix' => '',
  'region' => 'Texas',
  'region_id' => '57',
  'street' => '123 W. 29th Street',
  'suffix' => '',
  'telephone' => '5555555555',
  'is_default_billing' => false,
  'is_default_shipping' => false,
)
```

SOAP Example

```
// view customer address info for address_id '465'.
$address_id = '465';
// using SOAP method
$results = $client->call($session_id, 'customer_address.info',
    $address_id);
// view results
var_dump($results);
```

Note If you add the fix, the customer_id will be updated to the correct address_id within the return array.

Caution The 'is_default_billing' and 'is_default_shipping' data are broken in this API method, too. To fix the problem, you have to fix the info() method in Api.php.

Open this file:

`\app\code\core\Mage\Customer\Model\Address\Api.php`

Replace these lines under the info($addressId) method:

```
$result['is_default_billing']  =
       $customer->getDefaultBillingAddress() == $address->getId();
$result['is_default_shipping'] =
       $customer->getDefaultShippingAddress() == $address->getId();
```

with these lines:

```
$result['is_default_billing'] =
       $customer->getDefaultBillingAddress()->entity_id == $address->getId();
$result['is_default_shipping'] =
       $customer->getDefaultShippingAddress()->entity_id == $address->getId();
```

Method: customer_address.create ($customer_id, $data)

Description: Creates a new customer address.

Return: Int value representing the new address_id created.

Arguments:

- $customer_id (required). Creates new address for this customer_id.
- $data (required). Uses an array of key/value pairs to set data.

Available data keys:

- created_at
- updated_at
- increment_id
- city (required)
- company
- country_id (required; can be obtained by the the directory_country.list API)
- fax

- firstname (required)

- lastname (required)

- middlename

- postcode (required)

- prefix

- region (this is the state)

- region_id (required; can be obtained by using the directory_region.list API)

- street (required)

- suffix

- telephone (required)

- is_default_billing

- is_default_shipping

Zend XML-RPC Example

```
// Create new address for this customer_id
$customer_id = '324';
// Prepare information
$data = array(
    'firstname' => 'John',
    'lastname' => 'Doe',
    'street' => '123 Congress',
    'country_id' => 'USA',
    'city' => 'Austin',
    'region' => 'Texas',
    'region_id' => '57',
    'postcode' => '78704',
    'telephone' => '5555555555',
    'is_default_billing' => true,
    'is_default_shipping' => true
);
// using Zend XML-RPC method
        $address_id = $client->call('call', array($session_id,
    'customer_address.create', array($customer_id, $data)));
        // display new address id
echo $address_id;
```

Method: customer_address.update ($address_id, $data)

Description: Updates existing customer address data.

Return: Boolean; true if update was successful.

Arguments:

- $address_id (required). address_id to perform update.
- $data (required). Uses an array of key/value pairs to update data.

Available data keys:

- created_at
- updated_at
- increment_id
- city
- company
- country_id (can be obtained by the directory_country.list API)
- fax
- firstname
- lastname
- middlename
- postcode
- prefix
- region (this is the state)
- region_id (can be obtained by using the directory_region.list API)
- street
- suffix
- telephone
- is_default_billing
- is_default_shipping

Zend XML-RPC Example

```
// Prepare information to update
$address_id = '465';
$data = array(
    'street' => '456 Research Blvd',
    'postcode' => '78750'
);
// using Zend XML-RPC method
$result = $client->call('call', array($session_id,
    'customer_address.update', array($address_id, $data)));
```

```
// display true if successful
var_dump($result);
```

Method: customer_address.delete ($address_id)

Description: Deletes an existing customer address.

Return: Boolean; true if delete was successful.

Argument:

- $address_id (required). address_id to remove.

Zend XML-RPC Example

```
// Prepare information to remove
$address_id = '465';
// using Zend XML-RPC method
$result = $client->call('call', array($session_id,
    'customer_address.delete', array($address_id)));
// display true if successful
var_dump($result);
```

Directory API

The directory API is used only to list information on country and region codes. These values cannot be changed; they are required when inputting customer address information.

Directory Set

The only methods available are basic listings:

- directory_country.list()
- directory_region.list()

Method: directory_country.list ()

Description: Lists all countries and their country_id.

Return: Key/values array.

Argument: None.

Sample Return Set

```
array (
  0 =>
  array (
    'country_id' => 'AD',
    'iso2_code' => 'AD',
```

```
    'iso3_code' => 'AND',
    'name' => 'Andorra',
  ),
  1 =>
  array (
    'country_id' => 'AE',
    'iso2_code' => 'AE',
    'iso3_code' => 'ARE',
    'name' => 'United Arab Emirates',
  ),
  2 =>
  array (
    'country_id' => 'AF',
    'iso2_code' => 'AF',
    'iso3_code' => 'AFG',
    'name' => 'Afghanistan',
  ),
...
```

SOAP Example

```
// using SOAP method
$results = $client->call($session_id, 'directory_country.list');
// output results
var_dump($results);
```

Method: directory_region.list ($country)

Description: Lists all regions with country_id.

Return: Key/values array.

Argument:

- $country (required). Can be the two-letter acronym of country_id, iso2_code, or iso3_code; or the three-letter acronym of country_name pulled from the directory_country.list() API.

Sample Return Set

```
array (
  0 =>
  array (
    'region_id' => '1',
    'code' => 'AL',
    'name' => 'Alabama',
  ),
  1 =>
  array (
    'region_id' => '2',
    'code' => 'AK',
    'name' => 'Alaska',
```

```
  ),
  2 =>
  array (
    'region_id' => '3',
    'code' => 'AS',
    'name' => 'American Samoa',
  ),
  3 =>
  array (
    'region_id' => '4',
    'code' => 'AZ',
    'name' => 'Arizona',
  ),
  …
```

SOAP Example

```
// using SOAP method
$country = 'USA';
$results = $client->call($session_id, 'directory_region.list',
    $country);
// output results
var_dump($results);
```

Catalog API

The catalog API contains the largest list of available methods. Within this set, you can create, update, move, assign, and delete your categories, products, and attributes. They are useful if you need to perform multiple actions such as importing/exporting your products.

Category Set

The category set allows you to perform the same functions as Manage Categories from the Admin panel, but through code instead:

- catalog_category.currentStore

- catalog_category.tree

- catalog_category.level

- catalog_category.info

- catalog_category.create

- catalog_category.update

- catalog_category.move

- catalog_category.delete

- catalog_category.assignedProducts

- catalog_category.assignProduct

- catalog_category.updateProduct

- catalog_category.removeProduct

Method: catalog_category.currentStore ($store_view_code)

Description: Gets the store_id.

Return: Returns the store_id.

Argument:

- $store_view_code (optional). Select Admin Panel, System, Manage Stores; select a store under the Store View Name, and you'll find the code listed there.

Zend XML-RPC Example

```
// Set the store code
$store_view_code = 'dollarstore';
// using Zend XML-RPC method
$result = $client->call('call', array($session_id,
    'catalog_category.currentStore', array($store_view_code)));
// returns the store_id
echo $result;
```

Method: catalog_category.tree ($parent_category_id, $store_view_code)

Description: Returns an ordered array of categories.

Return: Array.

Arguments:

- $parent_category_id (optional). Limits the array returned to this parent category id.

- $store_view_code (optional). Select Admin Panel, System, Manage Stores; select a store under the Store View Name, and you'll find the code listed there.

Sample Return Set

```
array (
  'category_id' => '1',
  'parent_id' => '0',
  'name' => 'Root Catalog',
  'is_active' => NULL,
  'position' => '1',
  'level' => '0',
  'children' =>
  array (
    0 =>
```

```
array (
  'category_id' => '2',
  'parent_id' => '1',
  'name' => 'Default Category',
  'is_active' => '1',
  'position' => '1',
  'level' => '1',
  'children' =>
  array (
    0 =>
    array (
      'category_id' => '4',
      'parent_id' => '2',
      'name' => 'My Dollar Store',
      'is_active' => '1',
      'position' => '1',
      'level' => '2',
      'children' =>
      array (
      ),
    ),
...
```

SOAP Example

```
// using SOAP method
$results = $client->call($session_id, 'catalog_catgeory.tree');
// returns the tree
var_dump($results);
```

Method: catalog_category.level ($website_code, $store_view_code, $parent_category_id)

Description: Returns one level of categories. If no arguments are used, the root categories will be returned.

Return: Array.

Arguments:

- $website_code (optional). Limits the result to this web site. Select Admin Panel, System, Manage Stores; select a store under the Website Name, and you'll find the code listed there.

- $store_view_code (optional). Select Admin Panel, System, Manage Stores; select a store under the Store View Name, and you'll find the code listed there.

- $parent_category_id (optional). Limits the array returned to this parent category id.

Sample Return Set

```
array (
  0 =>
```

```
array (
  'category_id' => '2',
  'parent_id' => 1,
  'name' => 'Default Category',
  'is_active' => '1',
  'position' => '1',
  'level' => '1',
),
1 =>
array (
  'category_id' => '7',
  'parent_id' => 1,
  'name' => 'Second Site',
  'is_active' => '1',
  'position' => '2',
  'level' => '1',
),
)
```

Zend XML-RPC Example

```
// using Zend XML-RPC method
$results = $client->call('call', array($session_id,
    'catalog_category.level'));
// returns the parent level categories
var_dump($results);
```

Method: catalog_category.info ($category_id, $store_view_code, $attributes)

Description: Returns category information given the category_id.

Return: Key/values array.

Arguments:

- $category_id (required). The category_id to view.

- $store_view_code (optional). Select Admin Panel, System, Manage Stores; select a store under the Store View Name, and you'll find the code listed there.

- $attributes (optional). Limits the array to only these sets of attributes.

Sample Return Set

```
array (
  'category_id' => '7',
  'is_active' => '1',
  'position' => '2',
  'level' => '1',
  'increment_id' => NULL,
  'parent_id' => 1,
  'created_at' => '2009-06-02 20:51:25',
  'updated_at' => '2009-06-09 07:34:55',
```

```
'name' => 'Second Site',
'url_key' => 'test-root-cat',
'description' => '',
'image' => NULL,
'meta_title' => '',
'meta_keywords' => '',
'meta_description' => '',
'path' => '1/7',
'all_children' => '7,9,10',
'path_in_store' => NULL,
'children' => '9,10',
'url_path' => NULL,
'children_count' => '2',
'display_mode' => 'PRODUCTS',
'landing_page' => NULL,
'is_anchor' => '1',
'available_sort_by' => '',
'default_sort_by' => NULL,
'custom_design' => '',
'custom_design_apply' => '1',
'custom_design_from' => NULL,
'custom_design_to' => NULL,
'page_layout' => '',
'custom_layout_update' => '',
)
```

SOAP Example

```
// view data for this category_id
$category_id = '7';
// using SOAP method
$results = $client->call($session_id, 'catalog_category.info',
    $category_id);
// view results
var_dump($results);
```

Method: catalog_category.create ($parent_category_id, $data, $store_view_code)

Description: Creates a new child category under the parent_category_id.

Return: Newly created category_id.

Arguments:

- $parent_category_id (required). Places the new category under this parent_category_id.

- $data (required). Uses an array of key/value pairs to set data.

- $store_view_code (optional). Select Admin Panel, System, Manage Stores; select a store under the Store View Name, and you'll find the code listed there.

Available data keys:

- is_active
- increment_id
- name (required)
- url_key
- description
- image
- meta_title
- meta_keywords
- meta_description
- display_mode
- landing_page
- is_anchor
- available_sort_by (required)
- default_sort_by (required)
- custom_design
- custom_design_apply
- custom_design_from
- custom_design_to
- page_layout
- custom_layout_update

Zend XML-RPC Example

```
// Prepare the data
$parent_category_id = '7';
$data = array(
    'name'=>'Toys',
    'available_sort_by' => '',
    'default_sort_by' => ''
);
// using Zend XML-RPC method
$category_id = $client->call('call', array($session_id,
    'catalog_category.create', array($parent_category_id, $data)));
// returns the newly created category_id
echo $category_id;
```

Method: catalog_category.update ($category_id, $data, $store_view_code)

Description: Updates an existing category given a key/value array of data.

Return: Boolean; true if update was successful.

Arguments:

- $category_id (required). The category_id to update.

- $data (required). Uses an array of key/value pairs to set data.

- $store_view_code (optional). Select Admin Panel, System, Manage Stores; select a store under the Store View Name, and you'll find the code listed there.

Available data keys:

- is_active

- increment_id

- name (required)

- url_key

- description

- image

- meta_title

- meta_keywords

- meta_description

- display_mode

- landing_page

- is_anchor

- available_sort_by (required)

- default_sort_by (required)

- custom_design

- custom_design_apply

- custom_design_from

- custom_design_to

- page_layout

- custom_layout_update

Zend XML-RPC Example

```
// Prepare the data
$category_id = '15';
$data = array(
    'description' => 'Colors available on request!',
    'meta_keywords' => 'new colors'
);
// using Zend XML-RPC method
$result = $client->call('call', array($session_id,
    'catalog_category.update', array($category_id, $data)));
// returns true if update was successful
var_dump($result);
```

Method: catalog_category.move ($category_id, $parent_category_id, $after_category_id)

Description: Moves the category under a specific parent.

Return: Boolean; true if update was successful.

Arguments:

- $category_id (required). The category_id to move.

- $parent_category_id (required). The destination for this move.

- $after_category_id (optional). You can place the category behind this child category_id.

Zend XML-RPC Example

```
// Prepare the data
$category_id = '15';
$new_parent_category_id = '2';
// using Zend XML-RPC method
$result = $client->call('call', array($session_id,
    'catalog_category.move', array($category_id,
        $new_parent_category_id)));
// returns true if update was successful
var_dump($result);
```

■ **Note** Make sure that you do not move the category under one of its children. Magento won't halt the process. Both the category_id and the parent_category_id will be removed. There is no undoing once the move (or deletion) has occurred.

Method: catalog_category.delete ($category_id)

Description: Deletes the category.

Return: Boolean; true if delete was successful.

Argument:

- $category_id (required). The category_id to remove.

Zend XML-RPC Example

```
// Prepare the data
$category_id = '15';
// using Zend XML-RPC method
$result = $client->call('call', array($session_id,
    'catalog_category.delete', array($category_id)));
// returns true if delete was successful
var_dump($result);
```

Method: catalog_category.assignedProducts ($category_id, $store_view_code)

Description: Returns a list of assigned products under the given category_id.

Return: Array.

Arguments:

- $category_id (required). Lists assigned products for this category_id.
- $store_view_code (required). Select Admin Panel, System, Manage Stores; select a store under the Store View Name, and you'll find the code listed there.

Sample Return Set

```
array (
  0 =>
  array (
    'product_id' => '2',
    'type' => 'simple',
    'set' => '4',
    'sku' => 'SSS0003',
    'position' => NULL,
  ),
  1 =>
  array (
    'product_id' => '10',
    'type' => 'simple',
    'set' => '4',
    'sku' => 'SSS0004',
    'position' => NULL,
  ),
)
```

SOAP Example

```
// view assigned products for this category_id
$category_id = '9';
$store_view_code = 'dollarstore';
// using SOAP method
$results = $client->call($session_id,
    'catalog_category.assignedProducts',
    array($category_id, $store_view_code));
// view results
var_dump($results);
```

Note Because we had multiple stores, we had to pass the $store_view_code to avoid getting empty arrays. Also, this feature fails in 1.3.0. Fixes can be found here: www.magentocommerce.com/boards/viewthread/ 38307/.

Method: catalog_category.assignProduct ($category_id, $product_id, $position)

Description: Assigns a product under the given category_id.

Return: Boolean; true if update was successful.

Arguments:

- $category_id (required). The product will be assigned to this category_id.

- $product_id (required). You can input the product_id or SKU number of the product.

- $position (optional). Sets the position within the category.

Zend XML-RPC Example

```
// Prepare the data
$category_id = '15';
$product_id = 'SSS0004';
// using Zend XML-RPC method
$result = $client->call('call', array($session_id,
    'catalog_category.assignProduct', array($category_id,
        $product_id)));
// returns true if successful
var_dump($result);
```

Note If you run into problems after assigning products through the API, please see this thread for rebuilding the flat catalog product: www.magentocommerce.com/boards/viewthread/42770/.

Method: catalog_category.updateProduct ($category_id, $product_id, $position)

Description: Updates a product to the given category_id.

Return: Boolean; true if update was successful.

Arguments:

- $category_id (required). The product will be assigned to this category_id.

- $product_id (required). You can input the product_id or SKU number of the product.

- $position (optional). Sets the position within the category.

Zend XML-RPC Example

```
// Prepare the data
$category_id = '11';
$product_id = 'SSS0004';
// using Zend XML-RPC method
$result = $client->call('call', array($session_id,
    'catalog_category.updateProduct', array($category_id,
        $product_id)));
// returns true if successful
var_dump($result);
```

Method: catalog_category.removeProduct ($category_id, $product_id)

Description: Removes a product to the given category_id.

Return: Boolean; true if remove was successful.

Arguments:

- $category_id (required). The product will be removed from this category_id.

- $product_id (required). You can input the product_id or SKU number of the product.

Zend XML-RPC Example

```
// Prepare the data
$category_id = '11';
$product_id = 'SSS0004';
// using Zend XML-RPC method
$result = $client->call('call', array($session_id,
    'catalog_category.removeProduct', array($category_id,
        $product_id)));
// returns true if successful
var_dump($result);
```

Category Attribute Set

The category attribute set allows you to pull options and attributes assigned for all categories:

- catalog_category_attribute.currentStore
- catalog_category_attribute.list
- catalog_category_attribute.options

Method: catalog_category_attribute.currentStore ($store_view_code)

Description: Gets the store_id.

Return: Int, the store_id.

Argument:

- $store_view_code (optional). Select Admin Panel, System, Manage Stores; select a store under the Store View Name, and you'll find the code listed there.

SOAP Example

```
// Set the store code
$store_view_code = 'dollarstore';
// using SOAP method
$result = $client->call($session_id,
    'catalog_category_attribute.currentStore', $store_view_code);
// returns the store_id
echo $result;
```

Method: catalog_category_attribute.list ()

Description: Gets a list of category attributes

Return: Array.

Argument: None.

Sample Return Set

```
array (
...
  5 =>
  array (
    'attribute_id' => '32',
    'code' => 'is_active',
    'type' => 'select',
    'required' => '0',
    'scope' => 'store',
  ),
  6 =>
  array (
```

```
  'attribute_id' => '33',
  'code' => 'url_key',
  'type' => 'text',
  'required' => '0',
  'scope' => 'global',
),
7 =>
array (
  'attribute_id' => '34',
  'code' => 'description',
  'type' => 'textarea',
  'required' => '0',
  'scope' => 'store',
),
...
```

SOAP Example

```
// using SOAP method
$results = $client->call($session_id,
    catalog_category_attribute.list');
// view results
var_dump($results);
```

Method: catalog_category_attribute.options ($attribute_id, $store_view_code)

Description: Gets a list of attribute options given the attribute_id or attribute_code.

Return: Array.

Arguments:

- $attribute_id (required). You can input attribute_id or attribute_code.

- $store_view_code (optional). Select Admin Panel, System, Manage Stores; select a store under the Store View Name, and you'll find the code listed there.

Sample Return Set

```
array (
  0 =>
  array (
    'value' => 'PRODUCTS',
    'label' => 'Products only',
  ),
  1 =>
  array (
    'value' => 'PAGE',
    'label' => 'Static block only',
  ),
  2 =>
  array (
    'value' => 'PRODUCTS_AND_PAGE',
```

```
        'label' => 'Static block and products',
    ),
)
```

Zend XML-RPC Example

```
// Prepare the data
$attribute_id = 'display_mode';
// using Zend XML-RPC method
$result = $client->call('call', array($session_id,
    'catalog_category_attribute.options', array($attribute_id)));
// view the results
var_dump($result);
```

Product Set

The product set allows you to list, create, update, and delete products:

- catalog_product.currentStore
- catalog_product.list
- catalog_product.info
- catalog_product.create
- catalog_product.update
- catalog_product.setSpecialPrice
- catalog_product.getSpecialPrice
- catalog_product.delete

Method: catalog_product.currentStore ($store_view_code)

Description: Gets the store_id.

Return: Int, the store_id.

Argument:

- $store_view_code (optional). Select Admin Panel, System, Manage Stores; select a store under the Store View Name, and you'll find the code listed there.

SOAP Example

```
// Set the store code
$store_view_code = 'dollarstore';
// using SOAP method
$result = $client->call($session_id,
    'catalog_product.currentStore', $store_view_code);
// returns the store_id
echo $result;
```

Method: catalog_product.list ($filters, $store_view_code)

Description: Returns a list of products.

Return: Array.

Arguments:

- $filters (optional). Uses an array of key/value pairs to set filters.

- $store_view_code (optional). Select Admin Panel, System, Manage Stores; select a store under the Store View Name, and you'll find the code listed there.

Available filter keys:

- product_id

- sku

- name

- set

- type

- category_ids

- (to see a full list of filters, use the "sample return set" from catalog_product.info)

Sample Return Set

```
array (
  0 =>
  array (
    'product_id' => '1',
    'sku' => 'SSS3006',
    'name' => 'Product Red',
    'set' => '4',
    'type' => 'simple',
    'category_ids' =>
    array (
      0 => '4',
      1 => '9',
    ),
  ),
  1 =>
  array (
    'product_id' => '2',
    'sku' => 'SSS0003',
    'name' => 'Product Blue',
    'set' => '4',
    'type' => 'simple',
    'category_ids' =>
    array (
      0 => '6',
      1 => '10',
```

```
    2 => '11',
  ),
),
...
```

SOAP Example

```
// Prepare filters
$filters = array('type' => 'simple');
// using SOAP method
$results = $client->call($session_id, 'catalog_product.list',
    array($filters));
// returns the tree
var_dump($results);
```

Method: catalog_product.info ($product_id, $store_view_code, $attributes)

Description: Returns detailed info of a product.

Return: Array

Arguments:

- $product_id (required). You can input product_id or product_sku.

- $store_view_code (optional). Select Admin Panel, System, Manage Stores; select a store under the Store View Name, and you'll find the code listed there.

- $attributes (optional). Returns only these sets of attributes.

Sample Return Set

```
array (
  'product_id' => '1',
  'sku' => 'SSS3006',
  'set' => '4',
  'type' => 'simple',
  'categories' =>
  array (
    0 => '4',
    1 => '9',
  ),
  'websites' =>
  array (
    0 => '2',
    1 => '4',
  ),
  'type_id' => 'simple',
  'name' => 'Product Red',
  'description' => 'test test',
  'short_description' => test test',
  'weight' => '6.0000',
  'manufacturer' => NULL,
```

```
'old_id' => NULL,
'color' => NULL,
'news_from_date' => NULL,
'news_to_date' => NULL,
'status' => '1',
'url_key' => 'product-red',
'url_path' => 'product-red-2.html',
'visibility' => '4',
'category_ids' =>
array (
  0 => '4',
  1 => '9',
),
'required_options' => '0',
'has_options' => '0',
'image_label' => 'Product Red',
'small_image_label' => 'Product Red',
'thumbnail_label' => 'Product Red',
'gift_message_available' => '2',
'created_at' => '2009-03-08 00:20:56',
'updated_at' => '2009-07-03 08:18:08',
'price' => '49.9500',
'special_price' => NULL,
'special_from_date' => NULL,
'special_to_date' => NULL,
'cost' => NULL,
'tax_class_id' => '2',
'minimal_price' => NULL,
'tier_price' =>
array (
  0 =>
  array (
    'website_id' => '0',
    'all_groups' => '0',
    'cust_group' => '8',
    'price_qty' => '1.0000',
    'price' => '32.0000',
    'website_price' => '32.0000',
  ),
  1 =>
  array (
    'website_id' => '0',
    'all_groups' => '0',
    'cust_group' => '9',
    'price_qty' => '1.0000',
    'price' => '30.0000',
    'website_price' => '30.0000',
  ),
  2 =>
  array (
    'website_id' => '0',
    'all_groups' => '0',
```

```
          'cust_group' => '10',
          'price_qty' => '1.0000',
          'price' => '28.0000',
          'website_price' => '28.0000',
      ),
      3 =>
      array (
          'website_id' => '0',
          'all_groups' => '0',
          'cust_group' => '5',
          'price_qty' => '1.0000',
          'price' => '30.0000',
          'website_price' => '30.0000',
      ),
      4 =>
      array (
          'website_id' => '0',
          'all_groups' => '0',
          'cust_group' => '6',
          'price_qty' => '1.0000',
          'price' => '28.0000',
          'website_price' => '28.0000',
      ),
      5 =>
      array (
          'website_id' => '0',
          'all_groups' => '0',
          'cust_group' => '7',
          'price_qty' => '1.0000',
          'price' => '28.0000',
          'website_price' => '28.0000',
      ),
      6 =>
      array (
          'website_id' => '0',
          'all_groups' => '0',
          'cust_group' => '3',
          'price_qty' => '1.0000',
          'price' => '32.0000',
          'website_price' => '32.0000',
      ),
      7 =>
      array (
          'website_id' => '0',
          'all_groups' => '0',
          'cust_group' => '4',
          'price_qty' => '1.0000',
          'price' => '32.0000',
          'website_price' => '32.0000',
      ),
  ),
  'enable_googlecheckout' => '1',
```

```
    'meta_title' => '',
    'meta_keyword' => '',
    'meta_description' => '',
    'custom_design' => '',
    'custom_design_from' => NULL,
    'custom_design_to' => NULL,
    'custom_layout_update' => '',
    'options_container' => 'container2',
    'page_layout' => NULL,
)
```

Zend XML-RPC Example

```
// Prepare the data
$product_id = '1';
// using Zend XML-RPC method
$result = $client->call('call', array($session_id,
    'catalog_product.info', array($product_id)));
// view the results
var_dump($result);
```

Method: catalog_product.create ($type, $product_attribute_set_id, $sku, $data)

Description: Creates a product.

Return: Newly created product_id.

Arguments:

- $type (required). Defined under the catalog_product_type.list() API. Your choices are simple, grouped, configurable, virtual, bundle, or downloadable.

- $product_attribute_set_id (required). Defined under the catalog_product_attribute_set.list() API.

- $sku (required). Input the sku for this new product. Each sku must be unique, or else Magento will throw errors upon product creation.

- $data (required). Uses an array of key/value pairs to set data. Magento allows you to create a new product with no information, although it isn't wise to do so.

Available data keys:

- name

- websites (array of website ids)

- description

- short_description

- price

- (to see a full list, use the "sample return set" from catalog_product.info)

Zend XML-RPC Example

```
// Prepare the data
$type = 'simple';
$product_attribute_set_id = '4';
$sku = 'SSS12345';
$data = array(
    'name' => 'Product Green',
    'price' => 49.95
);
$new_product_id = $client->call('call', array($session_id,
    'catalog_product.create', array($type,
        $product_attribute_set_id, $sku, $data)));
// view the new product id
echo $new_product_id;
```

Method: catalog_product.update ($product_id, $data, $store_view_code)

Description: Updates product info.

Return: Boolean; true if remove was successful.

Arguments:

- $product_id (required). The product_id or product_sku to update.

- $data (required). Uses an array of key/value pairs to update data.

- $store_view_code (optional). Select Admin Panel, System, Manage Stores; select a store under the Store View Name, and you'll find the code listed there.

Available data keys:

- name

- websites (array of web site ids)

- description

- short_description

- price

- (to see a full list, use the sample return set from catalog_product.info)

SOAP Example

```
// Prepare filters
$product_id = '12';
$data = array(
    'name' => 'Product Dark Green'
);
// using SOAP method
$results = $client->call($session_id, 'catalog_product.update',
    array($product_id, $data));
```

```
// returns true if update was successful
var_dump($results);
```

Method: catalog_product.setSpecialPrice ($product_id, $special_price, $from_date, $to_date, $store_view_code)

Description: Sets special price for a product.

Return: Boolean; true if update was successful.

Arguments:

- $product_id (required). The product_id or product_sku to update.

- $special_price (optional). The price amount.

- $from_date (optional). Sets the start date for this special pricing.

- $to_date (optional). Sets the end date for this special pricing.

- $store_view_code (optional). Select Admin Panel, System, Manage Stores; select a store under the Store View Name, and you'll find the code listed there.

SOAP Example

```
// Prepare filters
$product_id = '12';
$special_price = 14.99;
// using SOAP method
$results = $client->call($session_id,
    'catalog_product.setSpecialPrice', array($product_id,
        $special_price));
// returns true if update was successful
var_dump($results);
```

Method: catalog_product.getSpecialPrice ($product_id, $store_view_code)

Description: Gets special price for a product.

Return: Array.

Arguments:

- $product_id (required). The product_id or product_sku to query.

- $store_view_code (optional). Select Admin Panel, System, Manage Stores; select a store under the Store View Name, and you'll find the code listed there.

Sample Return Set

```
array (
  'product_id' => '12',
  'sku' => 'SSS123456',
  'set' => '4',
```

```
  'type' => 'simple',
  'categories' =>
  array (
  ),
  'websites' =>
  array (
  ),
  'special_price' => '14.9900',
  'special_from_date' => '2009-09-05 00:00:00',
  'special_to_date' => NULL,
)
```

Zend XML-RPC Example

```
// Prepare the data
$product_id = '12';
$results = $client->call('call', array($session_id,
    'catalog_product.getSpecialPrice', array($product_id)));
// view the results
var_dump($results);
```

Method: catalog_product.delete ($product_id)

Description: Deletes the product.

Return: Boolean; true if delete was successful.

Argument:

- $product_id (required). The product_id or product_sku to remove.

SOAP Example

```
// Prepare filters
$product_id = '12';
// using SOAP method
$results = $client->call($session_id,
    'catalog_product.delete', $product_id);
// returns true if delete was successful
var_dump($results);
```

Product Attribute Set

The product attribute set allows you to pull options and attributes assigned for products:

- catalog_product_attribute.currentStore

- catalog_product_attribute.list

- catalog_product_attribute.options

Method: catalog_product_attribute.currentStore ($store_view_code)

Description: Gets the store_id.

Return: Int, the store_id.

Argument:

- $store_view_code (optional). Select Admin Panel, System, Manage Stores; select a store under the Store View Name, and you'll find the code listed there.

SOAP Example

```
// Set the store code
$store_view_code = 'dollarstore';
// using SOAP method
$result = $client->call($session_id,
    'catalog_product_attribute.currentStore', $store_view_code);
// returns the store_id
echo $result;
```

Method: catalog_product_attribute.list ($attribute_set_id)

Description: Returns a list of product attributes given the attribute_set_id.

Return: Array.

Argument:

- $attribute_set_id (required). This can be obtained through the catalog_product_attribute_set.list() API.

Sample Return Set

```
array (
  0 =>
  array (
    'attribute_id' => '56',
    'code' => 'name',
    'type' => 'text',
    'required' => '1',
    'scope' => 'store',
  ),
  1 =>
  array (
    'attribute_id' => '57',
    'code' => 'description',
    'type' => 'textarea',
    'required' => '0',
    'scope' => 'store',
  ),
  2 =>
  array (
    'attribute_id' => '58',
```

```
      'code' => 'short_description',
      'type' => 'textarea',
      'required' => '1',
      'scope' => 'store',
  ),
...
```

Zend XML-RPC Example

```
// Prepare the data
$attribute_set_id = '4';
$results = $client->call('call', array($session_id,
    'catalog_product_attribute.list', array($attribute_set_id)));
// view the results
var_dump($results);
```

Method: catalog_product_attribute.options ($attribute_id, $store_view_code)

Description: Returns a list of product attribute options.

Return: Array

Arguments:

- $attribute_id (required). The attribute_id or attribute_code to list options.

- $store_view_code (optional). Select Admin Panel, System, Manage Stores; select a store under the Store View Name, and you'll find the code listed there.

Sample Return Set

```
array (
  0 =>
  array (
    'value' => '',
    'label' => '- Please Select --',
  ),
  1 =>
  array (
    'value' => 1,
    'label' => 'Enabled',
  ),
  2 =>
  array (
    'value' => 2,
    'label' => 'Disabled',
  ),
)
```

SOAP Example

```
// Prepare the data
$attribute_id = 'status';
```

```
// using SOAP method
$result = $client->call($session_id,
    'catalog_product_attribute.options', $attribute_id);
// view the result
var_dump($result);
```

Product Attribute Set

The product attribute set lists the sets available on your store:

- catalog_product_attribute_set.list

Method: catalog_product_attribute_set.list ()

Description: Returns a list of product attribute sets.

Return: Array.

Argument: None.

Sample Return Set

```
array (
  0 =>
  array (
    'set_id' => '4',
    'name' => 'Default',
  ),
)
```

SOAP Example

```
// using SOAP method
$results = $client->call($session_id,
    'catalog_product_attribute_set.list');
// view the results
var_dump($results);
```

Product Type Set

The product type set lists the available product types in your store:

- catalog_product_type.list

Method: catalog_product_type.list ()

Description: Returns a list of product types.

Return: Array.

Argument: None.

Sample Return Set

```
array (
  0 =>
  array (
    'type' => 'simple',
    'label' => 'Simple Product',
  ),
  1 =>
  array (
    'type' => 'grouped',
    'label' => 'Grouped Product',
  ),
  2 =>
  array (
    'type' => 'configurable',
    'label' => 'Configurable Product',
  ),
  3 =>
  array (
    'type' => 'virtual',
    'label' => 'Virtual Product',
  ),
  4 =>
  array (
    'type' => 'bundle',
    'label' => 'Bundle Product',
  ),
  5 =>
  array (
    'type' => 'downloadable',
    'label' => 'Downloadable Product',
  ),
)
```

Zend XML-RPC Example

```
$results = $client->call('call', array($session_id,
    'catalog_product_type.list'));
// view the results
var_dump($results);
```

Product Attribute Media Set

The product attribute media set is used to handle all product images in your store:

- catalog_product_attribute_media.currentStore
- catalog_product_attribute_media.list
- catalog_product_attribute_media.info

- catalog_product_attribute_media.types
- catalog_product_attribute_media.create
- catalog_product_attribute_media.update
- catalog_product_attribute_media.remove

Method: catalog_product_attribute_media.currentStore ($store_view_code)

Description: Gets the store_id.

Return: Int, the store_id.

Argument:

- $store_view_code (optional). Select Admin Panel, System, Manage Stores; select a store under the Store View Name, and you'll find the code listed there.

SOAP Example

```
// Set the store code
$store_view_code = 'dollarstore';
// using SOAP method
$result = $client->call($session_id,
    'catalog_product_attribute_media.currentStore',
    $store_view_code);
// returns the store_id
echo $result;
```

Method: catalog_product_attribute_media.list ($product_id, $store_view_code)

Description: Returns a list of product images given the product_id.

Return: Array.

Arguments:

- $product_id (required). Pulls all images associated to this product_id or product_sku.
- $store_view_code (optional). Select Admin Panel, System, Manage Stores; select a store under the Store View Name, and you'll find the code listed there.

Sample Return Set

```
array (
  0 =>
  array (
    'file' => '/s/s/sse.jpg',
    'label' => 'Product Red',
    'position' => '0',
    'exclude' => '0',
    'url' => 'http://test.com/media/catalog/product/s/s/sse.jpg',
```

```
    'types' =>
    array (
    ),
  ),
  1 =>
  array (
    'file' => '/p/a/pancakes.jpg',
    'label' => 'Pancakes',
    'position' => '1',
    'exclude' => '0',
    'url' => 'http://test.com/media/catalog/product/p/a/pancakes.jpg',
    'types' =>
    array (
      0 => 'image',
      1 => 'small_image',
      2 => 'thumbnail',
    ),
  ),
)
```

Zend XML-RPC Example

```
// Prepare the data
$product_id = '1';
$results = $client->call('call', array($session_id,
    'catalog_product_attribute_media.list',
    array($product_id)));
// view the results
var_dump($results);
```

Method: catalog_product_attribute_media.info ($product_id, $file, $store_view_code)

Description: Lists detailed information of a product image.

Return: Array.

Arguments:

- $product_id (required). Pulls all images associated to this product_id or product_sku.

- $file (required). The file attribute from catalog_product_attribute_media_list().

- $store_view_code (optional). Select Admin Panel, System, Manage Stores; select a store under the Store View Name, and you'll find the code listed there.

Sample Return Set

```
array (
    'file' => '/p/a/pancakes.jpg',
    'label' => 'Pancakes',
    'position' => '1',
    'exclude' => '0',
```

```
    'url' => 'http://test.com/media/catalog/product/p/a/pancakes.jpg',
    'types' =>
    array (
      0 => 'image',
      1 => 'small_image',
      2 => 'thumbnail',
    ),
)
```

SOAP Example

```
// Prepare data
$product_id = '1';
$file = '/p/a/pancakes.jpg';
// using SOAP method
$results = $client->call($session_id,
    'catalog_product_attribute_media.info',
    array($product_id, $file));
// view the results
var_dump($results);
```

Method: catalog_product_attribute_media.types ($product_attribute_set_id)

Description: Returns a list of product image types.

Return: Array.

Argument:

- $product_attribute_set_id (required). Can be obtained through the catalog_product_attribute_set.list() API.

Sample Return Set

```
array (
  0 =>
  array (
    'code' => 'image',
    'scope' => 'store',
  ),
  1 =>
  array (
    'code' => 'small_image',
    'scope' => 'store',
  ),
  2 =>
  array (
    'code' => 'thumbnail',
    'scope' => 'store',
  ),
)
```

Zend XML-RPC Example

```
// Prepare the data
$product_attribute_set_id = '4';
$results = $client->call('call', array($session_id,
    'catalog_product_attribute_media.types',
    array($product_attribute_set_id)));
// view the results
var_dump($results);
```

Method: catalog_product_attribute_media.create ($product_id, $data, $store_view_code)

Description: Creates and uploads a new image.

Return: String, image file name.

Arguments:

- $product_id (required). product_id or product_sku to associate this image to.

- $data (required) .Uses an array of key/value pairs to set the data.

- $store_view_code (optional). Select Admin Panel, System, Manage Stores; select a store under the Store View Name, and you'll find the code listed there.

Available data keys:

- file (required)

- label

- position

- types (array containing: 'thumbnail', 'small_image', 'image')

- exclude

SOAP Example

```
// Prepare data
$product_id = '1';
$data = array(
    'file' => array(
        'content' => base64_encode(file_get_contents('pic.jpg')),
        'mime' => 'image/jpeg'
    )
);
// using SOAP method
$results = $client->call($session_id,
    'catalog_product_attribute_media.create',
    array($product_id, $data));
// view the results
var_dump($results);
```

Method: catalog_product_attribute_media.update ($product_id, $file, $data, $store_view_code)

Description: Updates image info.

Return: Boolean; true if update was successful.

Arguments:

- $product_id (required). product_id or product_sku to update.

- $file (required). The file attribute from catalog_product_attribute_media_list().

- $data (required). Uses an array of key/value pairs to update the data.

- $store_view_code (optional). Select Admin Panel, System, Manage Stores; select a store under the Store View Name, and you'll find the code listed there.

Available data keys:

- file (required)

- label

- position

- types (array containing: 'thumbnail', 'small_image', 'image')

- exclude

Zend XML-RPC Example

```
// Prepare the data
$product_id = '1';
$file = '/s/s/sse.jpg';
$data = array(
    'label' => 'New Red'
);
$results = $client->call('call', array($session_id,
    'catalog_product_attribute_media.update',
    array($product_id, $file, $data)));
// return true if successful
var_dump($results);
```

Method: catalog_product_attribute_media.remove ($product_id, $file)

Description: Removes the image.

Return: Boolean; true if delete was successful.

Arguments:

- $product_id (required). product_id or product_sku to remove.

- $file (required). The file attribute from catalog_product_attribute_media_list().

SOAP Example

```
// Prepare data
$product_id = '1';
$file = '/s/s/sse.jpg';
// using SOAP method
$results = $client->call($session_id,
    'catalog_product_attribute_media.remove',
    array($product_id, $file));
// return true if successful
var_dump($results);
```

Product Attribute Tier Price Set

The product attribute tier price allows you to view and update tier pricing:

- catalog_product_attribute_tier_price.info
- catalog_product_attribute_tier_price.update

Method: catalog_product_attribute_tier_price.info ($product_id)

Description: Views the tier pricing for a particular product.

Return: Array.

Argument:

- $product_id (required). product_id or product_sku to update.

Sample Return Set

```
array (
  0 =>
  array (
    'customer_group_id' => '8',
    'website' => 'all',
    'qty' => '1.0000',
    'price' => '32.0000',
  ),
  1 =>
  array (
    'customer_group_id' => '9',
    'website' => 'all',
    'qty' => '1.0000',
    'price' => '30.0000',
  ),
```

```
  2 =>
  array (
    'customer_group_id' => '10',
    'website' => 'all',
    'qty' => '1.0000',
    'price' => '28.0000',
  ),
...
```

Zend XML-RPC Example

```
// Prepare the data
$product_id = '1';
$results = $client->call('call', array($session_id,
    'catalog_product_attribute_tier_price.info',
array($product_id)));
// view results
var_dump($results);
```

Method: catalog_product_attribute_tier_price.update ($product_id, $tierPrices)

Description: Updates the tier pricing for a particular product.

Return: Boolean; true if delete was successful.

Arguments:

- $product_id (required). product_id or product_sku to update.

- $tierPrices (required). Key/value array of tier prices.

Available keys for tier prices:

- customer_group_id

- website

- qty

- price

SOAP Example

```
// We don't want to erase the current tier pricing, so let's grab
// that current set and append to it.
$product_id = '1';
// using SOAP method
$tierPrices = $client->call($session_id,
    'catalog_product_attribute_tier_price.info',
    array($product_id));
```

```
$tierPrices[] = array(
    'customer_group_id' => 'all',
    'website' => 'all',
    'qty' => '50',
    'price' => '24.99'
);
$results = $client->call($session_id,
    'catalog_product_attribute_tier_price.update',
    array($product_id, $tierPrices));
// return true if successful
var_dump($results);
```

Product Link Set

The product link set allows you to view, assign, update, and remove any product links such as cross sell, up sell, related, and grouped.

- catalog_product_link.list

- catalog_product_link.assign

- catalog_product_link.update

- catalog_product_link.remove

- catalog_product_link.types

- catalog_product_link.attributes

Method: catalog_product_link.list ($type, $product_id)

Description: Views any product links associated with this product_id.

Return: Array.

Arguments:

- $type (required). Can be 'cross_sell', 'up_sell', 'related', or 'grouped'.

- $product_id (required). product_id or product_sku to view.

Sample Return Set

```
array (
  0 =>
  array (
    'product_id' => '10',
    'type' => 'simple',
    'set' => '4',
    'sku' => 'SSA0004',
    'position' => '0',
    'qty' => NULL,
  ),
```

```
  1 =>
  array (
    'product_id' => '12',
    'type' => 'simple',
    'set' => '4',
    'sku' => 'SSS123456',
    'position' => '0',
    'qty' => NULL,
  ),
)
```

Zend XML-RPC Example

```php
// Prepare the data
$type = 'related';
$product_id = '1';
$results = $client->call('call',
    array($session_id,
        'catalog_product_link.list',
        array($type, $product_id)
    )
);
// view results
var_dump($results);
```

Method: catalog_product_link.assign ($type, $product_id, $linked_product_id, $data)

Description: Associates product_id to linked_product_id with the defined type.

Return: Boolean; true if assign was successful.

Arguments:

- $type (required). Can be 'cross_sell', 'up_sell', 'related', or 'grouped'.

- $product_id (required). target product_id or product_sku.

- $linked_product_id (required). linked product_id or product_sku.

- $data (optional). Assigns values to the relationship, such as position and qty.

SOAP Example

```php
// Prepare the data
$type = 'up_sell';
$product_id = '1';
$linked_product_id = '2';
// using SOAP method
$results = $client->call($session_id,
    'catalog_product_link.assign',
    array($type, $product_id, $linked_product_id));
// return true if successful
var_dump($results);
```

Method: catalog_product_link.update ($type, $product_id, $linked_product_id, $data)

Description: Updates product_id and linked_product_id to the defined type.

Return: Boolean; true if update was successful.

Arguments:

- $type (required). Can be 'cross_sell', 'up_sell', 'related', or 'grouped'.
- $product_id (required). target product_id or product_sku.
- $linked_product_id (required). linked product_id or product_sku.
- $data (optional). Updates values to the relationship, such as position and qty.

Zend XML-RPC Example

```
// Prepare the data
$type = 'up_sell';
$product_id = '1';
$linked_product_id = '2';
$data = array(
    'position' => '2'
);
$results = $client->call('call',
    array($session_id,
        'catalog_product_link.update',
        array($type, $product_id, $linked_product_id, $data)
    )
);
// view results
var_dump($results);
```

Method: catalog_product_link.remove ($type, $product_id, $linked_product_id)

Description: Removes the associated link from product_id to linked_product_id.

Return: Boolean; true if remove was successful.

Arguments:

- $type (required). Can be 'cross_sell', 'up_sell', 'related', or 'grouped'.
- $product_id (required). target product_id or product_sku.
- $linked_product_id (required). linked product_id or product_sku.

SOAP Example

```
// Prepare the data
$type = 'up_sell';
$product_id = '1';
$linked_product_id = '2';
// using SOAP method
```

```
$results = $client->call($session_id,
    'catalog_product_link.remove',
    array($type, $product_id, $linked_product_id));
// return true if successful
var_dump($results);
```

Method: catalog_product_link.types ()

Description: Lists the available link types.

Return: Array.

Argument: None.

Sample Return Set

```
array (
  0 => 'related',
  1 => 'up_sell',
  2 => 'cross_sell',
  3 => 'grouped',
)
```

Zend XML-RPC Example

```
// Using Zend XML-RPC
$results = $client->call('call',
    array($session_id,
        'catalog_product_link.types'));
// view results
var_dump($results);
```

Method: catalog_product_link.attributes ($type)

Description: Lists the available link type attributes for the given type.

Return: Array.

Argument:

- $type (required) Can be 'cross_sell', 'up_sell', 'related', or 'grouped'.

Sample Return Set

```
array (
  0 =>
  array (
    'code' => 'position',
    'type' => 'int',
  ),
)
```

Zend XML-RPC Example

```
// Prepare data
$type = 'cross_sell';
// Using Zend XML-RPC
$results = $client->call('call',
    array($session_id,
        'catalog_product_link.attributes',
        array($type)));
// view results
var_dump($results);
```

Sales API

The sales API is broken up into three main sets: orders, shipping, and invoice. Similar to the previous API sets, you are given the basic view, create, and update. You can use these methods to export your sales data into CSV, Excel, or even to another database.

Sales Order Set

In the sales order set, you can view, add comments, cancel orders, or place them on hold. Magento does not give you the ability to create orders through web services, which we believe is a valid architectural decision. It limits the chance for a hacker to maliciously place an order.

- sales_order.list
- sales_order.info
- sales_order.addComment
- sales_order.hold
- sales_order.unhold
- sales_order.cancel

Method: sales_order.list ($filters)

Description: Returns a list of sales orders.

Return: Array.

Argument:

- $filters (optional). Uses an array of key/value pairs to set filters.

Available filter keys:

- increment_id
- store_id
- created_at

- customer_id

- status

- (to see a full list of filters, use the following sample return set)

Sample Return Set

```
array (
  0 =>
  array (
    'increment_id' => '200000001',
    'parent_id' => '0',
    'store_id' => '2',
    'created_at' => '2009-06-12 14:28:38',
    'updated_at' => '2009-07-09 08:25:13',
    'is_active' => '1',
    'customer_id' => '13',
    'tax_amount' => '0.0000',
    'shipping_amount' => '8.9600',
    'discount_amount' => '0.0000',
    'subtotal' => '32.0000',
    'grand_total' => '40.9600',
    'total_paid' => '40.9600',
    'total_refunded' => '0.0000',
    'total_qty_ordered' => '0.0000',
    'total_canceled' => '0.0000',
    'total_invoiced' => '40.9600',
    'total_online_refunded' => '0.0000',
    'total_offline_refunded' => '0.0000',
    'base_tax_amount' => '0.0000',
    'base_shipping_amount' => '8.9600',
    'base_discount_amount' => '0.0000',
    'base_subtotal' => '32.0000',
    'base_grand_total' => '40.9600',
    'base_total_paid' => '40.9600',
    'base_total_refunded' => '0.0000',
    'base_total_qty_ordered' => '0.0000',
    'base_total_canceled' => '0.0000',
    'base_total_invoiced' => '40.9600',
    'base_total_online_refunded' => '0.0000',
    'base_total_offline_refunded' => '0.0000',
    'subtotal_refunded' => NULL,
    'subtotal_canceled' => NULL,
    'discount_refunded' => NULL,
    'discount_canceled' => NULL,
    'discount_invoiced' => '0.0000',
    'tax_refunded' => NULL,
    'tax_canceled' => NULL,
    'shipping_refunded' => NULL,
    'shipping_canceled' => NULL,
    'base_subtotal_refunded' => NULL,
```

```
'base_subtotal_canceled' => NULL,
'base_discount_refunded' => NULL,
'base_discount_canceled' => NULL,
'base_discount_invoiced' => '0.0000',
'base_tax_refunded' => NULL,
'base_tax_canceled' => NULL,
'base_shipping_refunded' => NULL,
'base_shipping_canceled' => NULL,
'subtotal_invoiced' => '32.0000',
'tax_invoiced' => '0.0000',
'shipping_invoiced' => '8.9600',
'base_subtotal_invoiced' => '32.0000',
'base_tax_invoiced' => '0.0000',
'base_shipping_invoiced' => '8.9600',
'shipping_tax_amount' => '0.0000',
'base_shipping_tax_amount' => '0.0000',
'shipping_tax_refunded' => NULL,
'base_shipping_tax_refunded' => NULL,
'billing_address_id' => '1',
'billing_firstname' => 'John',
'billing_lastname' => 'Doe',
'shipping_address_id' => '2',
'shipping_firstname' => 'Jane',
'shipping_lastname' => 'Doe',
'billing_name' => 'John Doe',
'shipping_name' => 'Jane Doe',
'status' => 'complete',
'store_to_base_rate' => '1.0000',
'store_to_order_rate' => '1.0000',
'base_to_global_rate' => '1.0000',
'base_to_order_rate' => '1.0000',
'weight' => '6.0000',
'remote_ip' => '10.0.1.1',
'customer_email' => 'jd@test.com',
'customer_prefix' => '',
'customer_firstname' => 'John',
'customer_middlename' => '',
'customer_lastname' => 'Doe',
'customer_suffix' => '',
'customer_taxvat' => '',
'global_currency_code' => 'USD',
'base_currency_code' => 'USD',
'store_currency_code' => 'USD',
'order_currency_code' => 'USD',
'applied_rule_ids' => '',
'shipping_method' => 'ups_GND',
'shipping_description' => 'United Parcel Service - Ground',
'state' => 'complete',
'store_name' => 'Store X',
'quote_id' => '3',
'customer_group_id' => '8',
'customer_note_notify' => '1',
```

```
    'customer_is_guest' => '0',
    'is_virtual' => '0',
    'email_sent' => '1',
    'order_id' => '1',
  ),
...
```

SOAP Example

```
// Pull only orders with status complete
$filters = array(
    'status' => 'complete'
);
// using SOAP method
$results = $client->call($session_id,
    'sales_order.list', array($filters));
// view the results
var_dump($results);
```

Method: sales_order.info ($order_increment_id)

Description: Returns detailed information on a specific order, including shipping, billing, and items purchased.

Return: Array.

Argument:

- $order_increment_id (required). This is the increment_id pulled from sales_order.list().

Sample Return Set

```
array (
    'increment_id' => '200000001',
    'parent_id' => '0',
    'store_id' => '2',
    'created_at' => '2009-06-12 14:28:38',
    'updated_at' => '2009-07-09 08:25:13',
    'is_active' => '1',
    'customer_id' => '13',
    'tax_amount' => '0.0000',
    'shipping_amount' => '8.9600',
    'discount_amount' => '0.0000',
    'subtotal' => '32.0000',
    'grand_total' => '40.9600',
    'total_paid' => '40.9600',
    'total_refunded' => '0.0000',
    'total_qty_ordered' => '0.0000',
    'total_canceled' => '0.0000',
    'total_invoiced' => '40.9600',
    'total_online_refunded' => '0.0000',
```

```
'total_offline_refunded' => '0.0000',
'base_tax_amount' => '0.0000',
'base_shipping_amount' => '8.9600',
'base_discount_amount' => '0.0000',
'base_subtotal' => '32.0000',
'base_grand_total' => '40.9600',
'base_total_paid' => '40.9600',
'base_total_refunded' => '0.0000',
'base_total_qty_ordered' => '0.0000',
'base_total_canceled' => '0.0000',
'base_total_invoiced' => '40.9600',
'base_total_online_refunded' => '0.0000',
'base_total_offline_refunded' => '0.0000',
'subtotal_refunded' => NULL,
'subtotal_canceled' => NULL,
'discount_refunded' => NULL,
'discount_canceled' => NULL,
'discount_invoiced' => '0.0000',
'tax_refunded' => NULL,
'tax_canceled' => NULL,
'shipping_refunded' => NULL,
'shipping_canceled' => NULL,
'base_subtotal_refunded' => NULL,
'base_subtotal_canceled' => NULL,
'base_discount_refunded' => NULL,
'base_discount_canceled' => NULL,
'base_discount_invoiced' => '0.0000',
'base_tax_refunded' => NULL,
'base_tax_canceled' => NULL,
'base_shipping_refunded' => NULL,
'base_shipping_canceled' => NULL,
'subtotal_invoiced' => '32.0000',
'tax_invoiced' => '0.0000',
'shipping_invoiced' => '8.9600',
'base_subtotal_invoiced' => '32.0000',
'base_tax_invoiced' => '0.0000',
'base_shipping_invoiced' => '8.9600',
'shipping_tax_amount' => '0.0000',
'base_shipping_tax_amount' => '0.0000',
'shipping_tax_refunded' => NULL,
'base_shipping_tax_refunded' => NULL,
'store_to_base_rate' => '1.0000',
'store_to_order_rate' => '1.0000',
'base_to_global_rate' => '1.0000',
'base_to_order_rate' => '1.0000',
'weight' => '6.0000',
'store_name' => 'Store X',
'remote_ip' => '10.0.1.1',
'status' => 'complete',
'state' => 'complete',
'applied_rule_ids' => '',
'global_currency_code' => 'USD',
```

```
'base_currency_code' => 'USD',
'store_currency_code' => 'USD',
'order_currency_code' => 'USD',
'shipping_method' => 'ups_GND',
'shipping_description' => 'United Parcel Service - Ground',
'customer_email' => 'jd@test.com',
'customer_prefix' => '',
'customer_firstname' => 'John',
'customer_middlename' => '',
'customer_lastname' => 'Doe',
'customer_suffix' => '',
'customer_taxvat' => '',
'quote_id' => '3',
'billing_address_id' => '1',
'shipping_address_id' => '2',
'is_virtual' => '0',
'customer_group_id' => '8',
'customer_note_notify' => '1',
'customer_is_guest' => '0',
'email_sent' => '1',
'order_id' => '1',
'shipping_address' =>
array (
  'increment_id' => '',
  'parent_id' => '1',
  'store_id' => NULL,
  'created_at' => '2009-06-12 14:28:39',
  'updated_at' => '2009-07-09 08:25:13',
  'is_active' => '1',
  'address_type' => 'shipping',
  'prefix' => '',
  'firstname' => 'Jane',
  'middlename' => '',
  'lastname' => 'Doe',
  'suffix' => '',
  'company' => '',
  'street' => '705 S Congress Apt. A',
  'city' => 'Austin',
  'region' => 'Texas',
  'postcode' => '78704',
  'country_id' => 'US',
  'telephone' => '5555555555',
  'fax' => '',
  'customer_id' => '13',
  'customer_address_id' => '9',
  'region_id' => '57',
  'address_id' => '2',
),
'billing_address' =>
array (
  'increment_id' => '',
  'parent_id' => '1',
```

```
      'store_id' => NULL,
      'created_at' => '2009-06-12 14:28:39',
      'updated_at' => '2009-07-09 08:25:13',
      'is_active' => '1',
      'address_type' => 'billing',
      'prefix' => '',
      'firstname' => 'Jane',
      'middlename' => '',
      'lastname' => 'Doe',
      'suffix' => '',
      'company' => 'ABC Corporation',
      'street' => '1234 Research Blvd',
      'city' => 'Austin',
      'region' => 'Texas',
      'postcode' => '78758',
      'country_id' => 'US',
      'telephone' => '5555555555',
      'fax' => '',
      'customer_id' => '13',
      'customer_address_id' => '9',
      'region_id' => '32',
      'address_id' => '1',
    ),
    'items' =>
    array (
      0 =>
      array (
        'item_id' => '1',
        'order_id' => '1',
        'parent_item_id' => NULL,
        'quote_item_id' => '4',
        'created_at' => '2009-06-12 14:28:39',
        'updated_at' => '2009-07-09 08:25:13',
        'product_id' => '1',
        'product_type' => 'simple',
        'product_options' => 'a:1:{s:15:"info_buyRequest";a:3:{s:4:"uenc";s:96:↵
"abcabc";s:7:"product";s:1:"1";s:3:"qty";s:1:"1";}}',
        'weight' => '6.0000',
        'is_virtual' => '0',
        'sku' => 'SSS3006',
        'name' => 'Product Yellow',
        'description' => NULL,
        'applied_rule_ids' => '',
        'additional_data' => NULL,
        'free_shipping' => '0',
        'is_qty_decimal' => '0',
        'no_discount' => '0',
        'qty_backordered' => NULL,
        'qty_canceled' => '0.0000',
        'qty_invoiced' => '1.0000',
        'qty_ordered' => '1.0000',
        'qty_refunded' => '0.0000',
```

```
    'qty_shipped' => '1.0000',
    'cost' => '0.0000',
    'price' => '32.0000',
    'base_price' => '32.0000',
    'original_price' => '32.0000',
    'base_original_price' => '32.0000',
    'tax_percent' => '0.0000',
    'tax_amount' => '0.0000',
    'base_tax_amount' => '0.0000',
    'tax_invoiced' => '0.0000',
    'base_tax_invoiced' => '0.0000',
    'discount_percent' => '0.0000',
    'discount_amount' => '0.0000',
    'base_discount_amount' => '0.0000',
    'discount_invoiced' => '0.0000',
    'base_discount_invoiced' => '0.0000',
    'amount_refunded' => '0.0000',
    'base_amount_refunded' => '0.0000',
    'row_total' => '32.0000',
    'base_row_total' => '32.0000',
    'row_invoiced' => '32.0000',
    'base_row_invoiced' => '32.0000',
    'row_weight' => '6.0000',
    'gift_message_id' => NULL,
    'gift_message_available' => '2',
    'base_tax_before_discount' => '0.0000',
    'tax_before_discount' => '0.0000',
    'weee_tax_applied' => 'a:0:{}',
    'weee_tax_applied_amount' => '0.0000',
    'weee_tax_applied_row_amount' => '0.0000',
    'base_weee_tax_applied_amount' => '0.0000',
    'base_weee_tax_applied_row_amount' => '0.0000',
    'weee_tax_disposition' => '0.0000',
    'weee_tax_row_disposition' => '0.0000',
    'base_weee_tax_disposition' => '0.0000',
    'base_weee_tax_row_disposition' => '0.0000',
    'ext_order_item_id' => NULL,
    'locked_do_invoice' => NULL,
    'locked_do_ship' => NULL,
  ),
),
'payment' =>
array (
  'increment_id' => '',
  'parent_id' => '1',
  'store_id' => NULL,
  'created_at' => '2009-06-12 14:28:39',
  'updated_at' => '2009-07-09 08:25:13',
  'is_active' => '1',
  'amount_ordered' => '40.9600',
  'base_amount_ordered' => '40.9600',
  'shipping_amount' => '8.9600',
```

```
  'base_shipping_amount' => '8.9600',
  'amount_paid' => '40.9600',
  'base_amount_paid' => '40.9600',
  'shipping_captured' => '8.9600',
  'base_shipping_captured' => '8.9600',
  'method' => 'purchaseorder',
  'po_number' => '123-1234567',
  'cc_type' => '',
  'cc_number_enc' => '',
  'cc_last4' => '',
  'cc_owner' => '',
  'cc_exp_month' => '0',
  'cc_exp_year' => '0',
  'cc_ss_start_month' => '0',
  'cc_ss_start_year' => '0',
  'payment_id' => '3',
),
'status_history' =>
array (
  0 =>
  array (
    'increment_id' => '',
    'parent_id' => '1',
    'store_id' => NULL,
    'created_at' => '2009-07-09 08:25:13',
    'updated_at' => '2009-07-09 08:25:13',
    'is_active' => '1',
    'comment' => '',
    'is_customer_notified' => '0',
    'status' => 'complete',
  ),
  1 =>
  array (
    'increment_id' => '',
    'parent_id' => '1',
    'store_id' => NULL,
    'created_at' => '2009-06-13 00:00:08',
    'updated_at' => '2009-07-09 08:25:13',
    'is_active' => '1',
    'comment' => '',
    'is_customer_notified' => '0',
    'status' => 'processing',
  ),
  2 =>
  array (
    'increment_id' => '',
    'parent_id' => '1',
    'store_id' => NULL,
    'created_at' => '2009-06-12 14:28:39',
    'updated_at' => '2009-07-09 08:25:13',
    'is_active' => '1',
    'is_customer_notified' => '1',
```

```
      'status' => 'pending',
   ),
  ),
)
```

Zend XML-RPC Example

```
// Prepare data
$order_increment_id = '200000001';
// Using Zend XML-RPC
$results = $client->call('call', array($session_id,
    'sales_order.info', array($order_increment_id)));
// view results
var_dump($results);
```

■ **Note** We are purposely listing all the output data so you can extract the exact bit of information that is required when building your third-party application.

Method: sales_order.addComment ($order_increment_id, $status, $comment, $notify)

Description: Adds comments into the order.

Return: Boolean; true if successful.

Arguments:

- $order_increment_id (required). This is the increment_id pulled from sales_order.list().

- $status (required). Can be pending, pending_paypal, processing, holded, complete, closed, or canceled.

- $comment (optional). Message to add into sales order.

- $notify (optional). Set to false if you don't want an e-mail sent to the customer.

SOAP Example

```
// Prepare data
$order_increment_id = '200000001';
$status = 'processing';
$comment = 'Your order has been shipped.';
$notify = true;
// using SOAP method
$results = $client->call($session_id,
    'sales_order.addComment',
    array($order_increment_id, $status,
        $comment, $notify));
// display true if successful
var_dump($results);
```

Note Sales statuses can be found in the config.xml file located here: /app/code/core/Mage/Sales/etc/config.xml.

Tip Because the comment argument is optional, you can use this method to update the status of an order. Set the notify argument to false and you have an updateStatus() method.

Method: sales_order.hold ($order_increment_id)

Description: Adds hold status to an order.

Return: Boolean; true if successful.

Argument:

- $order_increment_id (required). This is the increment_id pulled from sales_order.list().

Zend XML-RPC Example

```
// Prepare data
$order_increment_id = '200000001';
// Using Zend XML-RPC
$results = $client->call('call', array($session_id,
    'sales_order.hold', array($order_increment_id)));
// view results
var_dump($results);
```

Method: sales_order.unhold ($order_increment_id)

Description: Unholds an order.

Return: Boolean; true if successful.

Argument:

- $order_increment_id (required). This is the increment_id pulled from sales_order.list().

SOAP Example

```
// Prepare data
$order_increment_id = '200000001';
// using SOAP method
$results = $client->call($session_id,
    'sales_order.unhold', $order_increment_id);
```

```
// display true if successful
var_dump($results);
```

Method: sales_order.cancel ($order_increment_id)

Description: Cancels an order that has not been processed.

Return: Boolean; true if successful.

Argument:

- $order_increment_id (required). This is the increment_id pulled from sales_order.list().

Zend XML-RPC Example

```
// Prepare data
$order_increment_id = '200000001';
// Using Zend XML-RPC
$results = $client->call('call', array($session_id,
    'sales_order.cancel', array($order_increment_id)));
// view results
var_dump($results);
```

Sales Order Shipment Set

In the sales order shipment set, you can create shipment orders and record-tracking numbers. The available methods are as follows:

- sales_order_shipment.list()

- sales_order_shipment.info()

- sales_order_shipment.create()

- sales_order_shipment.addComment()

- sales_order_shipment.addTrack()

- sales_order_shipment.removeTrack()

- sales_order_shipment.getCarriers()

Method: sales_order_shipment.list ($filters)

Description: Returns a list of sales order shipments.

Return: Array.

Argument:

- $filters (optional). Uses an array of key/value pairs to set filters.

Available filter keys:

- order_increment_id
- store_id
- created_at
- (to see a full list of filters, use the following sample return set)

Sample Return Set

```
array (
  0 =>
  array (
    'increment_id' => '200000001',
    'parent_id' => '0',
    'store_id' => '2',
    'created_at' => '2009-07-03 03:58:32',
    'updated_at' => '2009-07-09 08:28:19',
    'is_active' => '1',
    'shipping_address_id' => '30',
    'shipping_firstname' => 'Jeff',
    'shipping_lastname' => 'Lowey',
    'order_id' => '5',
    'order_increment_id' => '200000004',
    'order_created_at' => '2009-06-16 14:34:01',
    'total_qty' => '6.0000',
    'shipment_id' => '169',
  ),
...
```

SOAP Example

```
// Pull only shipments created after June 1st
$filters = array(
    'created_at' => array('gt'=>'2009-06-01')
);
// using SOAP method
$results = $client->call($session_id,
    'sales_order_shipment.list', array($filters));
// view the results
var_dump($results);
```

Method: sales_order_shipment.info ($shipment_increment_id)

Description: Returns detailed information on a specific shipment order.

Return: Array.

Argument:

- $shipment_increment_id (required). This is the increment_id pulled from sales_order_shipment.list().

Sample Return Set

```
array (
  'increment_id' => '200000001',
  'parent_id' => '0',
  'store_id' => '2',
  'created_at' => '2009-07-03 03:58:32',
  'updated_at' => '2009-07-09 08:28:19',
  'is_active' => '1',
  'customer_id' => '18',
  'order_id' => '5',
  'billing_address_id' => '29',
  'shipping_address_id' => '30',
  'total_qty' => '6.0000',
  'shipment_id' => '169',
  'items' =>
  array (
    0 =>
    array (
      'increment_id' => '',
      'parent_id' => '169',
      'store_id' => NULL,
      'created_at' => '2009-07-03 03:58:32',
      'updated_at' => '2009-07-09 08:28:19',
      'is_active' => '1',
      'sku' => 'SSS3006',
      'name' => 'Product Red',
      'order_item_id' => '9',
      'product_id' => '1',
      'weight' => '6.0000',
      'price' => '32.0000',
      'qty' => '6.0000',
      'item_id' => '170',
    ),
  ),
  'tracks' =>
  array (
  ),
  'comments' =>
  array (
    0 =>
    array (
      'increment_id' => '',
      'parent_id' => '169',
      'store_id' => NULL,
      'created_at' => '2009-07-09 08:28:19',
      'updated_at' => '2009-07-09 08:28:19',
      'is_active' => '1',
      'comment' => 'Your items have been shipped',
      'is_customer_notified' => '1',
      'comment_id' => '359',
    ),
```

```
    1 =>
    array (
      'increment_id' => '',
      'parent_id' => '169',
      'store_id' => NULL,
      'created_at' => '2009-07-09 07:58:33',
      'updated_at' => '2009-07-09 08:28:19',
      'is_active' => '1',
      'comment' => 'Your items have been shipped',
      'is_customer_notified' => '1',
      'comment_id' => '294',
    ),
  ),
)
```

Zend XML-RPC Example

```
// Prepare data
$shipment_increment_id = '200000001';
// Using Zend XML-RPC
$results = $client->call('call',
    array($session_id,
        'sales_order_shipment.info',
        array($shipment_increment_id)));
// view results
var_dump($results);
```

▓ **Note** It can get confusing with the order_increment_id and the increment_id within the sales_order_shipment.list() API. Just keep track of which number represents the order id and which represents the shipment order id. There's also a shipment_id, which is not the same as the shipment order id.

Method: sales_order_shipment.create ($order_increment_id, $items, $comment, $email_send, $email_with_comment)

Description: Creates a shipment order.

Return: Int, newly created shipment_increment_id.

Arguments:

- $order_increment_id (required). This is the order number.
- $items (required). Key/value array of item_id and qty. See the following example.
- $comment (optional). Shipment comment message.
- $email_send (optional). True/false; sends an e-mail to the customer.
- $email_with_comment (optional). True/false; sends an e-mail with the comment.

Zend XML-RPC Example

```php
// Prepare the data
$order_increment_id = '200000004';
$product_id = '1234';
$qty_shipped = '4';
$comment = 'Four items have been shipped.';
$item_id = '';
// Pull sales_order.info
$results = $client->call('call', array($session_id,
    'sales_order.info', array($order_increment_id)));
// Extract the item_id
foreach ($results['items'] as $item)
{
    if ($item['product_id'] == $product_id)
        $item_id = $item['item_id'];
}
// Create the items array
$items = array($item_id => $qty_shipped);
// Create order shipment
$new_shipment_increment_id = $client->call('call',
    array($session_id,
        'sales_order_shipment.create',
        array(
            $order_increment_id,
            $items,
            $comment,
            true,
            true
        )
    )
);
// Display the new shipment increment id
echo $new_shipment_increment_id;
```

Method: sales_order_shipment.addComment ($shipment_increment_id, $comment, $email_send, $email_with_comment)

Description: Adds a shipment comment.

Return: Boolean; true if successful.

Arguments:

- $shipment_increment_id (required). This is the shipment increment id.
- $comment (required). Shipment comment message.
- $email_send (optional). True/false; sends an e-mail to the customer.
- $email_with_comment (optional). True/false; sends an e-mail with the comment.

SOAP Example

```
// Prepare data
$shipment_increment_id = '200000001';
$comment = 'Your item has left the factory.';
$email_send = true;
$email_with_comment = true;
// using SOAP method
$results = $client->call($session_id,
    'sales_order_shipment.addComment',
    array($shipment_increment_id,
        $comment,
        $email_sent,
        $email_with_comment
    ));
// return true if successful
var_dump($results);
```

Method: sales_order_shipment.addTrack ($shipment_increment_id, $carrier_key, $tracking_title, $tracking_num)

Description: Adds a tracking number to the shipment order.

Return: Int, newly created tracking id.

Arguments:

- $shipment_increment_id (required). This is the shipment increment id.

- $carrier_key (required). Can be obtained by the sales_order_shipment.getCarriers() API.

- $tracking_title (required). Title that will appear on tracking info.

- $tracking_num (required). Tracking number.

Zend XML-RPC Example

```
// Prepare the data
$shipment_increment_id = '200000001';
$carrier = 'fedex';
$tracking_title = 'Fedex Tracking Info';
$tracking_num = '111222333';
// Create tracking order
$new_tracking_id = $client->call('call',
    array($session_id,
        'sales_order_shipment.addTrack',
```

```
        array(
            $shipment_increment_id,
            $carrier,
            $tracking_title,
            $tracking_num
        )
    )
);
// Display the new tracking id
echo $new_tracking_id;
```

Method: sales_order_shipment.removeTrack ($shipment_increment_id, $tracking_id)

Description: Deletes a tracking number.

Return: Boolean; true if successful.

Arguments:

- $shipment_increment_id (required). This is the shipment increment id.

- $tracking_id (required). This is the tracking id.

SOAP Example

```
// Prepare data
$shipment_increment_id = '200000001';
$tracking_id = '237';
// using SOAP method
$results = $client->call($session_id,
    'sales_order_shipment.removeTrack',
    array(
        $shipment_increment_id,
        $tracking_id
    ));
// return true if successful
var_dump($results);
```

Method: sales_order_shipment.getCarriers ($order_increment_id)

Description: Gets a list of carriers from an order_increment_id.

Return: Array; returns only valid carriers that are associated with this order.

Argument:

- $order_increment_id (required). This is the order increment id.

Sample Return Set

```
array (
  'custom' => 'Custom Value',
  'dhl' => 'DHL',
  'fedex' => 'FedEx',
  'ups' => 'United Parcel Service',
  'usps' => 'United States Postal Service',
)
```

Zend XML-RPC Example

```
// Prepare the data
$order_increment_id = '200000004';
// Using Zend XML-RPC
$results = $client->call('call',
    array($session_id,
        'sales_order_shipment.getCarriers',
        array($order_increment_id)
    )
);
// View the results
var_dump($results);
```

Sales Order Invoice Set

In the sales order invoice set, you can view, create, cancel, and add comments to invoices:

- sales_order_invoice.list
- sales_order_invoice.info
- sales_order_invoice.create
- sales_order_invoice.addComment
- sales_order_invoice.capture
- sales_order_invoice.void
- sales_order_invoice.cancel

Method: sales_order_invoice.list ($filters)

Description: Returns a list of sales invoices.

Return: Array.

Argument:

- $filters (optional). Uses an array of key/value pairs to set filters.

Available filter keys:

- order_increment_id

- store_id

- created_at

- (to see a full list of filters, use the following sample return set)

Sample Return Set

```
array (
  0 =>
  array (
    'increment_id' => '200000001',
    'parent_id' => '0',
    'store_id' => '2',
    'created_at' => '2009-08-13 00:00:08',
    'updated_at' => '2009-08-13 00:00:08',
    'is_active' => '1',
    'billing_address_id' => '1',
    'billing_firstname' => 'John',
    'billing_lastname' => 'Doe',
    'order_id' => '1',
    'order_increment_id' => '200000001',
    'order_created_at' => '2009-08-12 14:28:38',
    'state' => '2',
    'grand_total' => '40.9600',
    'order_currency_code' => 'USD',
    'invoice_id' => '5',
  ),
...
```

SOAP Example

```
// Pull only invoices created after June 1st
$filters = array(
    'created_at' => array('gt'=>'2009-06-01')
);
// using SOAP method
$results = $client->call($session_id,
    'sales_order_invoice.list',
    array($filters)
);
// view the results
var_dump($results);
```

Method: sales_order_invoice.info ($invoice_increment_id)

Description: Returns detailed information about an invoice.

Return: Array.

Argument:

- $invoice_increment_id (required). This is the increment_id pulled from sales_order_invoice.list().

Sample Return Set

```
array (
  'increment_id' => '200000001',
  'parent_id' => '0',
  'store_id' => '2',
  'created_at' => '2009-08-13 00:00:08',
  'updated_at' => '2009-08-13 00:00:08',
  'is_active' => '1',
  'global_currency_code' => 'USD',
  'base_currency_code' => 'USD',
  'store_currency_code' => 'USD',
  'order_currency_code' => 'USD',
  'store_to_base_rate' => '1.0000',
  'store_to_order_rate' => '1.0000',
  'base_to_global_rate' => '1.0000',
  'base_to_order_rate' => '1.0000',
  'subtotal' => '32.0000',
  'discount_amount' => '0.0000',
  'tax_amount' => '0.0000',
  'shipping_amount' => '8.9600',
  'grand_total' => '40.9600',
  'base_subtotal' => '32.0000',
  'base_discount_amount' => '0.0000',
  'base_tax_amount' => '0.0000',
  'base_shipping_amount' => '8.9600',
  'base_grand_total' => '40.9600',
  'state' => '2',
  'order_id' => '1',
  'billing_address_id' => '1',
  'shipping_address_id' => '2',
  'invoice_id' => '5',
  'items' =>
  array (
    0 =>
    array (
      'increment_id' => '',
      'parent_id' => '5',
      'store_id' => NULL,
      'created_at' => '2009-08-13 00:00:08',
      'updated_at' => '2009-08-13 00:00:08',
      'is_active' => '1',
      'weee_tax_applied' => 'a:0:{}',
      'qty' => '1.0000',
      'cost' => '0.0000',
      'price' => '32.0000',
      'tax_amount' => '0.0000',
```

```
          'row_total' => '32.0000',
          'base_price' => '32.0000',
          'base_tax_amount' => '0.0000',
          'base_row_total' => '32.0000',
          'base_weee_tax_applied_amount' => '0.0000',
          'base_weee_tax_applied_row_amount' => '0.0000',
          'weee_tax_applied_amount' => '0.0000',
          'weee_tax_applied_row_amount' => '0.0000',
          'weee_tax_disposition' => '0.0000',
          'weee_tax_row_disposition' => '0.0000',
          'base_weee_tax_disposition' => '0.0000',
          'base_weee_tax_row_disposition' => '0.0000',
          'sku' => 'SSS3006',
          'name' => 'Product Red',
          'order_item_id' => '1',
          'product_id' => '1',
          'item_id' => '6',
        ),
      ),
      'comments' =>
      array (
        0 =>
        array (
          'increment_id' => '',
          'parent_id' => '5',
          'store_id' => NULL,
          'created_at' => '2009-08-13 00:00:08',
          'updated_at' => '2009-08-13 00:00:08',
          'is_active' => '1',
          'comment' => 'Invoice Created',
          'is_customer_notified' => '0',
          'comment_id' => '7',
        ),
      ),
  )
```

Zend XML-RPC Example

```
// Prepare data
$invoice_increment_id = '200000001';
// Using Zend XML-RPC
$results = $client->call('call',
    array($session_id,
        'sales_order_invoice.info',
        array($invoice_increment_id)
    )
);
// view results
var_dump($results);
```

Method: sales_order_invoice.create ($order_increment_id, $items, $comment, $email_send, $email_with_comment)

Description: Creates an invoice.

Return: Int, newly created invoice_increment_id.

Arguments:

- $order_increment_id (required). This is the order number.

- $items (required). Key/value array of item_id and qty. See the following example.

- $comment (optional). Invoice comment message.

- $email_send (optional). True/false; sends an e-mail to the customer.

- $email_with_comment (optional). True/false, sends an e-mail with the comment.

Zend XML-RPC Example

```
// Prepare the data
$order_increment_id = '200000004';
$product_id = '1234';
$qty_invoiced = '6';
$comment = 'New invoice creation.';
$item_id = '';
// Pull sales_order.info
$results = $client->call('call', array($session_id,
    'sales_order.info', array($order_increment_id)));
// Extract the item_id
foreach ($results['items'] as $item)
{
    if ($item['product_id'] == $product_id)
        $item_id = $item['item_id'];
}
// Create the items array
$items = array($item_id => $qty_invoiced);
// Create order invoice
$new_invoice_increment_id = $client->call('call',
    array($session_id,
        'sales_order_invoice.create',
        array(
            $order_increment_id,
            $items,
            $comment,
            true,
            true
        )
    )
);
// Display the new invoice increment id
echo $new_invoice_increment_id;
```

Method: sales_order_invoice.addComment ($invoice_increment_id, $comment, $email_send, $email_with_comment)

Description: Adds an invoice comment.

Return: Boolean; true if successful.

Arguments:

- $invoice_increment_id (required). This is the invoice increment id.

- $comment (required). Shipment comment message.

- $email_send (optional). True/false; sends an e-mail to the customer.

- $email_with_comment (optional). True/false, sends an e-mail with the comment.

SOAP Example

```
// Prepare data
$invoice_increment_id = '200000001';
$comment = 'Invoice has been setup.';
$email_send = true;
$email_with_comment = true;
// using SOAP method
$results = $client->call($session_id,
    'sales_order_invoice.addComment',
    array(
        $invoice_increment_id,
        $comment,
        $email_sent,
        $email_with_comment
    )
);
// return true if successful
var_dump($results);
```

Method: sales_order_invoice.capture ($invoice_increment_id)

Description: Captures an invoice.

Return: Boolean; true if successful.

Argument:

- $invoice_increment_id (required). This is the invoice number.

Zend XML-RPC Example

```
// Prepare the data
$invoice_increment_id = '200000001';
// Capture invoice
$result = $client->call('call',
    array($session_id,
```

```
        'sales_order_invoice.capture',
        array($invoice_increment_id)
    )
);
// Display true if successful
var_dump($result);
```

Method: sales_order_invoice.void ($invoice_increment_id)

Description: Voids an invoice.

Return: Boolean; true if successful.

Argument:

- $invoice_increment_id (required). This is the invoice number.

SOAP Example

```
// Prepare the data
$invoice_increment_id = '200000001';
// using SOAP method
$results = $client->call($session_id,
    'sales_order_invoice.void',
    array($invoice_increment_id));
// view the results
var_dump($results);
```

Method: sales_order_invoice.cancel ($invoice_increment_id)

Description: Cancels an invoice.

Return: Boolean; true if successful.

Argument:

- $invoice_increment_id (required). This is the invoice number.

Zend XML-RPC Example

```
// Prepare the data
$invoice_increment_id = '200000001';
// Capture invoice
$result = $client->call('call', array($session_id,
    'sales_order_invoice.cancel',
    array($invoice_increment_id))
);
// Display true if successful
var_dump($result);
```

Inventory API

The inventory API allows you to list and update item status and quantity. There are two methods at your disposal:

- cataloginventory_stock_item.list()
- cataloginventory_stock_item.update()

Method: cataloginventory_stock_item.list ($product_ids)

Description: Returns stock information on a set of products.

Return: Array.

Argument:

- $product_ids (required). An array of product_id or product_sku.

Sample Return Set

```
array (
  0 =>
  array (
    'product_id' => '1',
    'sku' => 'SSS3006',
    'qty' => '520.0000',
    'is_in_stock' => '1',
  ),
  1 =>
  array (
    'product_id' => '2',
    'sku' => 'SSS0003',
    'qty' => '1465.0000',
    'is_in_stock' => '1',
  ),
  2 =>
  array (
    'product_id' => '3',
    'sku' => ' SSS3007',
    'qty' => '96.0000',
    'is_in_stock' => '1',
  ),
)
```

SOAP Example

```
// Pull stock info for these product ids or skus
$product_ids = array(
    '1',
    '2',          // product_id
    'SSS3007'     // sku
);
```

```
// using SOAP method
$results = $client->call($session_id,
    'cataloginventory_stock_item.list',
    array($product_ids)
);
// view the results
var_dump($results);
```

Method: cataloginventory_stock_item.update ($product_id, $data)

Description: Updates stock information for a product_id or product_sku.

Return: Boolean; true if successful.

Arguments:

- $product_id (required). Can be product_id or product_sku.

- $data (required). Key/value array to update the stock data.

Available data keys:

- qty

- is_in_stock (1 = in stock, 0 = out of stock)

Zend XML-RPC Example

```
// Prepare the data
$product_id = '1';
$data = array(
    'qty' => '1000',
    'is_in_stock' => '1'
);
// Capture invoice
$result = $client->call('call',
    array($session_id,
        'cataloginventory_stock_item.update',
        array(
            $product_id,
            $data
        )
    )
);
// Display true if successful
var_dump($result);
```

Index

B

C